9/82

SYNGE
A CRITICAL STUDY OF THE PLAYS

SYNGE

A Critical Study of the Plays

NICHOLAS GRENE

First edition 1975
Reprinted 1979

Published by
THE MACMILLAN PRESS LTD
London and Basingstoke
Associated companies in Delhi
Dublin Hong Kong Johannesburg Lagos
Melbourne New York Singapore Tokyo

ISBN 0 333 17259 0

Printed in Great Britain by
LOWE AND BRYDONE PRINTERS LTD
Thetford, Norfolk

TO
ELEANOR

Contents

Preface   ix

Acknowledgements   xi

Abbreviations and Conventions   xii

1   The Landscape of Ireland   1

2   Synge's Aran   19

3   The Vision of *Riders to the Sea*   41

4   The Development of Dialect   60

5   In Wicklow: *The Shadow of the Glen*, *The Tinker's Wedding*   84

6   The Dramatic Structure of *The Well of the Saints*   110

7   Approaches to *The Playboy*   132

8   Unhappy Comedies   146

9   *Deirdre of the Sorrows*: Unfinished or Unsuccessful   160

10   Conclusion   183

Notes   187

Sources   194

Index   199

Preface

No one, starting a critical study of Synge, could claim a need for rehabilitation; Synge is not forgotten, he is not even a neglected figure, except perhaps in comparative terms. In the sixty-odd years since his death sufficient books, articles and newspaper pieces on him have accumulated to fill a full-length bibliography of published criticism – not in itself necessarily a testimony to a writer's greatness, but a sign at least of a continuing awareness of his work. In the past fifteen years, in particular, there have been a number of important publications; principally, a major biography by David H. Greene and Edward M. Stephens in 1959, followed by the definitive *Collected Works* (1962–8), both of which made use of a large body of manuscript material which had not been previously available. Synge's work is now, therefore, better known than it has ever been before. It may be that he has reached that stage in a writer's reputation when he can shed his initials. That, at any rate, is the significance of the title of this book, *Synge* rather than *J. M. Synge*. Its object is to provide the detailed criticism, analysis and evaluation which we accord to a recognised writer, who does not need to be introduced and whose canon of major works has been established. It is in some ways surprising how long it has taken Synge to reach this stage; surprising, for example, that this is the first full study to concentrate exclusively on the plays. Previous critical books have all been of a general scope, covering comprehensively everything that Synge wrote, the sort of 'man and his works' study which is appropriate to a lesser-known author. We can by now perhaps afford to neglect his poems, only a few of which are really successful, and to admit that most of his prose is interesting mainly for what it can tell us of his plays. When the hitherto unpublished juvenilia first appeared, it was exciting to look at what had been unearthed, but by now it can be allowed to fall back into its proper subordinate place. The Oxford edition has added enormously to our knowledge of Synge; it has not substantially changed or enlarged our sense of his creative achievement which remains centred on the six plays by which he made his name. No one has ever been in doubt that it was as a dramatist that Synge was important. It should now be possible to look closely at those six plays, to attempt to analyse the special success of his drama, without needing to explain who he was and where he lived when, what else he wrote and in which order.

With this as an objective, it may well seem inconsistent to have included chapters on Synge and the Irish background or his experience of Aran, subjects which have been commonly discussed in earlier more general critical works. Here I must admit to a personal bias. I grew up in Ireland in the area of Wicklow where Synge set three of his plays, and partly as a consequence of this I have a special interest in the relation between his work and the reality from which it was drawn. Synge seems to me a fascinating example of the workings of creativity and I have returned again and again to the use he makes of the Irish material, to try to define the nature of the changes by which it was transformed into drama. I think, however, that this interest is relevant to the main purpose of the book. To understand the character of the plays, we need to consider Synge's development as a dramatist and the origins of that development. Too many critics have given the impression that Synge's career hinges on a single turning-point – before and after Aran – and that once he found his medium there was little further change. I hope to show that the plays do differ one from another, and that as they derive from different experiences, they represent distinct phases in Synge's dramatic creation.

It may perhaps be added that in areas which have been very controversial – the authenticity of Synge's peasant characters and their language, his supposed satirical 'slanders' of Ireland – some first-hand knowledge of the background may legitimately be claimed as expertise. Alan Price, surveying the state of Synge criticism in 1969, remarked on the fact that Irishmen had written very little that was intelligent, dispassionate or appreciative on Synge. I would be very happy if this book went some way towards disproving that statement.

Liverpool   N. GRENE
December 1974

Acknowledgements

Grateful acknowledgement is made to Oxford University Press for permission to quote from J. M. Synge, *Collected Works*; to the Trustees of the Synge Estate for permission to quote from unpublished manuscripts, and to the Librarian of Trinity College, Dublin, for making those manuscripts available to me.

Parts of Chapters 2 and 4 have already appeared in somewhat different versions in *Modern Drama* and *Long Room*, and are here reprinted by permission of the editor of *Modern Drama*, and of the Friends of the Trinity College Library.

I would like also to thank several people for their contributions to this book.

First of all, I have to express my deep sense of gratitude to the late T. R. Henn, who supervised this study in its initial form, and who gave so generously of his time, his learning and most of all his friendship; I feel how great a privilege it was to have been one of his last pupils.

Thomas Cullen of Ballinaclash has supplied me over the years with a fund of fascinating local information, extremely valuable for anyone interested in Synge. William O'Sullivan, the Keeper of Manuscripts in the Library of Trinity College, Dublin, by inviting me to collaborate with him on a catalogue of the Synge manuscripts, first gave me the opportunity to study the collection in detail.

My mother and sister have both read parts of this study in various stages of completion, and by their criticism and encouragement, have stimulated its development. My father will recognise just how pervasive is his influence throughout.

My greatest dept of gratitude I can only express, inadequately, through the dedication.

Abbreviations and Conventions

All quotations from Synge's published work are taken from J. M. Synge, *Collected Works*, General Editor Robin Skelton, Vols I–IV (Oxford University Press, 1962–8). References are included in the body of the text, and the following abbreviations are used:

Poems   Vol. I, *Poems*, ed. Robin Skelton, 1962.
Prose   Vol. II, *Prose*, ed. Alan Price, 1966.
Plays I   Vol. III, *Plays*, Book 1, ed. Ann Saddlemyer, 1968.
Plays II   Vol. IV, *Plays*, Book 2, ed. Ann Saddlemyer, 1968.

Where I have quoted from manuscript material references are to the accession numbers in the Trinity College Library collection, see *The Synge Manuscripts in the Library of Trinity College Dublin*. I have left such manuscript quotations virtually unedited, indicating a passage crossed out by square brackets and italics, thus '[*the scattered fragments of my*] notes'. I have tried to give references to the Oxford text wherever the manuscript material has been included in that edition; where there are slight differences between my reading and that of the editors, I have added the manuscript reference as well.

I

The Landscape of Ireland

On the first night of The Playboy of the Western World, after the audience had rioted, Synge replied to nationalist criticisms with an irritated disclaimer: 'I wrote the play because it pleased me, and it just happens that I know Irish life best, so I made my methods Irish.'[1] He described satirically to his friend Stephen MacKenna the sort of questions which had annoyed him. '"Do you really think, Mr Synge, that if a man did this in Mayo, girls would bring him a pullet?" The next time it was, "Do you think Mr Synge, they'd bring him eggs?".'[2] Synge's reaction is understandable. Any artist thus faced with demands for verisimilitude which he regards as irrelevant, will be inclined to insist on the individuality of his vision. Obviously it is absurd to judge his work simply as a representation of Irish life, and to condemn it out of hand if it is considered inaccurate. Yet, it is not just accidental that Synge 'knew Irish life best', and his plays are more than incidentally Irish. What did being Irish mean to Synge? How did his attitude to Ireland and the Irish people affect his writing? How far did his artistic success depend upon his use of Irish material? These are important questions which are crucial to the understanding of his plays.

To say that Synge came from an Anglo-Irish Protestant family seems a simple enough definition of his class background, but the simplicity is deceptive. The peculiar position of the Anglo-Irish involved complexities which make generalisation and preconceptions almost always inaccurate. The Synges, for example, did not in the least resemble the 'hard-riding country gentlemen' celebrated by Yeats. Some of their income did come from land, and they had landed cousins, but they were themselves middle-class, professional people – barristers, land-agents, engineers. The Anglo-Irish were an Ascendancy not an aristocracy, including individuals of very different social standing, united by their common minority interests, rather than by any class uniformity. In the 1880s, when Synge was growing up, the two main political issues of the time, home rule and land reform, provided a joint threat which drew them together. With their church disestablished, they felt, quite rightly, that they were fighting a last-ditch stand against the growing power of the Catholic nationalists. In an embattled situation, their political and social views tended to be rigidly orthodox. Mrs Synge temporarily changed papers from the very conservative *Daily Express* to the moderate *Irish Times*. 'I took it to please Johnnie', she explained to her son Robert, 'but I find it a rebel paper and praises O'Connell, so I gave it up.'³ Daniel O'Connell, the Great Liberator, had been dead for forty years, and he was never a rebel in any ordinary sense of the word, but a newspaper that could include praise of the hero of Catholic emancipation was evidently seditious to Mrs Synge.

We can see that 'Johnnie', like so many liberal-minded adolescents, must have tried to enlighten his reactionary family. His mother was hardly a suitable case for 'enlightenment'. She was the daughter of a Northern Irish clergyman, and herself a strongly evangelical member of the Church of Ireland. Synge's announcement of his loss of faith when he was eighteen produced a family crisis. They made an effort – he was given serious talks from his brother Samuel who was training to be a medical missionary, his mother prayed for his recovery – but it was no use, and by degrees he was established as 'poor Johnnie', the only one of Mrs Synge's children who was a trouble to her. Synge himself regarded this as crucial in his estrangement from his own background. 'By it I laid a chasm between my present and my past and between myself and my kindred and friends. Till I was twenty-three I never met or at least knew a man or woman who shared my opinions.' (*Prose* p. 11) Synge's shyness and reserve, the lonely isolated life he led while at Trinity College Dublin, living at home, absorbed in music, must have accentuated his feeling of being odd man out in his surroundings. A photograph taken in 1900 at Castle Kevin, the house in County Wicklow where the Synges often spent their summers, splendidly catches the incongruity of his position: behind a group composed of his mother, in formal black, and two decorously dressed young ladies, sitting on rugs on the stone steps of the house, Synge squats in shabby country clothes with a tramp-like hat tilted back from his forehead.⁴ He lived with his mother in Dublin for many years after his return from the Continent, and they seem to have developed a tacit agreement of mutual toleration. She was less upset than he expected when he eventually revealed his engagement to the Catholic shop-girl turned actress, Molly Algood. But although Synge stayed very close to his family in many ways, the 'chasm' remained. None of them ever went to see his plays produced – Mrs Synge strongly disapproved of the theatre – and his success as a dramatist merely surprised and puzzled them. When Samuel Synge came to write a memoir of his brother, the plays were scarcely mentioned. Edward Stephens, Synge's nephew and biographer, tells us that at his uncle's funeral he did not know even by appearance Synge's colleagues from the Abbey.

No doubt the story of Synge's early development is ordinary enough. His conversion to Darwinism, for example, must have been a common path to intellectual liberation in the nineteenth century; Yeats, the last writer one would associate with scientific rationalism, speaks of a similar experience in *Autobiographies*. When Synge went to Germany to study music in 1893, his immediate purpose may have been merely to escape the uncongenial atmosphere of a conventional home background. But it was equally important for him to leave Ireland and the provincial culture it offered. Bernard Shaw, looking back with over forty years' hind-sight at his own decision to leave Dublin, put it emphatically: 'Every Irishman who felt that his business in life was on the higher planes of the cultural professions felt that he must have a metropolitan domicile and an international culture; that is, he felt that his first business was to get out of Ireland.'[5] Synge's visits to the Continent, like Shaw's first years in London, provided a period of international education.

'Silence, exile, and cunning', Dedalus proclaimed were the only weapons the artist had against the nets spread by his country to catch his soul. The formula looks odd applied to Synge, who was never cunning, and who had to escape very different nets from Joyce. But 'silence' was crucial. Synge needed a passive unpro-ductive time in which he could absorb sufficient European culture to give him a broader base of identity. It was one of his tempera-mental assets as an artist that he could continue to believe in his future throughout this barren period of development, that he could wait in silence without becoming discouraged. Attempts to establish a significant influence on Synge of this or that European writer may often look unconvincing. The more telling effects of his time on the Continent are perhaps the French tags with which he interlarded his speech, the assurance with which he spoke of

Ronsard, Petrarch or Goethe. These are the outward signs of a personality made confident by its cosmopolitanism.

The hero of Synge's first play, *When the Moon Has Set*, written around 1900–1, is an Anglo-Irish young man with artistic inclinations recently returned to Ireland from Paris – for Colm Sweeny read John Millington Synge. Yeats said that 'dramatic action is a fire that must burn up everything but itself'; *When the Moon Has Set* smoulders dismally round the uninflammable clinker of Synge's personal feelings and ideas. The emotional impetus for the play comes from the unhappy end to his relationship with Cherrie Mattheson, the girl with whom he had been in love for many years and who had refused to marry him on the grounds that he was a non-believer. Colm accordingly uses triumphantly successful anti-Christian arguments to persuade the nun, Sister Eileen, to leave her order and marry him. (Cherrie Mattheson, whose family were strict Plymouth Brethren, would hardly have liked being cast as a nun.) Throughout the play Synge is self-consciously defying the standards and attitudes of his background. The gloomy country house in which it is set, the dead uncle from whom Colm inherits the estate, provide symbols of frustration and repression. In one version of the play, Colm comments in a letter to a friend: 'The old-fashioned Irish conservatism and morality seemed to have evolved a melancholy degeneration worse than anything in Paris.' (*Plays* I p. 160) Or again, in Synge's worst pretentious style, he speaks of his uncle: 'What a life he has had. I suppose it is a good thing that this [Anglo-Irish] aristocracy is dying out. They were neither human nor divine.' (*Plays* I p. 162) Looking at his own class from his new European vantage-point, Synge saw nothing but repressiveness, hatred and decadence.

Only once in Synge's work do we find him expressing a sympathetic attitude towards the Anglo-Irish. In the essay 'A Landlord's Garden in County Wicklow', published in the *Manchester Guardian* in 1907 but written several years before, he describes the derelict garden of a big house and comments:

> Everyone is used in Ireland to the tragedy that is bound up with the lives of farmers and fishing people; but in this garden one seemed to feel the tragedy of the landlord class also, and of the innumerable old families that are quickly dwindling away. These owners of the land are not much pitied at the present day, or much deserving of pity; and yet one cannot quite forget that

they are the descendants of what was at one time, in the eighteenth century, a high-spirited and highly-cultivated aristocracy. (*Prose* pp. 230–1)

Synge regrets above all the decline in the cultural standards of the Anglo-Irish, and, like Yeats, looks back with nostalgia to the eighteenth century – 'that one Irish century that escaped from darkness and confusion'.[6] Yet Synge had reservations even about the great Ascendancy epoch before the Union. He added in a sentence which he did not include in the final text: 'Still, this class, with its many genuine qualities, had little patriotism, in the right sense, few ideas, and no seed for future life, so it has gone to the wall.' (*Prose* p. 231n) This is finely judicial – it is almost the same judgement which Maria Edgeworth passed on her contemporaries in *Castle Rackrent* at the time of the Union itself. With a shrug of indifference Synge left the Anglo-Irish dead to bury their dead and turned to those parts of Irish life where he still saw vitality.

Synge was unusual among Anglo-Irish writers in this capacity to leave aside the problems of his class. The familiar ambivalences of the Anglo-Irish situation – their split loyalties as England's colonial garrison', their uneasy position as landlords – tended to undermine the attempts of writers from an Anglo-Irish background to look steadily and dispassionately at the 'Irish question'. George Moore, for example, in *A Drama in Muslin* (1886) set out to produce a Zolaesque investigation of the crumbling social world which centred round Dublin Castle. He gives a satirical picture of the decadent Ascendancy of the 1880s, trying to continue with traditional frivolities, while in terror of their lives from the Land League and the secret societies. Yet Moore's own vision is from within the Ascendancy context. The characteristic image of the peasantry is the menacing silhouette seen from the carriage window, and Moore, who himself had an estate in Mayo, cannot exclude a note of outrage at the shooting of a fellow landlord. His next publication, *Parnell and his Island*, was a series of hysterically abusive vignettes of Irish life, in which the strenuous attempt at understanding gives way to undirected derision and hatred. 'The Irish race is one that has been forgotten and left behind in a bog hole; it smells of the wet earth, its face seems as if made of it, and its ideas are moist and dull, and as sterile as peat.'[7] Even Shaw in his characteristically quizzical look at Ireland in *John Bull's Other Island* betrays the uncertainty of his feelings. There are suggestions of self-portrait in Larry Doyle, the Irish exile, the professed admirer of England, who is emotionally crippled by his bitter reaction against the background of his youth.

For Synge these issues were not particularly significant. Yeats once said that Synge 'seemed by nature unfitted to think a political thought'.[8] This lack of interest in politics has been questioned by Greene and Stephens, who cite his views on the Irish situation as his mother reported them:

> I asked him in one letter how he could be mixed up with nationalists, and he said I was not to think he is a rebel, but he thinks Ireland will come to her own in years to come when socialistic ideas spread in England, but he does not at all approve of fighting for freedom. He thinks things will change by degrees in the world and there will be equality and no more grinding down of the poor . . .[9]

This seems reasonable enough, moderate liberal views – a Home Ruler, in terms of the Irish issues of the time. Yet such a statement does not really invalidate Yeats's point. No doubt Synge like anyone else had views on the current political situation, and if challenged, as in this instance, could express them. But he clearly did not *care* about politics. He did not naturally think in a political way; in his essays, much less in his plays, he rarely draws political implications. It is perhaps mistaken to describe Synge as a complete political naif, but a lack of interest in politics in an intensely political time and place is in itself striking.

A social identity, however, cannot be shed at will, and though Synge rejected the orthodox beliefs of his class, in the Irish context he remained an Anglo-Irish Protestant. An odd incident which he relates in the 'Landlord's Garden' essay suggests that he involuntarily retained some of the attitudes of his background. The 'garden' of the title was, we learn from Edward Stephens, the garden of Castle Kevin which had become overgrown since a boycott had forced the owners of the house to leave. Synge describes how he set out to catch an orchard thief, lying in wait one Sunday morning when all the household were at church. Most likely he had a sense of the ridiculousness of his position as landlord's watchdog guarding the fruit in a deserted garden; certainly the picture of him chasing the thief round and round the raspberry canes is thoroughly undignified. But there remains an instinct to defend the rights of property, a desire to protect the garden from the insult of

casual depredation. The description ends with a peculiarly humour-
less note. 'Yet it must not be thought that this young man was
dishonest; I would have been quite ready the next day to trust him
with a ten-pound note.' (*Prose* p. 233) Does anyone need to be told
that orchard-robbing is not necessarily a sign of dishonesty? This
reads like the disclaimer of a person who, at some level, still takes
his position as a property-owner quite seriously.

Particularly in Wicklow, it would have been difficult for Synge
to escape his class role. The Synges were a well-known Wicklow
family – the old man described in the essay 'The People of the
Glens' could trace back their genealogy and family history for a
hundred years – and anywhere in Wicklow he mentioned his name,
Synge would have been placed. People he talked to near Castle
Kevin, for example, would automatically use the forms of deference,
'your honour', 'sir', or 'Mr Synge'. On Aran he was more anony-
mous, a stranger rather than a familiar figure from the big house,
and a few friends like Martin MacDonough could even call him by
his Christian name. Synge caused indignation among nationalists
by the picture he gave of himself as the gentleman eavesdropper in
the Preface to *The Playboy*. 'When I was writing *The Shadow of
the Glen*, some years ago, I got more aid than any learning could
have given me, from a chink in the floor of the old Wicklow house
where I was staying, that let me hear what was being said by the
servant girls in the kitchen.' (*Plays* II p. 53)[10] No doubt the chink
was essential for him to learn how the girls talked among themselves, for they would never have spoken without constraint in his
presence. In fairness to Synge, however, we must bear in mind that
this is his home ground, and it is not entirely typical of his relation
to the people elsewhere in Ireland.

In one respect Synge's attitude was unmistakably that of his
class. There can be no doubt of the animus behind his remarks on
the Catholic middle classes. Shortly after the Playboy riots he
remarked in a letter to MacKenna (April 1907),

> the scurrility and ignorance and treachery of some of the attacks
> upon me have rather disgusted me with the middle-class Irish
> Catholic. As you know I have the wildest admiration for the
> Irish Peasants and for Irish men of known or unknown genius...
> but between the two there's an ungodly ruck of fat-faced, sweaty-
> headed swine. (*Prose* p. 283n)

Alan Price includes this passage in his edition of the *Prose*, and comments that it shows Synge's political acumen, his 'disdain for the man of money merely who manipulates the fruits of others' labours', his participation in Yeats's 'dream of the noble and the beggar man'. This is to speak in rhetorical euphemisms. Synge's outburst is founded not upon any ideal, but on instinctive class hatred. Hence, for example, the physical nature of the abuse, which we find also in Yeats's attacks on 'Paudeen' in *Responsibilities*:

> What need you, being come to sense,
> But fumble in a greasy till
> And add the halfpence to the pence
> And prayer to shivering prayer, until
> You have dried the marrow from the bone?[11]

Or, much later, in extreme form, in 'Under Ben Bulben':

> Scorn the sort now growing up
> All out of shape from toe to top,
> Their unremembering hearts and heads
> Base-born products of base beds.[12]

Unreasoning hatred, of class as of race, focuses upon physical characteristics. The attitudes of both Synge and Yeats are conditioned by the historical background, by the fact that it was the Catholic middle classes who, at the beginning of the twentieth century, succeeded in wresting power from the Anglo-Irish Ascendancy.

In the polemical pieces which Synge wrote against his nationalist critics we can see the intrusion of the same kind of social animus. In the fragmentary skit, 'National Drama', and the 'Letter to the Gaelic League', the ostensible purpose is to reveal the absurd narrow-mindedness of the nationalist ideals. In 'National Drama', a committee meets to discuss the 'Possibility, Origin and Future of an Irish National drama'. (It was written after the renewal in 1905 of the controversy over *The Shadow of the Glen*, which Arthur Griffith had claimed was not representative of the Irish national spirit.) The committee rejects as possible models Molière, Shakespeare, Ibsen and the Greeks for their immorality or decadence; Synge uses the great European writers – interesting that he includes Ibsen – to indicate the petty provincialism of the whole concept of 'national drama'. But it is by no means good-humoured satire, and the caricature traits attributed to the nationalists are suggestive. They are constantly gasping for a drink, anxious about the approach of closing time; although they protest loudly against the mention of sex in the drama, they have a prurient interest in chorus girls and dirty stories. It is a thoroughly unpleasant view of the Catholic nationalists with their ideals of national decency covering vices all the more sordid for being suppressed.

It was in the same vein that Synge, infuriated by the attacks on *The Playboy*, fulminated against the Gaelic League:

> I believe in Ireland. I believe the nation that has made a place in history by seventeen centuries of manhood, a nation that has begotten Grattan and Emmet and Parnell will not be brought to complete insanity in these last days by what is senile and slobbering in the doctrine of the Gaelic League. (*Prose* p. 399)

(Notice again the physical touch – senile and slobbering.) Though Synge is here supposedly defending the ancient Irish tradition, he selects as his examples of 'manhood' three Protestant patriots of the eighteenth and nineteenth century. We may guess that Synge, like many other Anglo-Irish liberals, hoped that the Ascendancy would continue to provide an intellectual and political élite for the new nationally independent Ireland. It was a shock when such leadership was rejected – Yeats's fury over the refusal of the Lane pictures is typical. Synge and Yeats both, nursing their bitten hands, turned violently on the nationalists whom they had tried to feed.

'I have the wildest admiration for the Irish peasants', Synge says in his letter to MacKenna. This admiration was perfectly genuine, and the charge of misrepresenting the Irish peasants in his plays was particularly grating. He prided himself on his knowledge of the people and his sympathy with them, and he refused to admit that his view could be mistaken. He wrote to Willie Fay, who was directing *The Well of the Saints*, about suggested changes, 'what I write of Irish country life I know to be true and I most emphatically will not change a syllable of it because A. B. or C. may think they know better than I do'. (*Plays* I p. xxiv) He was generous in acknowledging his dept to the people whose language he used in his plays. For him, the remote country areas of Ireland still held the values which he saw threatened by an urban culture; he disliked the Gaelic League partly because he saw it as one of the standardising urbanising influences in districts where there was a tradition of native Irish speaking. He was uneasy about the benefits of progress conferred on the people by a centralised government. In his articles for the *Manchester Guardian* on the distressed districts of Mayo and Galway, he was thorough and conscientious in suggesting remedies for the economic and social problems of the peasants. But privately in a letter to MacKenna he revealed his misgivings: 'In a way it is all heartrending, in one place the people are starving but wonderfully attractive and charming, and in another place where things are going well, one has a rampant, double-chinned vulgarity I haven't seen the like of' (*Prose* p. 283n).

Synge's attitude to the peasants has been a controversial issue, and it is perhaps worth stressing, therefore, how unusual it was for a man of his class and background. Compare, for example, *The Aran Islands* with an essay on Aran by Somerville and Ross, 'An Outpost of Ireland', which was published in 1906. It is written in the usual style of Somerville and Ross's travel pieces – ordinary enough description, with a sharp eye open for the ridiculous, for ludicrous scenes and characters, the material of anecdote. It is a professional job, and no doubt Edith Somerville and Violet Martin did not give it a great deal of thought, but the attitudes expressed are fairly typical. The people are observed with patronising amusement, with a genial mockery which is not intended to be unkind. They remark on the cooking facilities of Aran: 'To us, nurturing a sulky flame in a gloomy pile of turf, the truly Simple Life resolved itself into two words: good servants.'[13] This is, of course, a standard sort of joke, but it does suggest the complacency of their social attitude. In the face of the terrible poverty of Aran it even seems smug and heartless. Synge occasionally comments on the discomforts of his situation on Aran; apparently the people were very hurt by a remark he made in an article about giving him stewed tea. On the whole, however, he took things as he found them, and he was content to stay in the MacDonough's small cottage, to put up with the crying of the baby and the smoking of the fire. He could talk to people without self-consciousness or *gêne*, attend funerals, watch an eviction, listen to the story-tellers without causing embarrassment. Synge's presence was accepted frankly and simply. The observations of *The Aran Islands* or 'In West Kerry' show a really remarkable capacity for self-effacement.

For Daniel Corkery, a Gaelic writer and scholar and an ardent Irish nationalist, it was Synge's love of the people which saved him as a writer. Corkery's book, *Synge and Anglo-Irish Literature*, has been neglected and underrated because of its polemical bias. It starts with what is, admittedly, a provocative thesis – that Anglo-Irish literature, an Irish literature written in English, is an impossibility. All distinctive literature, according to Corkery, is national literature, and the Anglo-Irish, cut off by class, religion and culture from the Irish people, could produce only arid rootless work. Synge is the great, the portentous exception: 'to show how he stands apart from all his fellow Ascendancy writers, it is but necessary to state, that he, an Ascendancy man, went into the huts of the people and lived with them.'[14] Corkery argues that Synge must have been a nationalist, a 'cultural' rather than a political national-ist, although he admits that 'he never made himself familiar with all the tenets of that faith'.

Throughout *Synge and Anglo-Irish Literature* there is a striking conflict between polemic and aesthetic judgement. Corkery, we may guess, admired Synge's work almost in spite of his principles, and tried to rationalise his admiration accordingly. Hence the very doubtful argument about Synge's nationalism. Synge's genuine achievement is whittled down to *Riders* and *The Aran Islands*, the works of which an Irish nationalist can approve, and yet in Corkery's treatment of *The Playboy* or *The Shadow of the Glen*, both of which he attacks strongly, we can detect an undercurrent of appreciation. Even when Corkery considers Synge's feeling for the people, the basis of his 'cultural nationalism', he finds embar-rassing limitations. He distinguishes as 'the three great forces . . . working for long in the Irish national being [which] have made it so different from the English national being . . . (1) The Religious Consciousness of the People; (2) Irish Nationalism; (3) The Land.'[15] He remarks that of these three Synge never made any attempt to come to terms with the first, except in *Riders*. He sums up:

> If he failed to give us a true reading of the people . . . it was not from any want of sympathy with them. His sympathy with them was true and deep; but his range of mind was limited, and was not quite free from inherited prejudices. He saw in them what he had brought with him: he noted their delight in the miraculous, the unrestrained outbursts of emotion, they indulged in; he noted what their living so close to mother earth had made of them. He drenched himself in all the features of the physical world they moved in, but he made choice among the features of their mental environment. Of their spiritual environment he did not even do that same.[16]

This is well observed, and for any nationalist critic, even a sympathetic one like Corkery, it is inevitably seen as a weakness, a failure of understanding in Synge. To those less favourable, indeed, this selective vision amounts to deliberate exploitation of the people. Seamus Ó Cuisin in an article in *Sinn Fein* in 1909 was uneasy because 'we are not certain where the eavesdropper ends and the creator begins'.[17] The same sort of criticism was voiced by another nationalist writer, D. J. O'Donoghue, in his obituary of Synge, where he spoke of 'wondering at what appeared the exotic point of view of the writer' in *The Aran Islands*.[18] O'Donoghue expressed this criticism more forcibly in a later article:

> the whole of the plays seem to be so many experiments in a special vein, and essentially artificial. I have never been able to regard Synge as one who, living among a people, grows to be one of them, identifies entirely with them, and voices their thoughts and emotions, and interprets their every movement.[19]

This is undoubtedly correct. There were times when Synge, carried away by his admiration for the Aran islanders dreamed of becoming one of them. 'I told them I was going back to Paris in a few days to sell my books and my bed, and that then I was coming back to grow as strong and simple as they were among the islands of the west' (*Prose* p. 142). Much more often, however, he is conscious of his exclusion from their world.

> In some ways these men and women seem strangely far away from me. They have the same emotions that I have, and the animals have, yet I cannot talk to them when there is much to say, more than to the dog that whines beside me in a mountain fog. There is hardly an hour I am with them that I do not feel the shock of some inconceivable idea, and then again the shock of some vague emotion that is familiar to them and to me. On some days I feel this island as a perfect home and resting place; on other days I feel that I am a waif among the people. I can feel more with them than they can feel with me, and while I wander among them, they like me sometimes, and laugh at me sometimes, yet never know what I am doing. (*Prose* p. 113)

Synge speaks with regret, yet his position could not be changed; he remained as an observer among the peasants, a sympathetic outsider but an outsider nevertheless, unable to understand completely the people he observed and, at the deepest level, unable to communicate with them.

If then Synge's relations with the peasants were marred by what

Corkery calls his limited range of mind and 'inherited prejudices', could he, or did he share with them any sense of national identity? In 'National Drama' Synge speaks, through the character Jameson, of nationality in terms of landscape.

> An Irish drama that is written in Ireland about Irish people, and not on a foreign model will and must be national in so far as it exists at all. Our hope of it is that as Ireland is a beautiful and lovely country that the drama that Ireland is now producing may catch a little of this beauty and loveliness ... A beautiful art has never been produced except in a beautiful environment and nowhere is there one more beautiful than in the mountains and glens of Ireland. (Plays I pp. 224–5)

As an argument this looks fairly untenable – Wordsworthianism run mad – but it does suggest something of Synge's attitude to nationality. The Anglo-Irish commonly defined their feeling of difference from the English by allusions to the Irish scenery. Somerville and Ross, for example, write (in reproof of Kipling's Irishman in *Soldiers Three*), 'the very wind that blows softly over brown acres of bog carries perfumes and sounds that England does not know: the women digging the potato-land are talking of things that England does not understand'.[20] We may well doubt if Somerville and Ross themselves really understood the conversation of 'the women digging the potato-land', but the sense that they have a common ground, that they live in the same countryside, was perfectly genuine. For Synge, with his intense feeling for nature, the Irish landscape was of central importance.

A Russian analogy may be helpful here. Turgenev's *Huntsman's Sketches*, published between 1847 and 1851, is often considered a landmark in Russian literature as the first work in which the peasants were the main subject of interest. The collection of short stories is given unity by the narrator, who relates the incidents he has met with while out shooting. The stories often begin with a description of the weather and the terrain, setting out the circumstances of the day's sport. Characters and encounters are recorded by the way, and the most revealing glimpses of the peasants come when the narrator is disregarded, unseen or half asleep. Turgenev is consciously writing for a sophisticated audience; his role, or the role of the narrator rather, is that of the aristocrat/hunter mixing with the local people. 'Probably not many of my readers have had the chance to see the inside of a country pub; but we hunters –

we'll go anywhere.'[21] He realises that his presence may be an embarrassment to the peasants and tries therefore to be as un-obtrusive as possible. In 'Bezhin Meadow', for example, where he comes upon a group of boys spending the night round the camp-fire in charge of the village herd of horses, it is only after he pre-tends to fall asleep that they begin to tell their fairy-tales. He is an outsider, who is accidentally allowed a view of the life of the people as it really is.

Synge's position in the prose essays is very similar to the role Turgenev gives his fictional narrator. Synge also feels himself to be an intruder in the world of the peasants. He comments on his visit to the Blasket Islands: 'I know even while I was there I was an interloper only, a refugee in a garden between four seas.' (*Prose* p. 258) Synge, like the hunter, is to some extent without his class status, meeting the people in situations outside the normal area of social contact. But though class roles may be temporarily irrelevant, they are still there, and Synge is generally '*duine uasal*' – 'noble person' – just as Turgenev's hunter is addressed with the intimate feudal form, 'father'. They are accepted by the peasants as social anomalies, visitors from the world of the gentry who arouse brief curiosity but are otherwise received with indifference.

Turgenev and Synge are observers, observers who both have artistic interests. 'Bezhin Meadow' opens with a description of a July day, generalised to suggest the whole atmosphere of a hot summer's landscape. It is only after a protracted lyrical evocation that Turgenev returns to the particular instance of the story, the evening when he got lost and found himself in Bezhin meadow at the boys' camp-fire. Throughout the travel essays Synge uses the same counterpoint between description and narration, combining natural landscape with social observation and turning to specific anecdotes for illustration.

Synge and Turgenev want to show what it is like to live in a particular country. They see the relation between the natural environment and the people who live in it; they evoke local and national character through landscape. In the 'Bezhin Meadow' story Turgenev describes a typical hot summer day in a Russian province in order to prepare us to understand the atmosphere and spirit of the boys' Russian folklore. As he sets out in the morning, the dawn landscape has new meaning for the hunter:

Everywhere the heavy drops of dew reddened with diamonds of

light; towards me the sounds of bells were carried, fresh and clean, as if bathed in the morning cold. Suddenly, galloping past me after their night's rest, came the herd of horses, driven on by my friends the boys.[22]

The boys and all that he has learned about them are now a part of the scene. In the same way, Synge gives us the emotions aroused by contemplation of the Wicklow glens to suggest the character and ethos of those who live there.

For Turgenev, in contrast to Tolstoy, it is the landscape not the land which is the focus of attention. In *Anna Karenina* Levin's sense of national identity is based on the experience of the land which he shares with the peasants. It is while mowing with the workers in his meadows that he comes closest to identification with the people, and comes nearest to understanding them. For a time he is even tempted by the idea of joining a peasant community and giving up his estate. But he sees that this would be impossible, a false and sentimental decision, and that he must continue in his role as aristocratic master. He is divided from the people by immovable social barriers, and yet they can share a common feeling of the intimate relation to the land, even though such a sense is self-conscious only on Levin's side. The bond is the land which they work together. Turgenev's hunter is a landowner, but he apparently does not spend much time on his estate – for the purposes of the book he shoots all the year round. His meetings with the peasants are generally chance encounters, rather than part of the routine of his life as with Levin. The hunter is never directly identified, but we are given the impression of a youngish man who has spent a great deal of time abroad. Although he knows well, and can describe well, the varied appearance of the countryside, particular localities at particular times of year, he is not attuned to the ordinary continuum of the people's lives. To put it harshly, he is a dilettante. In 'The Singers', he is intensely moved by witnessing a singing contest in a village pub, where the singing of a folk-ballad seems to express the very spirit of the country. After hearing the song he leaves immediately, afraid of spoiling the impression. Sure enough when he looks in later, the poetic moment of the singing contest has developed into a regular drinking-bout. The hunter treasures the song as an 'epiphany', where for the peasants it is all in the day's drunk. *The Huntsman's Sketches* might have been sub-titled *Figures in a Russian Landscape*, for that is what we are given,

a series of striking tableaux of Russian life, pictorial if not picturesque.

It is worth emphasising here that Synge is closer to Turgenev
than to Tolstoy. Corkery stresses the importance of Synge's intimate knowledge of the countryside:

> Travelling through our quiet midland solitudes in a railway
> carriage I have often thought how different an experience it was
> from walking intimately in these same places, knowing whose
> the cattle were, what fair was to come or had come, whose
> cottage the spire of smoke was rising from in the distance; while
> all the time the nostrils were filled with the breathing of the
> earth and the ears with its stirrings. It is such essences of the
> landscape, of the people, of life itself, as will not pierce a
> sixteenth-inch pane of glass that makes the differences between
> national and what is now called international literature.[23]

Corkery's argument is that Synge was the only one of the
Ascendancy writers to get out of the train. But there is a further
distinction to be drawn. 'Knowing whose the cattle were, what fair
was to come' has a different significance for those who have owned
cattle or sold them at a fair, than for those who only look on.
Synge knew these things, but he knew them as a stranger. His
attitude to the countryside was not that of a man who had grown
up in it, had owned land or worked on it. It is rather that of the
naturalist, of the city child who from an early age is fascinated by
nature. The average 'countryman' – that is, the man who actually
works on the land – is frequently indifferent to the aesthetic effect
of landscape except at some subconscious level. It is the sportsman,
the angler or bird-watcher, those whose contact with the country
is in the nature of a holiday or escape, who most appreciate natural
phenomena in the aesthetic sense. All through his life Synge spent
alternate periods in urban and rural environments. In the years
between 1895 and 1902, he spent his winters in Paris, and returned
to Ireland for the summer; while he was director of the Abbey he
used to take off two to three months a year in Kerry, Connemara
or Wicklow. He was right to claim that he knew the Irish countryside, but he did not know it as an Irish countryman.

Yet in Synge, it is specifically a response to the Irish countryside,
as in Turgenev to the Russian landscape. A passage of 'In West
Kerry' in which he describes the people going to Mass in Bally-
ferriter is particularly interesting:

This procession along the olive bogs, between the mountains and the sea, on this grey day of autumn seemed to wring me with the pang of emotion one meets everywhere in Ireland – an emotion that is partly local and patriotic, and partly a share of the desolation that is mixed everywhere with the supreme beauty of the world. (*Prose* p. 240)

The response to beauty combined with the desolate feeling of its transience is to be found all through Synge's work, most of all in *Deirdre of the Sorrows* and in the poems. It is a personal 'theme'. But what are we to understand by 'local and patriotic'? Obviously it has nothing to do with 'public men and cheering crowds'. It cannot even include a reaction to the scene shared with other Irish people, for the people are a part of the scene. Indeed the very attitude suggests exclusion, watching from afar the community gathering for Mass – 'banned for ever from the candles of the Irish poor', as Louis McNeice puts it. In so far as this is a national emotion, we might describe it as aesthetic nationalism. It is the tenuous yet profound sense of an artist that his chosen subject is his in a very special way.

Irishmen have written well before Synge, but they have written well by casting off Ireland; but here was a man inspired by Ireland, a country that had not inspired any art since the tenth or twelfth century, a country to which it was fatal to return.[24]

This comment of George Moore's in *Hail and Farewell* is, in its way, a moving tribute from a failure to a success. Moore was himself of that older generation of Irish writers who felt that Ireland was a hazard to be escaped; for Moore, as for others, it had proved 'a country to which it was fatal to return'. Why did Synge succeed and in what way was he inspired by Ireland? It is possible to see some of the dangers he avoided. His rejection of his Anglo-Irish background, for example, enabled him to escape the problems of cultural identity which we find in Moore, or even in Shaw. With his European base, he by-passed the alternatives of allegiance either to England or Ireland which was the traditional Anglo-Irish dilemma. Yet, although he dissented from the stock social and political views of the Ascendancy, he remained a product of his background; he had much of the arrogance, the unconscious assumption of superiority of the upper class, and when this was challenged by middle-class Irish nationalists, his response was one of fury mingled with contempt. He was able, however, to centre his interest in Ireland away from the areas of social conflict altogether, in the remote country districts where issues of class or creed were not urgent.

It is here that we may begin to talk in positives rather than negatives, for if Synge was perhaps fortunate in avoiding problems of other Anglo-Irish writers, he was gifted with a unique feeling for what he saw among the Irish peasants. Here, indeed, we may fairly speak of inspiration. On Aran, and on the Blaskets, in Kerry, Connemara and Wicklow, he was passionately absorbed by the lives of the people. Where his imagination was caught he could watch them without self-consciousness or social embarrassment. But he watched from a centre of self which was tacitly acknowledged as wholly different and distinct from theirs. He looked at Ireland always, in his own phrase, 'with an eye that is aware of the arts also', that is, always with the detachment of an external vantage-point. In a situation of strong nationalist feeling this was inevitably seen as an 'exotic' view, the dilettante in search of the picturesque, or the satirist's caricature. However those who denied in Synge a sense of national identity wronged him. 'The national element in art', he claimed, 'is merely the colour, the intensity of the wildness or restraint of the humour.' (*Plays* I p. 225) Synge speaks here of his own experience of Ireland, of the intangibles which bound him to the scene he observed, which involved him with the life of the Irish people.

2
Synge's Aran

Give up Paris. You will never create anything by reading Racine, and Arthur Symons will always be a better critic of French literature. Go to the Aran Islands. Live there as if you were one of the people themselves; express a life that has never found expression. (*Plays* I p. 63)

Yeats's advice to Synge at their meeting in Paris in 1896 is one of the best publicised facts of modern literary history. Sceptical critics, suspicious of recollection coloured by hindsight, have questioned the authenticity of Yeats's account, but Synge himself let it stand in the Preface to *The Well of the Saints*, and in any case it hardly seems to matter whether the story is literally true. It is an appropriate myth. Yeats was an important influence on Synge's career, and the visit to Aran was a momentous turning-point. No one is likely to quarrel with the statement from the Greene and Stephens biography: 'Synge's visit to the Aran Islands in 1898 must be one of the most remarkable examples on record of how a sudden immersion in a new environment converted a man of ostensibly mediocre talent, a complete failure, in fact, into a writer of genius.'[1] But this change, though indeed astonishing, need not be regarded as an unaccountable miracle, a completely mysterious metamorphosis. We are in a position to look in detail at Synge's own description of the visits in *The Aran Islands* and at the notebooks he used on Aran, to try to analyse the reasons for the dramatic flowering of talent. We can watch from unusually close quarters the nature of this creative stimulus and attempt to define in what ways Aran was significant for Synge.

The first question to ask is, why did Synge go to Aran? He was urged by Yeats to 'express a life that has never found expression', but what form was such expression to take? We have to start by looking at what Synge may plausibly have thought he was going to find on the islands, the sort of factors which conditioned his decision to go. In 1898 he was a man of twenty-seven, of no fixed occupation, dabbling in the arts, living alone in Paris. In this life what can we relate to what followed?

The notebooks which Synge used in Paris show us a man putting himself through a conscientious course of self-education. He read a fair amount of contemporary literature – Mallarmé, Huysmans, Oscar Wilde, Anatole France are some of the names that recur – perhaps in preparation for a career as a literary journalist. He made use of what he read partly as a training for his own literary style. We find him, with characteristic literal-mindedness, copying down extracts, noting the number of words in individual sentences, and sentence structure within paragraphs. Where he has been reading Walter Pater's *The Renaissance*, he writes down his reaction in a passage headed 'Pater (Imitation)':

> You will find in him a fresh estimate of aesthetic things, perillous, it may be tinged (even) with (the most) harmful decadence, yet full of suggestion and spoken in a style . . . more flagrantly beautiful – more penetrated with the mysterious harmony of language than any other. He writes of Boticelli . . . Leonardo and many more drawing dreamy decadence from work, to us . . . natively robust. (MS 4378 f. 20v)

Synge was evidently attracted to the exotic elegance of Pater, and at the same time distrustful of his 'decadence'. The mixed emotions are equally characteristic of his attitude to modern French literature. Later on he dismissed scornfully 'Des Esseintes and all his ugly crew', but he must at one time have been interested in Des Esseintes' creator, Huysmans. There is an analysis of the colour symbolism of *La Cathédrale* in one of his notebooks, he reviewed *L'Oblat*, although without enthusiasm, for *The Speaker* in 1903, and there are echoes of *A Rebours* in his fragmentary 'Autobiography'. 'Etude Morbide', 'a morbid thing about a mad fiddler in Paris', as Synge described it to Yeats, is soaked in symbolist and decadent doctrine. Yet even in 'Etude Morbide', there is a reaction against the writers of the decadence:

> I have come out among the hills to write music again if I am able . . . All art that is not conceived by a soul in harmony with some mood of the earth is without value, and unless we are able to produce a myth more beautiful than nature – holding in itself

a spiritual grace beyond and through the earthly – it is better to
be silent . . . When I am here I do not think without a shudder
of the books of Baudelaire or Huysmans. (*Prose* p. 35)

Baudelaire and Huysmans are rejected as alien, artificial, unnatural.

Decadent French literature seems to have been one main pole of
Synge's interests around 1898; at the same time, perhaps in reaction,
he was drawn to the primitivism of Pierre Loti and the Breton folklore writer Anatole Le Braz. Loti and Le Braz in different ways
celebrate the virtues of the Breton peasant community at the
expense of the urban civilisation of the capital, the simple sanity of
the people living close to nature contrasted with the artifice and
hysteria of the metropolis. All this had an obvious appeal to Synge,
suffering from an overdose of introspective aestheticism. Much was
made at one time of the influence of Loti on Synge. However,
Synge's own remarks about Loti are contradictory, and the lushly
romantic *Pêcheur d'Islande* seems very unlike the austerity of
Synge's work. Anatole Le Braz may, perhaps, have been more
influential. Le Braz was the son of a village schoolmaster, a keen
Breton nationalist, who was best known for his collections of local
stories about the dead. We know that Synge heard him lecture in
1897, and in his 1899 Aran notebook there are notes on Le Braz's
La Légende de la Mort en Basse Bretagne. In an article written on
Le Braz for the Dublin *Daily Express* in January 1899, Synge gave
him the warmest praise and showed a considerable knowledge of his
work. In this article he refers indirectly to his own visit to Aran,
and it seems possible that Le Braz's Breton enthusiasm reawakened
his own college interest in the Celtic culture of Ireland.

Certainly the notebook Synge used on Aran in 1898 suggests a
similar purpose to that of Le Braz, for a principal object was the
recording of folklore. Pat Dirane, the old story-teller of Inishmaan,
supplied him with a series of tales, one of which he used as the
basis of *The Shadow of the Glen*. Synge's interest in these stories is
that of the folklorist, classifying, comparing and citing international
analogues. In his 1898 diary, on May 27 for example, he noted
'Histoire de P. Dirane Jack the Giant Killer and Perseus melangés'
(MS 4419 f. 66v). (The mixture of French and English is common
in the diary entries.) His first published article, which appeared in
The New Ireland Review in November 1898, was 'A Story from
Inishmaan', in which he glosses another of Pat Dirane's tables with
comments on its origins in European folklore.

Yet from the start Synge had literary ambitions for using the Aran experience; he had no notion of producing a semi-scientific collection of folklore as methodical as those of Le Braz. Even from his first visit Synge had some idea of publishing an account of Aran. We catch a glimpse of this intention in the remark with which he prefaces a description of one of the island 'duns' – the ancient forts – in the 1898 notebook: 'The antiquarian treasures of the islands are not strictly in the scope [of] my scattered . . . notes, and . . . have been often described' (MS 4385 f. 52v). This suggests that he had already a definite concept of the 'scope' of his work, with the deliberate exclusion of the archaeological material. This in itself seems a peculiar decision if the book was to appeal to readers for its description of a primitive culture. The modest reference to 'my scattered notes', the purple passages which turn up in the 1898 notebook, suggest that what Synge had in mind was a literary travel essay, where the interest is partly in the strangeness of the material, but partly also in the sensitivity of the observer and the beauty of his descriptions.

Here we can see that Synge did not altogether put aside his 'decadent' reading. He described his situation at the end of his first visit: 'A wet day with a close circumference of wet stones and fog showing only at my window and inside white wash, red petticoats, turf smoke, my long pipe and Maeterlinck.' (Prose p. 102n) (He was reading Pelléas et Mélisande.) Synge evidently savoured the incongruity of Maeterlinck's delicate refinement in the crude simplicity of his surroundings. He continued to express his reactions in highly literary, highly aesthetic terms – describing a striking girl he encounters: 'She is madonna-like, yet has a rapt majesty as far from easy exaltation as from the maternal comeliness of Raphael's later style' (Prose p. 54n) – or with a hyperaesthetic flight of fancy: 'What has guided the women of grey-brown western Ireland to clothe them in red? The island without this simple red relief would be a nightmare fit to drive one to murder in order to gloat a while on the fresh red flow of blood' (Prose p. 54n). When writing the first draft of the book in 1900–1, he included some passages which he omitted from the final text:

The charm I have found among these people is not easy to describe. Their minds have been coloured by endless suggestions from the sea and sky, and seem to form a unity in which all kinds of emotion match one another like the leaves or petals of a flower. When this atmosphere of humanity is felt in the place where it has been evolved, one's whole being seems to be surrounded by a scheme of exquisitely arranged sensations that has no analogue except in some services of religion or in certain projects of art we owe to Wagner and Mallarmé. (*Prose* p. 102n)

Synge is here still trying to describe the natural in terms of the artificial; he is the aesthete to whose cultivated senses nature gives the ultimate artistic sensation.

Synge went to Aran attracted by the ideal of the simple harmony of the lives of the peasants, to escape the decadent culture of Paris. He wrote of his first curragh trip to Inishmaan, 'It gave me a moment of exquisite satisfaction to find myself moving away from civilisation in this rude canvas canoe of a model that has served primitive races since man first went on the sea' (*Prose* p. 57). But even here, as he exults in his withdrawal from civilisation, his language is that of the decadence; the 'moment of exquisite satisfaction' is Pater's ideal in the famous 'Conclusion' to *The Renaissance*, it is the object of Des Esseintes' quest in *A Rebours*. Synge in 1898 was a dilettante, self-consciously cherishing his 'impressions', at his most imitative when he tried hardest to express his own reactions. Yeats's recollection of Synge's early work gives us an acute image of his failings: 'I have but a vague impression, as of a man trying to look out of a window and blurring all that he sees by breathing upon the window'.[2] Synge at this stage was indeed a prisoner of his own self-consciousness, and the window had to be shattered before he could develop into a creative artist.

It was a slow business learning to see on Aran. There is a curious mistake of perspective in the view of Synge's career which shows him transformed instantaneously into a writer of genius by his visit to Aran in 1898. It was not after all until 1902 that he wrote his first successful play, and throughout the period when he was working on *The Aran Islands* itself, he continued to write and revise the lamentable 'Etude Morbide', 'Vita Vecchia' and *When the Moon Has Set*. We can see, comparing the notebooks with the first draft of the book, the first draft with the final text, how gradually Synge found his way towards creativity. In view of the long-standing controversy about the origin of his dramatic dialect, the development of the language of the islanders is particularly interesting.

Writing in 1907 to the journalist Leon Brodzky, who was planning an article on his plays, Synge said,

> I look on *The Aran Islands* as my first serious piece of work – it was written before any of my plays. In writing out the talk of the people and their stories in this book, and in a certain number of articles on the Wicklow peasantry which I have not yet collected, I learned to write the peasant dialect and dialogue which I use in my plays. (*Prose* p. 47n)

It is worth looking in some detail at the stages in this learning process.

Among the collection of Synge manuscripts in Trinity College Dublin library there are some double sheets of foolscap which Synge used to copy down a story of Pat Dirane's, the story of Lady O'Conor which he gives in *The Aran Islands* (*Prose* pp. 61–4), and which he at one time tried to dramatise (*Plays* I pp. 208–14). This was the 'Story from Inishmaan' which he published in the *New Ireland Review*. In the article Synge claims that he has kept closely to the language of the story-teller, yet there are several differences between what he published and what he wrote down immediately after he heard the story. These changes are not, as we might expect, merely a matter of tidying up, but often involve an attempt to use more definitely Irish idioms than in the original. For example the published text reads:

> One day the son said to his father that he wished to marry his neighbour's daughter.
> 'Well', said the father whose name was O'Conor, 'try, if you think it good; but there is not gold enough with us to win her.'[3]

In the manuscript this final phrase was, quite simply, 'we are not rich enough to win her' (MS 4344 f. 403r). A characteristic Irish construction has been substituted for standard English. In the manuscript a man asks the young O'Conor, 'Are you wanting money?', which is, in fact, a turn of phrase often used in Ireland. But it was not Irish enough for Synge, who put in instead, 'Is it gold you might be wanting?'[4] Occasionally also there is a striking image in the article which does not appear in the manuscript, as when the neighbour's daughter is weighed against all the gold O'Conor can produce: 'Then they put them in the scales, the daughter in one side and the gold in the other, but the girl went down against the ground.'[5] In the original in place of this concrete description of the scales weighed down the last part of the sentence reads, 'the daughter was the heaviest' (MS 4344 f. 403r).

Of course it is possible that Synge wrote down the Lady O'Conor story in haste, and later recalled the actual phrases used and substituted them, but this seems unlikely, and one would expect the original manuscript to be closer to what he heard. The story was told to him in English, so he was not trying to catch the flavour of an Irish version. It is clear that, at this stage, he was not practised in the difficult technique of recording dialect accurately. Even in the published article the main style is standard literary English, and the Irish constructions seem oddly self-conscious. He wrote down the stories, when he heard them, in a language which at times is obviously not that of the speaker. For example, in one story recorded in manuscript, we find the patronising pomposity of a character who asks, 'Well my good man where may you be going?' (MS 4344 f. 399r) Elsewhere it is the pseudo-archaic style of the literary fairy-tale: 'He took out the sword and smote off at one [*pull*] blow the giant's head' (MS 4344 f. 399v). When preparing the Lady O'Conor story for publication, however, Synge probably realised that this style did not adequately represent the language of the *shanachie*, and consequently made a deliberate attempt to Gaelicise. In 1898 Synge was interested primarily in the stories he heard as folklore, in their content rather than their style, and no doubt he did not try particularly hard to capture the exact words of the story-tellers. But the principle of altering what he had recorded in the direction of a more evidently Irish style is a significant one, and it was to be applied much more thoroughly later on.

One of the most attractive features of *The Aran Islands* is its immediacy, the journal form which gives us the sense of Synge's experience as it happens. We can imagine him writing up his notes at the end of each day. In fact, this style was deliberately adopted when he was already at work on his draft of the book. On the sixth page of his typescript (MS 4344 f. 365r) he crossed out the sentence 'Late the next afternoon the rain cleared off', and substituted 'The rain has cleared off'. The rest of the text was then brought into line with this decision. Throughout the typescript, we can see Synge altering and revising always with a view to making his narrative more direct, more spontaneous, more dramatic. He imposed a discipline on his style, and tried never to use language which was out of character with the material he was describing. Vocabulary and syntax which tended to bring out the disparity between himself and the Aran people was excluded. Thus, for example, 'accompanying' becomes 'going with', 'rebuke' becomes 'check', and a reference to 'a relative of mine who was resident here for a while' is changed to 'who passed some time on the islands'. Synge's object in the great majority of stylistic changes is self-effacement. He wants to present Aran directly, to enable his readers to imagine themselves meeting and talking with the people. Words and phrases which draw attention to an educated and sophisticated narrator can only obscure and distance the vivid impression he is trying to convey.

Synge worked hard to achieve the effect of authenticity. Nowhere is this more striking than in the comparison of the notebook and the typescript versions of the story of the holy well, the source for *The Well of the Saints* (see *Prose* pp. 56–7). The opening of the story in the notebook reads as follows:

> A woman of Sligo had one son who was blind. [*One n*]
>   ed
> She dream [*ing*] of a well that held water potent to
> cure [*move with hope*] so she took boat with her
>   and came after long sailing   and she saw the shore
> son following the course of her dream, and reached Arran.
> She came to the house of my informant's father . . .
>
> (MS 4385 ff. 9r–9v, Plays I p. 263)

This was typed out with a few changes:

> She brought her son down by the coast of Galway, and took him out in a curragh [*going the way she had seen in her dream till she reached Aran. When she landed she came up to the house of the old man who was telling me the story which then belonged to his father*] MS 4344 f. 358r).

Clearly Synge saw that he was getting tied up in knots with explaining who was who, and he turned the whole passage into direct speech. The bracketed passage was crossed out, and instead he wrote in:

> landing below where you see a bit of a cove. She walked up to the house belonging to my father – god r. h. soul . . .

The final text reads like a direct transcription of the story in the original words, but all the 'authenticating' details – the gesture of 'below where you see a bit of a cove', the traditional blessing on the dead, 'God rest his soul' – these are afterthoughts of Synge. This is already the imagination of a dramatist rather than the description of a reporter.

Throughout the transcription of the Aran stories we can see Synge developing the dialect of his plays, actually learning to write it, as he himself said to Brodzky. Compare the opening of the Lady O'Conor story in the *New Ireland Review* with *The Aran Islands* text.

> There were two farmers in County Clare with farms not far apart. The one had a son, and the other, who was richer, a daughter.
> One day the son said to his father that he wished to marry his neighbour's daughter.
> 'Well', said the father whose name was O'Conor, 'try, if you think it good'.[6]

> There were two farmers in County Clare. One had a son, and the other, a fine rich man, had a daughter.
> The young man was wishing to marry the girl, and his father told him to try and get her if he thought well. (*Prose* p. 61)

In the first version relevant information is given as economically as possible; relative clauses are tucked away in the middle of sentences – 'the other, who was richer', 'the father, whose name was O'Conor'. In the revised form a phrase in apposition is substituted for one clause, 'a fine rich man', and the other relative is omitted, which makes necessary a parenthesis giving the young man's name later on in the story. Synge was aware that Irish syntax was mainly paratactic, using conjunction rather than subordination, and so when he tried to suggest the speaking voice of the story-teller, he cut out standard English subordinate clauses.

The process of change is the same elsewhere, as with the opening of the story which Synge referred to as Jack the Giant-Killer:

> There was once a poor widow who lived out in a wood with [*one*] her only son. (MS 4344 f. 399r)

This version from the manuscript is altered in the published text:

> There was once a widow living among the woods, and her only son living along with her. (*Prose* p. 84)

This participial construction, 'and' + noun + participle in place of a subordinate clause, is taken over from Irish. It was a favourite with Synge, and he used it again and again in the plays. A selection of examples show how the style of the stories was changed. (The specifically Irish forms are italicised.)

> they saw a ship coming in straight upon the rocks, and there were no sails on her at all. (*New Ireland Review* p. 153)
> . . . a ship coming in on the rocks, *and no sails on her* at all.
> > (*Prose* p. 62)

> so that he was not able to free himself (MS 4344 f. 399v).
> *the way he was not able* to free himself (*Prose* p. 85).

> the people saw the likeness of his raiment and wonder if he were the same man as fought on the day before (MS 4344 f. 401v).
> when the people saw him coming *there was great wonder on them* to know if it was the same man they had seen the day before (*Prose* p. 87).

> the ship was wrecked upon the rocks, and her load was tea and coffee and silk (*New Ireland Review* p. 153).
> She was wrecked on the rocks, *and it was* tea that was in her, and fine silk (*Prose* p. 62).

Not all of Synge's alterations, however, involved the substitution of Irish idioms for standard English forms. We can find examples where the change was in the opposite direction. In his typescript draft of the book he describes his enquiry for a dying woman:

> 'And how is the woman?' I said.
> 'It is only a little bit but lost she is.' (MS 4344 f. 305r)

This reply, though it is a literal translation of an Irish form, was clearly too clumsy, so Synge crossed it out and put in 'Nearly lost'. In the Jack the Giant-Killer story, when the young hero is asked where he is going, he answers: 'It is some where I am looking for where I can be given work to do for my living' (MS 4344 f. 399r). In Irish any word can be brought forward to the beginning of the sentence and introduced by the copula, 'It is'; but 'It is some where . . .' in this sentence was impossibly awkward in English, so it was changed to, 'I'm looking for some place where I can work for my living'. The habitual or frequentative, the 'do be' tense, is characteristic of Irish, and causes problems for all translators. In the version of a story given in Synge's notebook, a man looking for an 'officer' of the fairies 'came to where he did often used to frequent'

(MS 4385 f. 29v). This becomes in *The Aran Islands*, 'The poor man went down to the place where they used to see the officer' (*Prose* p. 82).

What appears in the original manuscripts of the tales Synge heard on Aran is a peculiar combination of story-book English with occasional barbaric-looking pieces of translation from Irish. The language in *The Aran Islands* is much more consistent. The uglier of the Irish phrases have been eliminated, while the staple constructions have been changed from literary English to colloquial Anglo-Irish. The speech sounds much more authentic, but it is a created authenticity. The language of the people is fashioned by Synge, not by transcribing what he heard, but by reworking it in accordance with his theoretical knowledge of Irish grammar and syntax, his sense of the genuineness of some phrases, his personal preferences for others. What emerges is the distinctive, the unique dialect of Synge's plays, the appropriate medium for his dramatic expression.

This development of language provides us with a pattern for understanding Synge's creative development as a whole. Just as the language of the stories is a version of the language he heard, so the picture he gives us of the islands is a version of Aran. 'In the pages that follow I have given a direct account of my life on the islands, and of what I met with among them, inventing nothing, and changing nothing that is essential' (*Prose* p. 47). There is no reason to question the accuracy of this statement of Synge's in his Introduction to *The Aran Islands*. He was no romancer, he had a great respect for factual truth, and much of the book is drab uncoloured description. But he saw Aran as it was significant for himself, and the normal selectivity of any individual's impressions is heightened to the level of artistic vision. John C. Messenger, assessing *The Aran Islands* as a source of anthropological data, remarks that 'it suffers from primitivism, a lack of concern with the importance of Catholicism in the lives of the folk, and the projection of the author's tragic view of life into his interpretations'.[7] Considering these distortions and omissions by comparison with other accounts of life on the islands may take us some way towards defining Synge's personal view of Aran.

'Primitivism' Messenger defines as 'the idealisation of past or future cultural estates or of contemporary primitive and folk cultures'.[8] It is the attitude which Synge shared with Loti and Le Braz. Throughout *The Aran Islands*, 'primitive', 'simple', 'ancient' are the characteristic words of praise, just as 'modern' is a term of disapproval. One of Synge's primitivist ideals is the islander as all-round man:

> Each man can speak two languages. He is a skilled fisherman, and can manage a curagh with extraordinary nerve and dexterity. He can farm simply, burn kelp, cut out pampooties, mend nets, build and thatch a house, and make a cradle or a coffin. His work changes with the seasons in a way that keeps him free from the dulness that comes to people who have always the same occupation. The danger of his life on the sea gives him the alertness of a primitive hunter, and the long nights he spends fishing in his curagh bring him some of the emotions that are thought peculiar to men who have lived with the arts. (*Prose* pp. 132–3)

This is an attractive picture of versatile self-sufficiency, and we can see a trace of personal identification in Synge's final sentence. But it is not quite accurate. Messenger points out that 'many men choose not to fish because they are unable to develop the requisite talents, are prone to severe sea-sickness, or are overly wary of the dangers associated with fishing'.[9] No doubt the majority of islanders would have tried their hand at all the occupations Synge mentions, but Tom O'Flaherty in *Aranmen All* tells us that most of them had one specialty, fishing, farming or kelp-burning. The point is obviously not an important one, but it does suggest the spirit of Synge's interpretation. Modern man in a developed society is increasingly helpless, an incompetent who depends on a sustaining web of technology; primitive man by contrast is the master of his own environment.

Messenger speaks of a 'lack of concern with the importance of Catholicism in the lives of the folk'. It is the same complaint which Corkery made against Synge, his inability to understand the 'spiritual environment' of the people. In this context there are striking omissions. Synge mentions very few of the churches on Aran, not even the churchyard in Killeany which is supposed to contain the bodies of 128 saints. The only church he even alludes to, in fact, is the Teampal Ceathair Aluinn – the Church of the Four Beautiful Persons – which he was to use for its resonant name in *The Well of the Saints*. The ordinary religion of the people he regarded as uninteresting or even vaguely distasteful. He tells of a conversation with Old Mourteen in which 'he gave the Catholic theory of fairies'. This, a vivid piece of imaginative folk belief,

Synge recounts with evident interest, but switches off when Mourteen moves to more orthodox material. 'From this he wandered off into tedious matters of theology, and repeated many long prayers and sermons in Irish that he had heard from the priests.' (*Prose* p. 56) He comments on the 'cheap religious pictures – abominable oleographs' which a pedlar who visits Aran has for sale; he is pleased to note that they did not find many buyers (*Prose* p. 139). Such pictures are to be seen everywhere in Catholic Ireland and they very often evoke this sort of Protestant reaction of disgust. The reaction is rationalised – the pictures are 'cheap', they are in sentimental bad taste – but perhaps at a deeper level they remind Protestants of the 'superstitious idolatry' in their neighbours' lives which they would prefer to forget.

Synge is not anti-Catholic in *The Aran Islands*. He speaks with admiration of the local curate, and describes a typically genial encounter with him:

> A couple of Sundays ago I was lying outside the cottage in the sunshine smoking my pipe, when the curate, a man of the greatest kindliness and humour came up, wet and worn out, to have his first meal. He looked at me for a moment and then shook his head.
> 'Tell me,' he said, 'did you read your Bible this morning?'
> I answered that I had not done so.
> 'Well, begob, Mr. Synge,' he went on, 'if you ever go to Heaven you'll have a great laugh at us.' (*Prose* pp. 162–3)

This sort of good humour between Protestant and Catholic has always been a common feature of Irish life, but it is based on mutual tolerance rather than mutual understanding. Synge was often aware of the barrier of religion between himself and the people. He speaks of the recurring 'shock of some inconceivable idea', and goes on to describe a young girl with whom he used to talk. 'Below the sympathy we feel there is still a chasm between us. "Musha," she muttered as I was leaving her this evening, "I think it's to hell you'll be going by and by."' (*Prose* p. 114) Synge felt great sympathy for the people of Aran, admired them and identified with them. Profoundly agnostic himself, he wanted to see them not as the devout Catholics they no doubt were, but as people whose orthodox Catholicism barely covered primitive pagan attitudes. At the first funeral he attended on Aran, when they had finished keening, an old man kneeled down by the grave and repeated a simple prayer for the dead'. Synge commented that 'there was an irony in these words of atonement and Catholic belief spoken by voices that were still hoarse with the cries of pagan desperation'. (*Prose* p. 75) It is an irony especially apparent to Synge, and it is clear that he felt that the 'cries of pagan desperation' came from a deeper source of feeling than the 'words of atonement and Catholic belief'.

The 'tragic view' of Aran in *The Aran Islands* and *Riders* is so compelling that few readers have stopped to consider whether it is accurate. Messenger tries to correct a common image of life on the islands: 'A recurring motif in writing about Inis Beag is the threatening sea and heavy loss of life among fishermen with its attendant psychological depression. In the past century, only four sea accidents have occurred in the island with the loss of 12 lives.'[10] Synge himself acknowledges at one point in *The Aran Islands* that 'accidents are rare'. It is presumably unlikely, therefore, that Maurya should lose six sons, her husband and father-in-law in sea accidents. Strictly speaking Synge is exaggerating when he describes his emotions after a funeral:

> As they talked to me and gave me a little poteen and a little bread when they thought I was hungry, I could not help feeling that I was talking with men who were under a judgement of death. I knew that every one of them would be drowned in the sea in a few years and battered naked on the rocks, or would die in his own cottage and be buried with another fearful scene in the graveyard I had come from. (*Prose* p. 162)

With the qualifying reference to those who might die in their beds, Synge just stops himself from claiming that all Aran men die by drowning.

Of course this is not to say that Synge 'got it all wrong', or that we can disregard *Riders* because it is founded on mistaken statistics. But it is worth reminding ourselves that there were other ways of looking at life on the islands. The description of the keen, for example, is one of the most eloquent passages in *The Aran Islands*:

> The grief of the keen is no personal complaint for the death of one woman over eighty years, but seems to contain the whole passionate rage that lurks somewhere in every native of the island. In this cry of pain the inner consciousness of the people seems to lay itself bare for an instant, and to reveal the mood of

beings who feel their isolation in the face of a universe that wars on them with winds and seas. They are usually silent, but in the presence of death all outward show of indifference or patience is forgotten, and they shriek with pitiable despair before the horror of the fate to which they are all doomed. (*Prose* p. 75)

Contrast this with the account of a keen at another old woman's funeral, on the Blasket islands, observed by the young Maurice O'Sullivan in *Twenty Years A'Growing*:

It was for Kate Joseph's voice I listened, for she was reputed to be like a banshee for keening.
'Oh, musha, Kate,' she began with a fine tune on the words, 'isn't it you were the graceful woman, and it is little profit for me to live after you, olagón! olagón! olagón!'
When they had finished keening I saw them laughing merrily with one another.
'Musha, Tomás,' said I, 'do you think they are lonesome at all after old Kate Liam?'
'Yé, my sorrow, no more than the seal-cow back in Bird Cove.'[11]

The two descriptions are not incompatible; Synge like O'Sullivan comments on the abrupt change back to everyday behaviour, the men after the funeral, 'talking of anything, and joking of anything, as if merely coming from the boat-slip, or the pier' (*Prose* p. 75). It is the difference of viewpoint which is striking. O'Sullivan is attending a virtuoso performance, with a boy's delight in watching the grown-ups and detecting their hypocrisy. To Synge it is intensely serious, and he gives to the keen an imaginative interpretation. If this is not necessarily the people's conception of keening, or what they intend by it, it is nevertheless for Synge what the keen expresses.

We can pick out now the outstanding features of Synge's Aran, the image of the islands which moved and inspired him so deeply. The Aran islands lie off the west coast of Ireland, at the extremest edge of the continent of Europe. They are cut off from the mainland, and this isolation was obviously one of their main attractions for Synge. But at the same time Aran could be seen as related to Europe. Synge comments at the end of the story of Lady O'Conor:

It gave me a strange feeling of wonder to hear this illiterate native of a wet rock in the Atlantic telling a story that is so full of European associations.

The incident of the faithful wife takes us beyond Cymbeline to the sunshine on the Arno, and the gay company who went out from Florence to tell narratives of love. It takes us again to the low vineyards of Würzburg on the Main, where the same tale was told in the middle ages, of the 'Two Merchants and the Faithful Wife of Ruprecht von Würzburg.' (*Prose* p. 65)

Synge's feeling of wonder is partly just the surprise of seeing patterns familiar to him from his reading reappear in this popular illiterate context. At the same time, he is struck by the idea of one essential European culture, diffused even to this 'wet rock in the Atlantic'. What is exciting is not that Pat Dirane tells a story which appears in Shakespeare and Boccaccio, but that the story is so universal, so archetypal in the European imagination. Arthur Griffith was quite wrong to argue that Synge foisted on the Irish in *The Shadow* a decadent literary version of the Widow of Ephesus tale out of Petronius. In dramatising a folk-story which he not only knew in its literary form but had actually heard on Aran, Synge could feel that he was basing his work on a representative, an aboriginal fable.

The Aran islanders were conscious of their isolation, interested in what was happening on the mainland. 'Is there any war in the world at this time, noble person', Synge is asked repeatedly. Beyond Aran is *an domhain mor*, the big world, which can be contrasted and compared with the little world of the islands. 'In the big world', says Maurya, 'the old people do be leaving things after them for their sons and children, but in this place it is the young men do be leaving things behind for them that do be old.' (*Plays* I p. 13) They are surprised when Synge, an experienced traveller in the world outside, can find something new to him on Aran. 'One of them said to me yesterday ... "isn't it a great wonder that you've seen France, and Germany, and the Holy Father, and never seen a man making kelp till you come to Inishmaan?"' (*Prose* p. 77)

Aran is quite literally a microcosm, a small world. In it Synge could see the basic human situation without the irrelevancies of a high civilisation, or the complication of an elaborate social structure. It was small enough to be perceptible as a whole, it offered images which were primary, representative, central. Synge's emphasis on the primitive quality of life on Aran is not just naïve idealisation of the 'noble savage'. By a return to a primitive milieu, he felt that he escaped from the accidental features of contemporary urban life, and reached essential truths. In Aran he found a community relatively untouched by the standard concepts of the 'big world' – progress, modernity, centralisation. He valued it accordingly, not only as it was archaic, traditional and picturesque, but as it showed 'the thing itself, unaccommodated man'.

Aran certainly affords little 'accommodation' to the men who live there. 'A bare starving rock' the Saint calls it in *The Well of the Saints*, and it is almost incredible that people should survive in the terrain Synge describes:

> Aran came in sight. A dreary rock appeared at first sloping up from the sea into the fog; then as we drew nearer a coastguard station and the village.
>
> A little later I was wandering out along the one good roadway of the island, looking over low walls on either side into small flat fields of naked rock. I have seen nothing so desolate. Grey floods of water were sweeping everywhere upon the limestone, making at times a wild torrent of the road, which twined continually over low hills and cavities in the rock or passed between a few small fields of potatoes or grass hidden away in corners that had shelter. Whenever the cloud lifted I could see the edge of the sea below me on the right, and the naked ridge of the island above me on the other side. (*Prose* p. 49)

The 'small flat fields of naked rock' are normal on Aran, tiny little plots fenced with stone walls which are constructed simply to get rid of the stones. The land for cultivation had to be made; seaweed and sand were collected, mixed and spread in order to create soil. Natural clay was rare and extremely precious, and Synge describes how 'a slight bank of earth under the wall of the yard' at the cottage he lived in was transported on donkey-panniers to a 'field' which was about to be made. On Aran in Synge's time, an industry which was almost equally laborious was the production of kelp, the fertiliser made from burned sea-weed:

> The work needed to form a ton of kelp is considerable. The seaweed is collected from the rocks after the storms of autumn and winter, dried on fine days, and then made up into a rick, where it is left till the beginning of June. It is then burnt in low kilns on the shore, an affair that takes from twelve to twenty-four hours of continuous hard work. (*Prose* p. 77)

The struggle to survive on Aran meant enormous work for tiny returns.

Synge may have exaggerated the frequency of accidents, but the dangers of fishing from light canoes in the Atlantic were undoubtedly real. Many of the accidents in fact happened because men were careless or drunk, and Synge's own account of travelling in a curragh brings home to us what a slight lapse of concentration it would take to be fatal. An old man explained to him the value of caution: ' "A man who is not afraid of the sea will soon be drownded," he said, "for he will be going out on a day he shouldn't. But we do be afraid of the sea, and we do only be drownded now and again".' (*Prose* p. 117)

There is more here than commonsense. The sea is a terrible enemy to be mollified with awe and respect, not challenged by arrogant pride. The intimate desperate battle with the sea was an essential part of Synge's image of Aran.

The alternative to fishing or farming under these conditions was emigration. It may be statistically implausible that Maurya should have lost six sons at sea, yet many Aran mothers must have seen all their children leave for America, a loss often as absolute as death. 'The maternal feeling is so powerful on these islands that it gives a life of torment to the women. Their sons grow up to be banished as soon as they are of age, or to live here in continual danger on the sea' (*Prose* p. 108). Emigrants do come back, but often in unhappy circumstances, as in the case of the 'native who had spent five years in New York', whose return Synge described:

> He came on shore with half a dozen people who had been shopping on the mainland, and walked up and down the slip in his neat suit, looking strangely foreign to his birthplace, while his old mother of eighty-five ran about on the slippery seaweed, half crazy with delight, telling every one the news. When the curaghs were in their place the men crowded round to bid him welcome. He shook hands with them readily enough, but with no smile of recognition.
> He is said to be dying. (*Prose* p. 96)

The stark irony of the final sentence, so characteristic of Synge's style, makes us realise with a jolt the attitude of the emigrant who only comes home to die.

In the Aran islands Synge saw men in a continual struggle for life and livelihood. Their adversary was the natural universe itself, not only the sea which threatened death, but the barren rock which forced them to leave or starve. In such a setting, man is constantly confronted with the harshest facts of his condition, his helplessness and his mortality. Synge understood this as an essentially pagan situation. In the underlying mournfulness of the people, in their fierce outbursts in the face of death, he saw the primitive response to the tragedy of human existence.

But if nature was man's enemy on Aran, if frequently he seemed to be alone in a hostile natural universe, it was also what gave beauty and distinction to the lives of the islanders. 'I cannot say it too often, the supreme interest of the island lies in the strange concord that exists between the people and the impersonal limited but profound impulses of the nature that is round them.' (*Prose* p. 75n) Their fight with the sea itself is a form of communion. Synge describes a curragh trip between two of the islands.

> Our lives depended upon the skill and courage of the men, as the life of the rider or swimmer is often in his own hands, and the excitement of the struggle was too great to allow time for fear. I enjoyed the passage. Down in this shallow trough of canvas, that bent and trembled with the motion of the men, I had a far more intimate feeling of the glory and power of the waves than I have ever known in a steamer. (*Prose* p. 120)

The Aran islanders have a more direct and immediate sense of their natural environment than people in a developed society. They tell the time by the sun – Synge's gift of a clock caused a sensation – and the change of the wind turns around the life within the cottages. Synge comments on how wearing pampooties, the cow-hide mocassins of the island, taught him 'the natural walk of man'. 'The absence of the heavy boot of Europe has preserved to these people the agile walk of the wild animal, while the general simplicity of their lives has given them many other points of physical perfection.' (*Prose* p. 66)

Synge is always on the verge of sentimentalism here, sometimes over the verge:

> Every article on these islands has an almost personal character, which give this simple life, where all art is unknown, something of the artistic beauty of mediaeval life. The curaghs and spinning-wheels, the tiny wooden barrels that are still much used in the place of earthenware, the home-made cradles, churns, and baskets,

are all full of individuality, and being made from materials that are common here, yet to some extent peculiar to the islands, they seem to exist as a natural link between the people and the world that is about them. (*Prose* pp. 58–9)

This is Synge's reaction to what is 'quaint' and picturesque; it is improbable that it would be the feeling of the islanders who make the cradles, churns and baskets. There are passages which are even more self-indulgent:

these men of Inishmaan seemed to be moved by strange archaic sympathies with the world. Their mood accorded itself with wonderful fineness to the suggestion of the day, and their ancient Gaelic seemed so full of divine simplicity that I would have liked to turn the prow to the west and row with them for ever.

(*Prose* p. 142)

This is completely spurious. It is the feeling of someone impressed by the unfamiliar sounds of a language he only partly understands, for who ever thinks of the language they speak normally as 'full of divine simplicity' or even 'ancient'? Synge is so brimful of his own emotion that it sloshes over on to the men, the day, even their ordinary conversation.

Synge is constantly trying to find in the islanders an emotion comparable to his own in the appreciation of nature, but they have none of his self-conscious awareness. Although he can find analogies between his own sort of emotions and those of the Aran people, it is only occasionally and intermittently.

The continual passing in this island between the misery of last night and the splendour of to-day, seems to create an affinity between the moods of these people and the moods of varying rapture and dismay that are frequent in artists, and in certain forms of alienation. Yet it is only in the intonation of a few sentences or some old fragment of melody that I catch the real spirit of the island, for in general the men sit together and talk with endless iteration of the tides and fish, and of the price of kelp in Connemara. (*Prose* p. 74)

Synge speaks almost as if the talk of the men was deliberately trivial, a perverse attempt to conceal their own deepest interests. But presumably the tides and the fish, the price of kelp are the day-to-day subjects of concern, and the superior 'reality' of the melodic fragments is Synge's own judgement. The 'real spirit of the island' is what he finds significant, the spirit of a people whose lives have the dignity, grace and harmony of those in simple and profound relation to their natural environment. The life he sees is the life he imagines, if we are clear that to imagine is not to invent, but to shape and select images from the available range of phenomena.

In a passage of his 1898 notebook Synge described the impact of the Aran experience:

> If a man could come with a full power of appreciation and stand for the first time before a woman – a woman perhaps who was very beautiful – what would he suffer? If a man grew up knowing nothing of death or decay and found suddenly a grey corpse in his path what would [he] suffer? Some such emotion was in me the day I looked first on these rising magnificent waves towering in dazzling white and green before the cliff. (*Prose* p. 97n)

Aran was enormously important to Synge because it represented this sort of primary contact with reality. The reaction here is an aesthetic one, but it is an aesthetic reaction to what is undeniably, unmistakably out there. It made it possible for him to reject the solipsist view of the decadents, most eloquently expressed by Pater:

> Experience, already reduced to a group of impressions, is ringed round for each of us by that thick wall of personality through which no real voice has ever pierced on its way to us, or from us to that which we can only conjecture to be without. Every one of those impressions is the impression of the individual in his isolation, each mind keeping as a solitary prisoner its own dream of a world.[12]

Aran was not merely Synge's dream of a world, it was really real. After the visit to Aran Synge could say with the certainty of Gautier, 'Je suis un homme pour qui le monde extérieur existe.'

This was all-important, because for Synge the artistic vision had to be underwritten by what he knew to be reality. He commented in a late notebook:

> Man has gradually grown up in this world that is about us, and I think that while Tolstoy is wrong in claiming that art should be intelligible to the peasant, he is right in seeking a criterion

for the arts, and I think this is to be found in testing art by its compatibility with the outside world and the peasants or people who live near it. (*Prose* p. 351)

The experience of a primitive community was significant as it provided an ultimate test of reality. The people were closer to basic truth in that they were closer to nature, and they lived their lives without self-consciousness. Where Synge found his own deeply-felt ideas and beliefs supported by the intuitive experience of a community, they were verified into absolutes. At such points it became possible for him to withdraw almost completely from the narrative; his 'opinions' became unnecessary, and he could concentrate on the sustained effort of making the life he saw live before the eyes of his readers. It was a crucial transition in the development of a dramatist.

3
The Vision of *Riders to the Sea*

We carry in our minds models of a writer's development – graphs on which we trace parabolas of gradual change with marked stages for juvenilia, increasingly successful experimentation, maturity and decline. In the case of *Riders to the Sea*, the graphs have to be scrapped altogether. It was written in the summer of 1902, at the very beginning of Synge's career as a working dramatist, and therefore it ought to have been an apprentice-work, in which Synge could be seen learning his trade. It is, of course, no such thing; to many people's way of thinking it is Synge's most perfect play, literally a masterpiece, the first accomplished work of a master craftsman. It is one of the two plays by which Synge's name is known, and it is performed perhaps even more often than *The Playboy*. Not only in technique, but in mood and theme, it seems an extraordinarily mature work to come from a novice.

However, it is not only the play's success which is striking, but also the uniqueness of that success. *Riders* is unlike Synge's other plays, certainly very unlike the four comedies which were to come immediately after it. We are conditioned into thinking of it as representative of his work, if only because it is so well known, although in form and spirit it is quite different from *The Shadow*, *The Playboy*, even from *Deirdre of the Sorrows*. It is the only play Synge set on Aran, a fact which is seldom emphasised. When he went to Aran for the fifth time just after completing *Riders*, he can have had no idea that it would be his last visit, and he planned several trips later which did not come off. Yet looking at the whole pattern of his career, it seems significant that he never returned to the islands. After 1902 Synge turned his attention towards other parts of Ireland – Wicklow, Kerry, Connemara. At the same time he concentrated on writing a particular sort of bitter comedy very different from the one-act tragedy he had achieved in *Riders*. If we cannot place *Riders* on a climbing graph of artistic development, we can perhaps set it in perspective in Synge's career as the appropriate expression of one phase of his experience before a change to other fields and other forms.

Synge was meticulous about the authenticity of the props used in the first production of *Riders* in 1904. He wrote to Michael Costello on Inishere asking about flannel and pampooties, and wanted to be certain that the clothing he was being sent was the same that was worn on Inishmaan. (The unnamed 'island off the West of Ireland' of *Riders* is definitely Inishmaan.) He was very anxious that the spinning-wheel used in the production should be brought along when the play was put on in London. Later he suggested that Sarah Algood, who played Cathleen, should be taught to spin, so that there would be 'no fake about the show' (*Plays* I p. xix). There is good reason for insisting on realism, for the props are peculiarly important in the play. Imagine the items on a stage-manager's list:

bread	flannel shirt
spinning-wheel	stick (blackthorn?)
turf	sail
bundle (bit of	plank
shirt and stocking)	jug (holy water)
boards	new rope

In the course of the play we have our attention drawn to all of these things, many of them several times, and they must be sufficiently real to sustain scrutiny. There are only a few objects in the cottage, but each one has its function in the dramatic structure. At the centre of the play are the two deaths of Michael and Bartley and the props which weave in and out of the action constantly direct us towards an awareness of these two figures. One way to approach *Riders* is to follow such lines of attention through the play, and to show how they help to create its dramatic texture.

The play opens with Cathleen alone on stage: she 'finishes kneading cake, and puts it down in the pot-oven by the fire; then wipes her hands, and begins to spin at the wheel' (*Plays* I p. 5). The moment's activity before Nora's entry gives the audience time to take in the scene, and the actions themselves, baking bread by an open fire and working at a spinning-wheel, establish the routine which is about to be interrupted. Nora carries in a bundle, and Cathleen's concentration on her spinning stops abruptly when she is told that it contains 'a shirt and a plain stocking were got off a drowned man in Donegal'. They are to try to see whether the shirt and stocking can be identified, whether the dead man is their brother Michael. The door blowing open, thoughts of Michael's loss, Nora's mention of the young priest, lead Cathleen on to her present fears for Bartley – will the young priest 'stop Bartley going this day with the horses to the Galway fair?' For a moment attention turns outward to the state of the wind and the sea, but then back in to the immediate problem, the bundle on the table in front of the girls. They cannot look at it now as their mother may interrupt them at any time, so Cathleen hides it up in the turf-loft. We follow Cathleen's glance round the set as she searches for a hiding-place, and we realise fully the bare poverty of the cottage where a stray parcel would be immediately obvious.

As Maurya comes in, Cathleen is forced to cover up her action:

Maurya (looking up at Cathleen and speaking querulously). Isn't it turf enough you have for this day and evening?
Cathleen. There's a cake baking at the fire for a short space (throwing down the turf), and Bartley will want it when the tide turns if he goes to Connemara. (*Plays* I p .7)

We saw the cake go into the oven, we hear now why it is needed, and we are back with the question of whether Bartley will go to Connemara. When Bartley himself enters he is looking for 'the bit of new rope' which he needs to make a halter for the mare, to ride down to the pier. (Synge comments in *The Aran Islands* on the islanders' way of riding without a bridle, with only a bitless halter.)

Maurya.   You'd do right to leave that rope, Bartley, hanging by the boards. (Bartley takes the rope.) It will be wanting in this place, I'm telling you, if Michael is washed up tomorrow morning, or the next morning, or any morning in the week, for it's a deep grave we'll make him by the grace of God. (*Plays* I p. 9)

The rope hangs beside the boards, which we notice now for the first time, and the two go together. Maurya uses Michael as an argument against Bartley's going; for if Bartley is away, who will make the coffin from the white boards, and without the rope how will he be lowered into his grave. Maurya pleads, but Bartley will not listen and continues with his work knotting the rope. As he gives detailed instructions to Cathleen for the farm-work in his absence, he concentrates on the halter with the exaggerated air of business-like hurry of someone who is deliberately avoiding an emotional scene.

He makes himself ready for the journey – 'lays down the halter, takes off his old coat, and puts on a newer one of the same flannel' – without another word addressed directly to his mother. Maurya's complaints from the fireside are all the more poignant for Bartley's deaf activity. 'Isn't it a hard and cruel man won't hear a word from an old woman, and she holding him from the sea?' (*Plays* I p. 11)

Cathleen reproaches her mother for sending Bartley off 'with an unlucky word behind him, and a hard word in his ear' but she pays no attention, she is lost in her misery. 'Maurya takes up the tongs and begins raking the fire aimlessly without looking round' (*Plays* I p. 11). Once again the girls' attention, and with them the audience's, is drawn back from an uneasy awareness of Bartley's exit to the focal point of the fire – and from the fire to the bread. Nora scolds Maurya:

> *Nora* (turning towards her).   You're taking away the turf from the cake.
> *Cathleen* (crying out).   The Son of God forgive us, Nora, we're after forgetting his bit of bread. (She comes over to the fire.)
> (*Plays* I p. 11)

After a moment's dismay, Maurya is sent off to pursue Bartley and give him the bread. We hardly know whether to admire the ingenuity of Cathleen in devising a satisfactory pretext for getting her mother out of the house so that she and Nora can examine the bundle, or the deft skill of Synge in making every link in the dramatic sequence so convincing. As Maurya moves towards the door to carry the bread to Bartley, she supports herself on the stick her dead son Michael left behind. Once again the direct attention to one brother is echoed by the allusion to the other.

The girls are left to themselves, and after they have checked to make sure Maurya is not returning, the bundle is taken down. Their talk circles round the circumstances – what the young priest said, how the body was found and how far away – but all the time the bundle itself is the centre of uneasy attention. We can feel the strain as Cathleen fumbles with the knot, the mixture of eagerness, anxiety and dismay as they take out the 'bit of a shirt and a stocking'.

> *Cathleen* (in a low voice).   The Lord spare us, Nora! Isn't it a queer hard thing to say if it's his they are surely? (*Plays* I p. 15)

Nora goes to look for Michael's shirt to compare the material but it is not on the hook, and Cathleen guesses that Bartley must have taken it, 'for his own shirt was heavy with the salt in it'. The shirt does correspond to 'a bit of a sleeve was of the same stuff' as Michael's, but this is not decisive. Final certainty comes when Nora identifies the stocking:

> Nora (who has taken up the stocking and counted the stitches, crying out).   It's Michael, Cathleen it's Michael; God spare his soul, and what will herself say when she hears this story, and Bartley on the sea?
> Cathleen (taking the stocking).   It's a plain stocking.
> Nora.   It's the second one of the third pair I knitted, and I put up three score stitches, and I dropped four of them. (Plays I p. 15)

Suddenly with these pathetic scraps of clothing in front of them the physical absence of Michael fills the room; the clothes vividly realise the loss of his everyday life among them: 'isn't it a pitiful thing when there is nothing left of a man who was a great rower and fisher, but a bit of an old shirt and a plain stocking?' (Plays I p. 17)

Maurya is heard coming back, the bundle is hastily stowed in the chimney corner, and a normal scene is recomposed with Cathleen once again at the spinning-wheel. Bartley has never been far from our minds throughout the preceding scene, but now with the recurrent switch of attention from Michael to Bartley we expect to hear news of him from Maurya. Maurya comes in silently. The girls notice that she still has the bread in her hands, the bread she was sent to give to Bartley. She ignores their questions to her, and begins 'to keen softly, without turning round', until Cathleen is finally provoked:

> God forgive you; isn't it a better thing to raise your voice and tell what you seen, than to be making lamentations for a thing that's done? Did you see Bartley, I'm saying to you. (Plays I p. 17)

Unconsciously Cathleen betrays her knowledge; the death of Michael, for which she imagines Maurya is keening, is now 'a thing that's done'. But Maurya has something else to lament. Cathleen, anxious for the safety of Bartley, looks out the window and is reassured: 'God forgive you; he's riding the mare now over the green head, and the grey pony behind him'. But the reassuring sight of Bartley alive and well is turned into terror:

> Maurya (starts, so that her shawl falls back from her head and shows her white tossed hair. With a frightened voice). The grey pony behind him . . . (Plays I p. 19)

The vision which Maurya now describes is the centre of the play; it is at once climax and catastrophe. Everything that has gone before has prepared us for it, everything that comes after is foreseen in it:

> Maurya. I went down to the spring well, and I stood there saying a prayer to myself. Then Bartley came along, and he riding on the red mare with the grey pony behind him (she puts up her hands, as if to hide something from her eyes). The Son of God spare us, Nora!
> Cathleen. What is it you seen?
> Maurya. I seen Michael himself.

It is a surprise, a shock – Michael is dead and buried in the far north, the clothing taken from his body is lying in a corner of the cottage. And yet at some deeper level it is immediately accepted that Michael, who has shadowed Bartley in our attention throughout, should have appeared behind his brother.

> I'm after seeing him this day, and he riding and galloping. Bartley came first on the red mare; and I tried to say 'God speed you', but something choked the words in my throat. He went by quickly; and 'the blessing of God on you', says he, and I could say nothing. I looked up then, and I crying, at the grey pony, and there was Michael upon it – with fine clothes on him and new shoes on his feet. (Plays I p. 19)

The 'fine clothes', such clothes as Michael perhaps never possessed in his life, are the appropriate signs of his ghostliness. At the same time there are associations from what we have already seen: the 'bit of an old shirt and a plain stocking' which identified Michael's body, the shirt of Michael's which Bartley put on in the morning, which he is wearing at that moment. It is not simply ominous that Bartley has donned the garb of the dead. A succession of images are offered – the clothes a man puts on going out to sea, the clothes stripped from a drowned man, and the spectral clothes of the returning dead.

Maurya now begins the long threnody which continues almost unbroken until the end of the play. In it the threads remain the same, and the familiar objects complete the pattern. The white boards, which were intended for Michael, Maurya now orders for her own coffin. 'Bartley will be lost now, and let you call in Eamon and make me a good coffin out of the white boards, for I won't live after them.' (*Plays* I p. 21) Eamon and Colum are asked to make a coffin at the end, but it is for Bartley not his mother. The men at work on the coffin will eat the new cake of bread which Cathleen was baking when the action started. At one point Maurya will not believe that Michael is certainly dead:

> There does be a power of young men floating round in the sea, and what way would they know if it was Michael they had, or another man like him, for when a man is nine days in the sea, and the wind blowing, it's hard set his own mother would be to say what man is in it. (*Plays* I p. 23)

(There is a horror in hearing the colloquial 'his own mother wouldn't know him' with literal meaning.) So the clothes are produced from the chimney corner to prove the identification. In the scene that follows, they represent Michael in Maurya's last blessing on her dead sons:

> Maurya drops Michael's clothes across Bartley's feet, and sprinkles the Holy Water over him ...
> Maurya stands up again very slowly and spreads out the pieces of Michael's clothes beside the body, sprinkling them with the last of the Holy Water. (*Plays* I p. 25)

Before they identified his dead body; here they symbolise his soul.

There is a simple satisfaction in the economy principle by which *Riders* is constructed, where every object serves a multiple function and the most casual stage properties are used as pivots for the action. Yet the props are never given the artificial emphasis of melodrama – Lady Windermere's fan style. They serve their normal purposes, and neither the characters nor the audience regard them as unnaturally significant. Michael's stocking is a plain stocking, only identifiable because Nora can remember knitting it. The clothes of the household are interchangeable – Bartley takes Michael's shirt when his own is wet. The rope which Bartley is looking for is hanging up out of the way of the pig with the black feet who was eating it. The function of the bread, the spinning-wheel, the white boards is to establish the ordinary reality of the lives we are watching, as much as to provide a focus for a particular sequence of events. It is the very ordinariness of these objects, their unchanging actuality, which gives them their strength. There is a special poignance in the simple objects which remain there before us, like rocks with the tides of human emotion eddying round them.

The action of the play is, at once, a day in the life of an Aran family, and a quite exceptional, a unique event. An ordinary time-scale is transcended by the single moment of quite extraordinary drama. The protagonist, Maurya, sees with a different vision, lives according to a different rhythm from those around her. When Bartley leaves, she cries out in despair: 'He's gone now, God spare us, and we'll not see him again. He's gone now, and when the black night is falling I'll have no son left me in the world.' (*Plays* I p. 11) This is not just the pessimism of extreme fear; it has a finality – enforced by the suggestiveness of the 'black night' – which cannot be resisted. Nora and Cathleen are anxious for Bartley's safety, Maurya *knows* that he will be lost. The vision itself brings together the past death of Michael with the future death of Bartley. From Maurya's point of view, indeed, Bartley's death is not in the future. She has seen two dead sons riding to the sea, and for all Cathleen's glimpse of Bartley through the window, his continuing life is more of an illusion than the image of death she has witnessed. From Michael and Bartley Maurya moves back in reverie to the other sons she has seen drowned, and as she recalls the death of Patch, we see the actions she describes repeated in mime:

There was Patch after was drowned out of a curagh that turned over. I was sitting here with Bartley, and he a baby, lying on my two knees, and I seen two women, and three women, and four women coming in, and they crossing themselves, and not saying a word. I looked out then, and there were men coming after them, and they holding a thing in the half of a red sail, and water dripping out of it – it was a dry day, Nora – and leaving a track to the door.
(She pauses again with her hand stretched out towards the door. It opens softly and old women begin to come in, crossing themselves on the threshold, and kneeling down in front of the stage with red petticoats over their heads.)

Maurya (half in a dream, to Cathleen).   Is it Patch, or Michael, or what is it at all? (*Plays* I p. 21)

The flash-back fades into the present and through Maurya's eyes we see the dead Bartley carried in representing all the other deaths.

With the body of Bartley in front of her, Maurya speaks 'as if she did not see the people around her'. She is, in fact, alone with her dead. She remembers all her suffering, and she looks ahead to rest, thinking of the anxious winter months of the past and the empty winters of the future:

> They're all gone now, and there isn't anything more the sea can do to me. . . . I'll have no call now to be up crying and praying when the wind breaks from the south, and you can hear the surf is in the east, and the surf is in the west, making a great stir with the two noises, and they hitting one on the other. I'll have no call now to be going down and getting Holy Water in the dark nights after Samhain, and I won't care what way the sea is when the other women will be keening. (*Plays* I pp. 23–5)

In her final speech she asks a blessing not only for Bartley and Michael, and her other dead sons, but for 'everyone is left living in the world'. Maurya is no longer simply a mother mourning the death of her sons; she is a visionary facing death itself, resentful and angry, terrified, bitter, and finally resigned.

But at the same time Synge sketches in the ordinary world of the islanders against which the figure of Maurya, made extraordinary by her situation, is set. At the opening of the play, Maurya has been in a stupefied state of grief since the loss of Michael nine days before, but for Nora and Cathleen and for Bartley, the concerns of everyday living continue. If Bartley is going to sea, he will need to take food with him. The pig with the black feet should be sold if there is a good price going. Michael's death means that there is only one man in the household and the girls will have to work all the harder. No one else in the play can sustain the concentrated passion of grief which absorbs Maurya; for the younger people there must be the occasional relief of irrelevance. Nora, although very distressed by Michael's death, yet takes a story-telling interest in rehearsing the details the priest told her of how the body was found. ' "There were two men", says he, "and they rowing round with poteen before the cocks crowed, and the oar of one of them caught the body, and they passing the black cliffs of the north." '

(*Plays* I pp. 13–15) Later she is naïvely surprised at Maurya's apparent indifference to Bartley's death:

> She's quiet now and easy; but the dày Michael was drowned you could hear her crying out from this to the spring well. It's fonder she was of Michael, and would any one have thought that? (*Plays* I p. 25)

Cathleen, the elder of the two girls, is very much in charge of the household, directing, deciding, arranging everything that goes on. She manages her mother with slight impatience at her old woman's ways, and her characteristic tone of voice is half scolding: 'You didn't give him his bit of bread? . . .' 'Did you see him riding down? . . .' 'God forgive you; isn't it a better thing to raise your voice and tell what you seen, than to be making lamentation for a thing that's done?' (*Plays* I p. 17) On both sides it is the bickering relationship of a mother with the daughter who is superseding her. We can imagine how habitual is the niggling attack on Cathleen's management in Maurya's opening words: 'Isn't it turf enough you have for this day and evening?' When Bartley is giving Cathleen instructions, Maurya breaks in petulantly:

> *Bartley.* Let you go down each day, and see the sheep aren't jumping in on the rye, and if the jobber comes you can sell the pig with the black feet if there is a good price going.
> *Maurya.* How would the like of her get a good price for a pig? (*Plays* I p. 9)

Maurya no longer lives in the normal world of the island, but in a world apart. She pleads with Bartley, 'If it was a hundred horses, or a thousand horses you had itself, what is the price of a thousand horses against a son where there is one son only?' (*Plays* I p. 9) Her plea is brushed aside as irrelevant or unrealistic, and it is answered indirectly by Cathleen: 'It's the life of a young man to be going on the sea, and who would listen to an old woman with one thing and she saying it over?' (*Plays* I p. 11) There is scarcely a positive feeling here that it is fitting that a young man should go to sea, as an appropriately manly life. It has rather the blank neutrality of a statement of fact. It is just as valid as Maurya's complaint; the two attitudes belong to different orders of truth. Again in the little incident of the nails, towards the end of the play, we recognise a similar duality:

Cathleen (to an old man kneeling near her).   Maybe yourself and Eamon would make a coffin when the sun rises. We have fine white boards herself bought, God help her, thinking Michael would be found, and I have a new cake you can eat while you'll be working.

The Old Man (looking at the boards).   Are there nails with them?

Cathleen.   There are not, Colum; we didn't think of the nails.

Another Man.   It's a great wonder she wouldn't think of the nails, and all the coffins she's seen made already.

Cathleen.   It's getting old she is, and broken. (*Plays* I p. 25)

This comes between Maurya's two great speeches, and its triviality is used to place her in perspective. What we, the audience, experience as a visionary communion with death, the other characters in the play see as a loss of touch with reality. Neither we nor they are mistaken.

For the ordinary people of Aran there is an expected and accepted pattern to their lives. Men must continue to work in spite of accidents; if there is likely to be a good horse fair in Connemara, one cannot hold back simply because there may be bad weather; a woman grows old having children and running a household, and at a certain stage she can no longer manage. Things are accepted in their order, not with a particularly deep sense of significant pattern, or with any very sharp resentment at their harshness. But in moments of extraordinary intensity, a more profound awareness is revealed. Synge dramatises one such moment in which the image of death is seen in all its timeless power against the normal sequence of events, in which Maurya through a life-time's suffering is brought to an absolute vision standing free of the individual event. While this vision makes its full dramatic impact, it is given reality and force by the everyday life of the community in which it is rooted, and yet which it transcends.

The success of *Riders* has been so seldom questioned that it is interesting to read the dissenting view of Malcolm Pittock, who argues that the play fails just because of its use of Maurya's vision. 'It is . . . one thing for Maurya to see a vision and to believe that vision fulfilled, but quite another for a modern audience, formed in a different cultural pattern, to believe in such superstition with any real seriousness.'[1] For Pittock the emotional response which we are expected to give to the vision is at odds with the detached and objective reality of Aran as we are shown it in the rest of the play. 'As a result the play is a mixture of tragedy and melodrama, that is to say it offers two incompatible attitudes to the experience it presents: one that takes it seriously and one that exploits it sensationally.'[2] This is a plausible argument, yet it conflicts with the experience of most readers, audiences and critics of *Riders*. The play does not fail in the way Pittock suggests, but his article is helpful in making us consider why it should succeed. How does Synge make us believe in a central incident which in cold blood we might call folk-superstition? Why does the vision not interfere with our sense of the reality of the drama? Why ultimately does a play concerned with a life which is alien and peripheral to our experience engage us with an immediate and profound sense of tragedy?

One way to answer these questions has been to look beneath the surface realism of *Riders* for images of mythical, religious or literary origin. For many critics, the strength of the play and its effectiveness depends not only on the skill of its construction, but on symbolic echoes which relate it to basic sources in our culture. The bare simplicity of the action is amplified by a network of oblique references which extend it in the minds of the audience to universal proportions. The 'grey pony', for example, on which Michael appears is frequently identified with the 'pale horse' of *Revelation*. 'And I looked, and behold, a pale horse: and his name that sat on him was Death, and Hell followed with him.'[3] Or again from *Revelation* there is the description of the bride of the Lamb: 'And to her was granted that she should be arrayed in fine linen, clean and white'; did Synge have this passage in mind when he described the ghostly figure of Michael 'with fine clothes on him, and new shoes on his feet'?[4] The bread which appears so often in the play is thought to have sacramental significance, or at least 'Maurya's failure to give it to her son has in it something of the negation of a sacrament'.[5]

This sort of approach seems not quite appropriate to the play. There is a literal reality about the action in *Riders* which is intractable to allegorical or symbolic interpretation. The very physical difference between the cake of coarse home-made soda bread and the communion wafer makes an identification of the bread as the sacrament implausible. As we have seen, an audience is conscious of the bread throughout the play, from the time Cathleen puts it down to bake in the opening moments, to the final scene where it is offered to the men who are to make Bartley's coffin. But it is

important as it is representative of the ordinary continuum, and it
has no special or heightened significance. We must retain a distinction between the dramatic representation of the theatre and the
very specialised drama of ritual.

In some cases it seems unnecessary to look for a Biblical source
for the images of *Riders*, where we have clear evidence of their
origin in *The Aran Islands*. A boy on Inishmaan told Synge several
stories of ghostly apparitions, including one of a man 'away' with
the fairies: 'A little while ago Patch Ruadh saw him going down the
road with broga arda (leather boots) on him and a new suit.' (*Prose*
p. 165) (On Aran where everyone normally wore pampooties, *broga
arda* in themselves would be a rarity.) There can be little doubt that
Synge had this story in mind in his description of Michael, or if
there was any, it is removed by a manuscript draft of the play in
which he has 'fine clothes and strong boots on his feet'. (*Plays* 1
p. 239)

Again the source of the 'grey pony' which Michael rides has
often been pointed out in a story Synge heard about a woman taken
by the fairies. She returned home to feed her child, and described a
'hosting' which was about to take place where her friends might
rescue her:

> she told them [the fairies] would all be leaving that part of the
> country on the Oidhche Shamhna, and that there would be four
> or five hundred of them riding on horses, and herself would be on
> a grey horse, riding behind a young man. (*Prose* p. 159)

It seems very probable that the detail of the horse's colour stuck in
Synge's mind. However it is always possible to invoke the slippery
concept of multiple source, and argue that he may also have recol-
lected the 'pale horse' of the Apocalypse, and that the figure of
Michael is thus associated with Death itself. But it seems a mistaken
context for Maurya's vision, and the association feels incongruous.
The grey pony is too literally a horse which Bartley is taking to sell
at the fair in Connemara to make it easy to accept it as an analogue
of the phantasmal allegorical figure of *Revelation*. The imaginative
mode of the two images is totally different.

The supernatural in Synge is oddly matter-of-fact and un-
mysterious. Stephen MacKenna, who was very interested in the
occult, was surprised to find Synge, the 'lean and hungry sceptic',
more certain of the existence of occult phenomena than he was
himself.[6] In *Riders* he presented Maurya's vision as though there

could be no doubt that she actually saw what she said she saw. No one in the play questions its reality; the level-headed and practical Cathleen immediately accepts the implication of the vision – 'It's destroyed we are from this day. It's destroyed, surely.' It is accepted that the apparition of Michael means the death of Bartley. Significantly it is the grey pony which Michael rode that causes Bartley's death. Bartley does not die, as all his brothers have, in the course of his work, as a result of the natural hazards of the fisherman's life. His death, though by the sea, is an exceptional accident. It is as though Michael were responsible, helping to bring his brother to death. If we are looking for analogues here, we should not be thinking in terms of the apocalyptic image of the four horsemen, but of the folk concept of the conspiracy of the dead. The dead are commonly thought to return to claim the living – hence the elaborate precautions of St John's Eve or Hallowe'en to placate the dead souls and prevent them from doing mischief. Michael passes into the service of the 'great majority of souls', and he comes to force Bartley to join all his other brothers. In the conflict with the sea, every defeat adds another enemy to those fighting for their lives. The apparition of Michael is not an arbitrary omen, ominous merely in that it is uncanny – a piece of folk-superstition exploited for sensational effect; nor, however, is it an archetypal figure for Death. It is a sharply realised image of the active malevolence of death which grows out of a particular dramatic context.

Far-reaching symbolic associations are rare in Synge, and in *Riders* his dramatic imagination works wholly within the realm of the life and culture of the Aran people. The simple action has an inviolable actuality which cannot be translated into the grand but shadowy world of symbols. If he has to overcome the problem of making folk-belief plausible to a sophisticated audience, he does not achieve it by the use of depth-imagery which is mythologically respectable. Where the Aran community have the unthinking belief of faith, Synge wins from his audience the willing suspension of disbelief by the strength and actuality of his dramatic image. The mystery and terror surrounding death are concentrated into a single moment, to which the audience are forced to accede, not as a piece of superstition experienced by a primitive community, but as a completely immediate and certain dramatic truth. We not only believe that Maurya saw Michael on the grey pony, we believe Michael was there.

*   *   *

The success of *Riders*, however, is not a purely technical achievement, the manipulation of the Aran experience for dramatic effect. Although it is not a symbolic work which takes us beyond its own reality, it does depend for its effectiveness on factors extrinsic to the life it represents. Synge's sophistication involves a familiarity with ideas and attitudes beyond the range of the island situation. The relationship between Christian and pagan becomes an issue of the play; variations of resentment and resignation make up a complex of emotions aligning it with the great tragedies. Synge and his audience share a cultural frame of reference which gives to the bare action of *Riders* the depth and resonance of a major work of art.

The final scene illustrates the way in which Synge keeps close to the reality he has observed, and yet makes of it a dramatic experience which lives within the world of artistic universals. The source of the play's famous last line is to be found in an Irish letter from Martin Macdonough, which translates literally as follows:

> it fell out that the wife of my brother Seaghan died, and she was buried the last Sunday of the month of December and look! that it is a sad story to tell, but if it is itself, we must be satisfied because nobody can be living forever. . .[7]

In spite of the similarity of the wording, however, this is different in spirit and effect to Synge's version. Martin's remark is a commonplace backed up by his Catholicism. If one believes in the afterlife, one must show resignation in the face of death and be satisfied, not only because death is inescapable, but because death is the beginning of everlasting life. All this is lightly present in Martin's comment, not personally felt but casually accepted. But in *Riders*, this easy Christianity is troubled by the deeply pagan emotion which Synge was always quick to detect beneath the surface of Aran Catholicism. The representative of orthodoxy in the play is the unseen 'young priest', who is obviously a controlling authority on the island. He is in charge of the identification of Michael's clothes; he is in a position to stop Bartley going to Connemara; his words of consolation, as Nora recounts them, are felt to have a special, an almost oracular force: 'let you not be afraid. Herself does be saying prayers half through the night, and the Almighty God won't leave her destitute . . . with no son living.' (*Plays* I p. 5) But to Maurya, he is no more than an ignorant young man speaking empty words of comfort – 'It's little the like of him knows of the sea' (*Plays* I p. 21). The terrible fact of the sea's hostility leaves no room for a pious hope in the justice of a Christian God. The conflict between Maurya and the Sea can end only in her bitter acknowledgement of defeat: 'They're all gone now, and there isn't anything more the sea can do to me.'

And yet the conclusion of the play is Christian in tone:

> May the Almighty God have mercy on Bartley's soul, and on Michael's soul, and on the souls of Sheamus and Patch, and Stephen and Shawn . . . and may He have mercy on my soul, Nora, and on the soul of everyone is left living in the world. (*Plays* I p. 27)

The blessing with the last drops of holy water is a moving and fully felt expression of devotion. But this is a Christian resignation which has been hard-won, much more impressive than the words of Martin's letter because it has been seen to overcome the pagan feeling of bitter resentment. Synge could not easily accept the Christian attitude, for struggling against it is his intense awareness of the finality of death. We see in Maurya not the serenity of the simple believer, but a peace which is close to emotional exhaustion, literally 'calm of mind, all passion spent'.

Again and again critics have compared the effect of the play's ending to that of classical tragedy. There seems to be a danger here of establishing *Riders* as an imitation Greek tragedy in little, dressed up in peasant outfit. In a play written in dialect, any hint of literary influence tends to suggest artificiality, and to say that the final line of *Riders* recalls Milton, Sophocles or Aristotle makes it look as though Maurya has been spuriously manipulated by her creator to achieve a literary effect. The ending of the play can come to seem too perfect an instance of 'catharsis', a text-book application of the Aristotelian principles.

Milton and Sophocles do hover around the final lines of the play, but they do not compromise the authenticity of Maurya. Resonance is added to Maurya's words by their congruence with the *loci classici* of literature, but the words are Maurya's own. She arrives by her own path at the same attitude expressed by Milton at the end of *Samson Agonistes*, or by Sophocles at the end of *Oedipus at Colonus*. The force of generations of human experience distilled as literature is added to her spontaneous expression, and we are aware as she speaks her simple words that she speaks also for all those before her in the same situation. The recurrent pattern of tragedy is re-enacted with the intense sense of loss met by the sorrowful mood of resignation. The great commonplaces of literature draw strength from one another, they do not grow banal from repetition.

Not everyone, however, has agreed that *Riders* is successful in recreating the form and spirit of Greek tragedy. Several critics, beginning with James Joyce, have argued that it lacks the just dimensions of classical tragedy – it has an end and a beginning but no middle. After some slight exposition, indeed, it is all catastrophe. It has neither conflict nor development, and should therefore be considered pathetic rather than tragic. Bluntly, *Riders to the Sea* is thought to be too short.

However, *Riders* depends for its success on its shortness. It is not a potential three-act tragedy undeveloped, for at its centre there is a single image which dominates the whole play and which could not be expanded. There is a necessary proportion between the frozen moment of Maurya's vision and the brief span of action which surrounds it. *Riders* could not be made to last for five minutes more without running into morbid sentimentality. It appears as though a great deal has been compressed into a short space of dramatic action, but without such compression the play could not exist at all. A woman's last two sons are killed at sea. In the sense of the series of deaths she has witnessed, for one moment we feel that we are given an epitome of all man's experience. But it is, and it can be, for a moment only.

The issue in *Riders* is life against death, or rather death against life – that simply and no more. Life is seen as passive endurance, its activity barely sketched in to provide a ground for the dominant figure of death. The play's stark austerity has been celebrated as one of its most classical features, but the overall effect here is very different from that of a full-length Greek tragedy. Thus far the neo-Aristotelian criticisms are justified. Aeschylus and Sophocles have a complex and fully religious vision of man's life, concerned not only with the fact of death, but with the vain efforts which man makes to understand his fate, and his mysterious relationship with the supernatural powers. Such a sense is present only vestigially in *Riders*, certainly not as the continuing and developing experience we find in Greek tragedy. The Greek tragic pattern involves a gradual process of understanding in which the audience, through the chorus, live out the god-given way from bewilderment to illumination. Synge's play presents instead a single powerful instant of revelation, a vision of men as riders to the sea.

*   *   *

The composition of *Riders* is a unique moment of balance in Synge's career, in which mind and materials coalesced without strain or friction. Sudden death seemed omnipresent on Aran, with disease as well as drowning a constant threat. Yet its very actuality, the fact that the islanders lived with it from day to day, made it impossible for Synge to dramatise it with the morbid hysteria that we find in the early poems. He loved and admired the Aran people, even to the point of idealisation. But whereas in *The Aran Islands* this admiration occasionally runs over into sentimentality, in *Riders* it is fittingly expressed through the simplicity, grace and dignity of the characters' words and actions. The Christian faith of the people, which Synge normally rejected, in this context was modulated into a mood of tragic resignation to which he could give his real sympathies. This is the balance of creative harmony, where vision finds embodiment in reality, and reality is shaped into vision.

But the perfection of *Riders* is achieved within limits, limits of range which Synge applied nowhere else in his work. He never again wrote a play so entirely consistent in tone, so completely unified round a single theme and a single image. *Riders* could not be imitated or repeated. Daniel Corkery shrugs his shoulders regretfully:

> To ask why Synge let this theory of the overwhelming importance of the imagination waylay him into cheap things when he had it in him to create *Riders to the Sea*, is very much like asking why John M. Synge was John M. Synge. Even had his advisers bidden him to write more plays like this masterpiece, and fewer plays like *The Tinker's Wedding*, one cannot feel that any good would have come of it.[8]

No, indeed. The theme of the imagination and the ironic satiric techniques of the comedies were essential to Synge's creativity and they could not be accommodated within the Aran setting of *Riders*. For Corkery *Riders* is on a level far above Synge's other work – 'If he had not written *Riders to the Sea* he would not only have been a less great writer, but he would have been an infinitely less great writer' – but he recognises that it is unique, out of character with the rest of the plays. We may perhaps contest his view that *The Shadow, The Well of the Saints* or *The Playboy* are cheap things, and argue that the move from *Riders* on to the comedies was necessary to the fulfilment of Synge's capacity as a dramatist.

Riders, in a sense, exhausted the possibilities of Aran for Synge. It was the perfect setting for the one-act tragedy, in which no idiosyncracies of temperament, no particularities of situation complicated the stark image presented. Its very perfection, however, the idyllic life of unified social harmony which he saw there, made it unsuitable as a setting for the sort of comedy Synge went on to write, in which social variation and conflict are often crucial. His view of the peasant community in the comedies is much more complex and more critical; it includes elements of mockery and satire of which he was incapable with the Aran people. In turning from Aran to other parts of Ireland, to areas far less 'unspoiled', he found different sorts of affinity and different kinds of inspiration. In the comedies which were created out of his experience in Wicklow and Kerry, he reveals a capacity for cool irony, a taste for the grotesque, and an exuberant delight in gaiety which are only partially present in the solemn, sombre Aran works.

4

The Development of Dialect

It was while at work on *The Aran Islands* in 1900–1 that Synge first learned to write the language of his plays, and by 1902 when he completed his first peasant plays the basic structure of the dialect was established. From then on, during the period he was working on the comedies, he was always on the look-out for words and phrases which he could use as a playwright, and his notebooks nearly all have a sprinkling of Anglo-Irish idioms. Many of these do reappear in the plays – so many, in fact, that it seems as if Synge's well-known boast was justified: 'In writing *The Playboy of the Western World*, as in my other plays, I have used one or two words only, that I have not heard among the country people' (*Plays* II p. 53). However there were also phrases which he invented, and when he entered these in his notebook he was careful to distinguish them from those he had actually heard by signing or initialling them. Thus for example, in a notebook used on his visit to Kerry in 1905, we find, ' "That seven thousand + seventy devil may play goals with your scull" J. M. Synge.' (MS 4401 f. 11r) This was clearly too many devils even for Synge, and in *The Playboy* Christy was made to curse his father somewhat less hyperbolically: 'May I meet him with one tooth and it aching, and one eye to be seeing seven and seventy divils in the twists of the road' (*Plays* II p. 125).

Such studies in dialect are on the same principle as the little 'imitations' of the style of the decadents which appear in the early reading notebooks, and they highlight the ambiguous character of Synge's dramatic dialogue. From one point of view the language is naturalistic, in that the characters frequently use the very words of their real-life counterparts. And yet, at the same time, the dialect is a studied artifact, exploited by Synge for poetic and dramatic purposes. This is a very special version of the commonplace paradox of all forms of realism, where artifice is used to simulate reality.

There was some truth behind the accusation of Synge's early critics that his dialogue was a fake. In so far as his dramatic language purports to be authentic – and this is the obvious implication of *The Playboy* preface – the invention and elaboration of dialect phrases can be condemned as faking. More interesting than the controversial arguments over authenticity, however, is the variation between the original dialect forms and the uses Synge made of them. This is a central critical issue, and deserves some detailed consideration.

*   *   *

It is universally granted that Synge's characters do not talk the ordinary language of Irish countrymen, but what relation does their speech bear to that of their originals? In *The Aran Islands* we saw that Synge imaginatively recreated the stories he had heard, using basic syntactic patterns which he thought of as character- istically Irish. These patterns remained virtually constant through- out all his plays, whether his characters were Aran islanders, Mayo men or Wicklow sheep-farmers. A speech, for example, from *The Tinker's Wedding* shows the typical forms which Synge borrowed from Irish:

> It's gone they are, *and I with my feet that* weak under me you'd knock me down with a rush, *and my head with a noise* in it the like of what you'd hear in a stream, *and it running* between two rocks *and rain falling*. (*Plays* II p. 25)

Wicklow is one of the areas in which Irish died out early on, and there is no likelihood that even Mary Byrne's mother would have spoken it, yet she is made to use an Irish construction four times within a single sentence.[1] Although the Irish substratum did and does survive surprisingly strongly in non Irish speaking areas, there was clearly a difference between the dialect of Aran, where English was still a second language, and the dialect of Wicklow, where English only was spoken. It is a difference which Synge never tried to reproduce.

And yet the language of Synge's plays is not completely homo- geneous. The spare style of *Riders*, for example, is very different from the language of *The Playboy*, in which every speech is indeed 'as fully flavoured as a nut or apple'. Much of this 'fully-flavoured' effect is gained by the use of unusual idioms or archaic vocabulary some of which has survived from seventeenth-century English.[2]

But these are not included to differentiate the Mayo dialect from the more purely Irish Aran speech. In fact most of the striking phrases in *The Playboy* Synge heard in Kerry. He spent comparatively little time in Mayo; apart from his official tour of it with Jack Yeats when writing articles for the *Manchester Guardian*, he only visited the district once, in September 1904 just when he was first planning *The Playboy*, and this is no doubt why it was set in Mayo rather than in one of the areas with which he was more familiar. It is not surprising, therefore, that in writing the supposedly Mayo dialect of *The Playboy* he should have borrowed from his Kerry notebooks. All the following phrases and incidents picked up in Kerry reappear in *The Playboy*: 'Daneen Sullivan . . . a great warrant to tell stories' (MS 4392 f. 12r); 'It is no harm if the poor die but the big wealthy nobles! it'd make the green stones cry to think of it' (MS 4392 f. 10r); 'in face of hog, dog or devil' (MS 4402 f. 1v); 'mule kicking the stars' (MS 4407 f. 4v).

Clearly Synge did not select the language of his characters on the basis of geographical representation. His dialogue is literally synthetic, in that he brings together dialect features from various parts of the country to suit his dramatic purposes. The mood and character of the play rather than its setting determine the style. In the austere atmosphere of *Riders*, the language is consistently simple and dignified, whereas in the comedies generally, and in *The Playboy* in particular, passages of heightened lyricism alternate with fantastic or grotesque comic speeches. Synge was not interested in creating characters who were identifiably Wicklow or Kerry men – he made it a rule, for example, not to try to render accent in writing dialogue. Indeed he was not interested in reproducing dialect simply because it was the speech of the people. Its authenticity was important to him, but he was quite prepared to alter the form and direction of dialect usage for the sake of the artistic effects he wanted.

This is particularly obvious in the instances where he is experimenting with invented phrases. 'As naked as an ash-tree in the moon of March (J.M.S.)' he noted down (MS 4391 f. 8r), and eventually used the simile in *The Playboy* where Christy describes his father, 'rising up in the red dawn, or before it maybe, and going out into the yard as naked as an ash-tree in the moon of May' (*Plays* II p. 83). 'Moon' in place of 'month' is certainly not a common usage in Anglo-Irish, and it does not seem to have an equivalent in Irish. However Synge evidently found its ambiguity effective. It has a pleasantly archaic flavour recalling the origin of the word 'month' itself, while at the same time we are given the visual image of the ash shining white under the moon. Christy's speech continues at this point, 'shying clods again the visage of the stars till he'd put the fear of death into the banbhs and the screeching sows' (*Plays* II p. 85). 'Pegging clods' appears in one of the notebooks (MS 4401 f. 1v), but Synge preferred to use the commoner English 'shying', probably because the Anglo-Irish 'pegging' for 'throwing' might have been misunderstood. *Banbhs* – commonly corrupted to 'bonhams' – are piglets in Irish, and 'again' in place of 'against' is still current in Anglo-Irish. 'Visage', however, is doubtfully genuine. It is not recorded in *The English Dialect Dictionary* or in the Anglo-Irish glossaries,[3] and in Standard English it has had only literary currency for several centuries. It is possible that Synge recalled the seventeenth-century transferred use of the word applied to 'the face or visible side of sun or moon'. The O.E.D. cites, for example, *A Midsummer Night's Dream*:

> Tomorrow night, when Phoebe doth behold
> Her silvery visage in the watr'y glass (I i ll. 209–10).

It may be that the contiguity of 'the moon of May' suggested to Synge the extended use of 'visage' for stars. The force of the word is to present a Titanic Old Mahon not just hurling clods up into the sky, but throwing them full in the face of the stars. Synge's intended effect is slipped unobtrusively into the camouflage of dialect.[4]

'The star of knowledge' was early recognised as one of Synge's few direct borrowings from Irish poetry. The phrase recurs four times in Hyde's *Love Songs of Connaught*, as a traditional image of the beloved: 'And I thought after that, That you were a lamp from God, Or that you were the star of knowledge Going before me and after me'.[5] Hyde glosses the phrase as follows:

> we find the . . . expression 'star of knowledge' and a lovely expression it is. It is making us understand it is, that there be's double knowledge and greatly increased sharp-sightedness to him who is in love. The love is like a star, and it is like a star of knowledge on account of the way in which it opens our senses, so that we be double more light, more lively and more sharp than we were before. We understand the glory and beauty of the world in a way we never understood it until then.[6]

This seems unnecessarily elaborate; the 'star of knowledge' is surely a nautical metaphor, the star by which one guides one's life, like the English 'cynosure'. (The Irish word used, *eolas*, is the perfectly ordinary word for 'knowledge'.) Synge includes the phrase in Christy's impassioned speech to Widow Quin in *The Playboy*:

> Amn't I after seeing the love-light of the star of knowledge shining from her brow, and hearing words would put you thinking on the holy Brigid speaking to the infant saints (*Plays* II pp. 125–7).

The image is made more complex than in the original by focusing on the light given off by the star. By placing it on Pegeen's brow Synge transforms it into a sort of halo. This, however, effectively destroys the meaning of the conceit, and the phrase degenerates into a purely decorative image. What is striking is not just this local failure, where Synge can fairly be accused of overstrained rhetoric, but the principle by which he is prepared to change the structure of the language as he found it.

Synge's 'plays of peasant life' were written for a middle-class audience of urban people to whom that life was basically unfamiliar. Though his language is drawn from a virtually illiterate society, his effects are aimed at the educated. This is partly why his plays were so immediately successful outside Ireland where his dialect, by its archaisms or associations with the Elizabethan writers, delighted English-speaking audiences. To those accustomed to a norm of 'joyless and pallid words' in the theatre, his 'fully-flavoured' language seemed infinitely refreshing. The nationalist critics were surely right to suspect this reaction. From an Irish standpoint, to be patronised for one's popular imagination may be little better than to be mocked for one's brogue. In fact, it must be admitted that Synge does sometimes verge on the deliberately picturesque, the exploitation of the dialect for its 'local colour'. But his more profound aim in the use of Anglo-Irish was that revitalisation of language which is an integral part of the poetic process. Unfamiliar constructions and archaic vocabulary may appear superficially picturesque; but at the highest level of Synge's craftsmanship they serve to renew the very springs of meaning. To do Synge justice we must go beyond our initial admiration for the 'poetic' quality of the dialect. We need to analyse his meaning and elucidate his effects as we would those of any other poetic dramatist.

*   *   *

Most critics of Synge have mentioned the outstanding features of his dialect, and detailed research has been done on the particular constructions which he favours. Jiro Taniguchi's book on Irish English, and Nicholas Newlin's dissertation on the Irish element in the language of the plays are the most comprehensive studies, from which the overall pattern of his dialect may be established.[7] It is clear that Synge had definite preferences for certain forms, and it is worth listing here those which he uses and those which he significantly rejects. This may take us some way towards understanding the main characteristics of the dialect and the sort of effects which Synge was specifically seeking.

1. The nominal group

The commonest instance of this form is the phrase 'the like of' in place of 'like', but it appears also in the use of 'the way . . .' as a conjunction introducing a clause of purpose where Standard English would have 'so that', and in the interrogative 'what way?' replacing 'how?'

> Maybe cold would be no sign of death with *the likes of him* (*Plays* I p. 35).
> I'm wanting him this night, *the way* he can go down into the glen (*Plays* I p. 41).
> *What way* would I live and I an old woman if I didn't marry . . . (*Plays* I p. 49).

'The like(s) of' can replace an adjective, adverb or conjunction, and it is extremely common in Synge's work. Together with its alternative forms 'his likeness' or 'his like', Taniguchi notes some sixty-three examples of it in *The Playboy* alone, and in his table of comparative frequency he shows that Synge favours the phrase far more than other writers of Anglo-Irish dialect (Taniguchi p. 4).

2. The suppressed relative pronoun

Newlin remarks on the preference for 'that' over 'who' or 'which' in Anglo-Irish, and on the tendency to omit the relative pronoun altogether. This is apparently a habit derived from Irish in which there is no true relative capable of inflection. Many of Synge's sentences have a relative pronoun suppressed, for example, 'It's a shirt and plain stocking were got off a drowned man in Donegal' (*Plays* I p. 5), where Standard English would require 'which' after 'stocking'. Newlin suggests that Synge is exaggeratedly fond of this habit, and Taniguchi points out that in *Deirdre* 'no relatives are used except in a few cases' (Taniguchi p. 35).

3.   *Progressive forms*
In Anglo-Irish the progressive form of the verb – 'I am going' rather than 'I go' – is used much more often than in Standard English, and in Synge this preference is particularly noticeable. In *The Shadow*, according to Taniguchi, the expanded form is used twice as often as in a comparable play of Lady Gregory, and over four times as often as in Standard English. As Newlin points out, the overall impression of a high incidence of continuous forms ending in '-ing' is increased by the common use of the present participle in clauses beginning with 'and' or 'after' (see 4 and 7 below). With certain verbs Synge almost never uses the simple forms:

> Did you see Bartley, *I'm saying* to you? (*Plays* I p. 17)
> *I'm thinking* many would be afeard (*Plays* I p. 37).

It is always 'I'm thinking', or 'I'm saying', never 'I think' or 'I say'.

4.   *'And' construction*
This construction which Synge uses constantly is taken over directly from Irish, where a subordinate clause may be loosely related to the main clause by *'agus'* – 'and' – followed by a noun and participle. (We have already seen instances in the passage from *The Tinker's Wedding* quoted earlier on.) The construction can be used to express various sorts of subordination, but very frequently it replaces a temporal clause:

> Was there anyone on the last bit of the road, stranger, *and you coming* from Aughrim? (*Plays* I p. 39)

In many cases the participle is omitted:

> how would I go out into the glen and tell the neighbours *and I a lone woman* with no house near me? (*Plays* I p. 37)

Newlin points out that there has been an increased incidence of this *'agus'* construction in Modern Irish, but even so, normal subordinate clauses are used as well, whereas Synge almost always uses this construction.

5. The copula

In Irish there are two forms of 'to be', the substantive verb '*tá*' and the copula '*is*'. Irish sentences normally place the verb first, unless some part of the predicate requires emphasis, in which case it can be moved forward and preceded by the copula. As P. L. Henry remarks, the phonetic similarity between 'It's' and '*is*' must 'have lightened the task of the early bilingual speaker when he instinctively sought to reproduce the Irish construction in English.'[8] This construction with prefatory 'It's' is a favourite with Synge. It occurs in over twenty per cent of all sentences in *Riders* (Taniguchi p. 148), and Newlin suggests that it is so common as to have lost its emphatic function altogether. It is particularly useful in dialogue where a word or phrase used by one speaker is picked up by the next.

> *Michael.* That's a poor coat you have, God help you, and I'm thinking *it's a poor tailor* you are with it.
> *Tramp.* If it's a poor tailor I am, I'm thinking it's a poor herd does be running back and forward after a little handful of ewes the way I seen yourself running this day, young fellow, and you coming from the fair. (*Plays* I pp. 45–7)

(Such echo clauses are especially common because the Anglo-Irish dialect follows Irish in almost always using a responsive sentence in place of 'yes' or 'no'.)

6. Reported questions

In Standard English a question in reported speech is preceded by 'if' or 'whether' and it has the normal word-order for a statement. 'I asked him if he was going to the fair.' In Irish, however, no distinction in form is made between direct and indirect questions, and consequently in Anglo-Irish the reported question is given as though in direct speech: 'I asked him was he going to the fair.' Alan Bliss points out that Synge uses both the 'correct' Anglo-Irish form, and the 'incorrect' English one in *Riders*:

> We're to find out if it's Michael's they are (*Plays* I p. 5).
> Did you ask him would he stop Bartley going this day with the horses to the Galway fair? (*Plays* I p. 5)

After Synge's first two plays, this inconsistency was apparently eliminated and he used only the Anglo-Irish form.[9]

7. The 'after' construction

This is again a translation of an Irish construction – 'after' + gerund – and in Anglo-Irish it often replaces the Standard English perfect.

> I'm *after putting him down* in the sports below (*Plays* II p. 99).
> I'm *after going down* and reading the fearful crimes of Ireland (*Plays* II p. 113).

Newlin points out that this most commonly translates the English perfect with 'just' – 'I have just put him down in the sports', 'I have just gone down and read . . .' Synge likes to use this form together with the 'and' construction (4), as, for example, in Michael Dara's speech at the end of *The Shadow*.

> And it's very dry I am surely, with the fear of death you put on me, *and I after driving* mountain ewes since the turn of day. (*Plays* I p. 59)

These then are the main forms which recur regularly in Synge's Anglo-Irish, and which are nearly all derived from Irish habits of speech. But equally noticeable are certain features of the dialect which he omits.

1. The 'Kiltartan infinitive'

In Anglo-Irish, subject + infinitive is sometimes used to render an Irish gerund in a subordinate clause. This provides the basis for a construction which occurs so frequently in Lady Gregory's work that it became known as the 'Kiltartan infinitive'.

> It would be a pity *you to be passing*, and I *not to be spreading* the news![10]
> Isn't it a hard case, Mike McInerney, *myself and yourself to be left* here in the bed.[11]

The infinitive is also often used in an exclamatory context, as in *Hyacinth Halvey*:

> I wonder, indeed, you to say a thing like that! I *to steal* your sheep or your rack or anything that belongs to you or your trade![12]

There is one instance of this usage in *The Tinker's Wedding*:

> *You to be going* beside me a great while, and rearing a lot of them, and then *to be setting off* with your talk of getting mar-

ried, and your driving me to it, and I not asking it at all. (*Plays* II p. 7)

Nowhere else in his plays does Synge use the Kiltartan infinitive.

2. *Colloquial forms*
Various colloquial forms of speech common in the dialect appear very seldom in Synge. Neither he nor Lady Gregory give the spelling 'me' for 'my', which is used by most other writers of Anglo-Irish. Synge also avoids one of Lady Gregory's mannerisms, 'sure' as a preface to a sentence. For example, in *Spreading the News*, Tim Casey does not believe Bartley Fallon has taken up with Mrs Jack Smith:

> How can he take charge of her? Sure he has a wife of his own. Sure you don't think he'd turn souper and marry her in a Protestant church?[13]

An irregular second person plural pronoun 'yous' is common in Anglo-Irish. 'O, yous are all nicely shanghaied now' screeches Bessie Burgess in *The Plough and the Stars*.[14] Newlin comments that 'We might expect to find this use of "yous" ("yez", "yiz") more often in Synge than we do, since it is the recognised mark of popular Anglo-Irish and particularly of Dublin speech.' (Newlin p. 111) But this is almost certainly the reason we do not find it in Synge any more than we find 'me' or 'sure'. Synge's object was to exclude expressions associated with popular stage-Irish, and in the manuscripts we can see him steadily removing the favourite forms of Boucicault and Lever from the early drafts of his plays.[15]

What is immediately striking about this outline of Synge's language is its consistency. Those constructions which he favours, he uses in almost every case far more than other writers of the dialect, while those which he avoids, he avoids completely. This restricts the range of his language, but it has compensating advantages. The frequent repetition of a relatively few constructions make it more readily comprehensible than it would otherwise be, so that to a non-Irish audience it is unfamiliar but not obscure. Certain staple rhythms are established and recur regularly, so that the ear is quickly accustomed to the texture of the dialogue. At the same time, the limited linguistic range enables Synge to build up structural patterns of words and phrases which act as key-notes for the play's meaning.

Most of Synge's preferred constructions contribute to a single general effect – that of a free-flowing, full-winded speech with the lightest possible grammatical punctuation. We saw earlier how Standard English forms of subordination were removed from the drafts of *The Aran Islands* stories, and of the seven dialect features listed here, four contribute to this same paratactic tendency. Instead of a precisely defined subordinate clause there is the loose 'and' construction; formal discrimination between direct and indirect speech is removed in reported questions; relative pronouns are omitted and the conjunctions 'when' and 'how' replaced with the substantive 'the time', 'the way'. All of this helps to make easier the flow of continuous verb forms, present participles and gerunds which Synge constantly uses. It may be, in fact, that the reason he avoids the Kiltartan infinitive is that its jerky rhythm – 'you to say', 'I to steal' – and its awkward disjunction would have interfered with the smoothly running sentences.

A single passage from *The Shadow of the Glen* can be used to illustrate some of the effects of this style. Nora Burke reflects on her past life, while Michael Dara counts what is from his point of view her dowry:

> Isn't it a long while I am sitting here in the winter, and the summer, and the fine spring, with the young growing behind me and the old passing, saying to myself one time, to look on Mary Brien who wasn't that height (holding out her hand), and I a fine girl growing up, and there she is now with two children, and another coming on her in three months or four (she pauses). *Michael* (moving over three of the piles). That's three pounds we have now, Nora Burke.
> *Nora* (continuing in the same voice). And saying to myself another time, to look on Peggy Cavanagh, who had the lightest hand at milking a cow that wouldn't be easy, or turning a cake, and there she is now walking round on the roads, or sitting in a dirty old house, with no teeth in her mouth, and no sense, and no more hair than you'd see on a bit of a hill and they after burning the furze from it. (*Plays* I pp. 49–51)

Michael's speech serves as a dramatic interruption to Nora's train of thought, and it points up ironically the disparity between them, but it does not break the linguistic sequence of Nora's words. Her two speeches are all one sentence, dependent on the initial rhetorical question: 'Isn't it a long while I am sitting here . . .' The poetic structure of the passage is carefully elaborated. There is

Synge's favourite triad with the rhythmic differentiation of the third part, 'the winter, and the summer, and the fine spring'. The exact balancing of the phrases, 'milking a cow' – 'or turning a cake', is made less obvious by the intervention of 'that wouldn't be easy'. Synge makes use of 'passing' instead of the ordinary 'passing away' to give a subtle suggestion of the race of time to 'the young growing behind me, and the old passing'. Above all there is the structural parallel between the two main clauses round which the whole speech is built – 'saying to myself one time, to look on . . . and there she is', 'saying to myself another time, to look on . . . and there she is . . .'

And yet none of these effects are obtrusive. The speech can present vividly and naturally a reverie within a reverie, Nora recollecting past recollections. The actual grammatical sequence is often vague. It is, for example, difficult to analyse the use of the infinitive 'to look', or to explain the jump to the indicative with 'there she is now'. P. L. Henry points out that Anglo-Irish concentrates on aspect and state rather than tense,[16] and here it is natural for Nora to shift her past thoughts forward into the present. This long and complicated sentence seems hardly out of place in the mouth of an uneducated peasant woman, because the normal forms of grammatical subordination are absent, and no more sophisticated connective than 'and' is used. Each clause seems to depend solely on the preceding one as the thoughts occur to Nora, and yet the whole pattern is controlled.

Synge's preference for long sentences caused problems for the actors who were required to speak them. Maire Nic Shiublaigh, who created the part of Nora Burke, commented:

> At first I found Synge's lines almost impossible to learn and deliver . . . It was neither verse nor prose. The speeches had a musical lilt, absolutely different to anything I had heard before. Every passage brought some new difficulty until the tempo in which they were written was finally discovered.[17]

It may be that the difficulty for the (largely Dublin) actors was partly one of accent. The speaker of Synge's language is drawn two ways. To suit the character he tries to assume an inarticulate or uneducated manner of speech, and yet the cadence of the poetry is constantly forcing him towards lyrical eloquence. The result is often a curious conflict between two accents, that of the East of Ireland, especially Dublin, which has come to represent the comic or vulgar aspect of Anglo-Irish, and that of the West which is still associated with poetry and lyricism. The sentences are difficult to speak because they are full and complex in rhythm and meaning. For all their lack of the paraphernalia of grammatical subordination they are never merely series of main clauses strung together, as, for example, those of O'Casey's Dubliners frequently are. Synge's achievement was to create a poetic period in the full rhetorical sense, without losing the basic verisimilitude of his dramatic situation.

The main features of Synge's dialect considered so far contribute to an overall effect which runs fairly consistently through all the plays. But, especially in the comedies, he also makes use of specific types of popular speech for a range of dramatic and poetic purposes. The syntactic and grammatical patterns of the dialect provided an essential structure, but within that structure he was free to culti-vate particular effects – lyrical, comic or grotesque. When consider-ing these effects it is interesting to see how they diverge from normal usage where that can be established, how far they belong to the 'popular imagination that is fiery and magnificent and tender' and how far they are Synge's own.

Similes must be one of the most primitive poetic tropes. They are common in almost any popular speech, and where traditional they harden into proverbs. P. W. Joyce, in his book *English As We Speak it in Ireland*, cites, for example, the pejorative phrase 'He has an eye like a questing hawk'. The comparison is, no doubt, commonplace, but when Synge develops it in *The Well of the Saints* he visualises the 'questing hawk'. The holy water, according to Timmy the smith, would 'make the blind see as clear as the grey hawks do be high up, on a still day, sailing the sky'. (*Plays* I p. 81) As Grattan Freyer puts it of some other examples, 'While the thought which first provoked the comparison was imaginative and even abstract, the impact on the hearer is immediate and tangible'.[18] With Michael James's image of the jackass in *The Playboy*, we can compare the original from *The Aran Islands*:

> What's a single man, I ask you, eating a bit in one house and drinking a sup in another, and he with no place of his own, like an old braying jackass strayed upon the rocks? (*Plays* II p. 157)

> Listen to what I'm telling you: a man who is not married is no better than an old jackass. He goes into his sister's house, and

into his brother's house; he eats a bit in this place and a bit in another place, but he has no home for himself; like an old jackass straying on the rocks. (*Prose* p. 121)

All that Synge actually adds is the epithet 'braying', but this brings the ass vividly before us, and helps to emphasise the sexual implications of the image which are only latent in the original. The Tramp in *The Shadow* speaks as an experienced traveller who has seen the sights of the town when he refers to 'a towering church in the city of Dublin'. In the context, Synge uses it as the culminating image in a series of three similes:

crossing the hills when the fog is on them, the time a little stick would seem as big as your arm, and a rabbit as big as a bay horse, and a stack of turf as big as a towering church in the city of Dublin (*Plays* I p. 37).

The successive images are controlled so that each object is bigger and each comparison is more complicated; we feel the frightening atmosphere in which the objects grow continually out of the mist. The colourful visual similes which are so common in Synge's plays are in many cases derived from comparisons he has heard, but he realises them and gives them point so that they become more than merely picturesque.

Many of Synge's comic effects depend on uses of language which are unfamiliar to his readers or audience. An obvious example is the Anglo-Irish use of the points of the compass. The speaker of Irish imagines himself facing the east; he therefore speaks of the left hand as the north, the right as the south, and east and west are front and back. This convention is used quite correctly in *The Shadow* when Dan asks the Tramp to 'bring me a black stick you'll see in the west corner by the wall.' (*Plays* I p. 43) But in Christy's account of his fight with his father it is purely comic:

He gave a drive with the scythe, and I gave a lep to the east. Then I turned around with my back to the north, and I hit a blow on the ridge of his skull . . . (*Plays* II p. 103)

This is an unlikely use of 'east' and 'north', but we can see what Synge intends by it. In suggesting a cosmic scale for the fight, like one of the great battles of the giants, he ridicules Christy's 'heroism'. The passage is only effective because we are not accustomed to hear the cardinal points used in this way.

In the final act of *The Playboy*, Pegeen dismisses Shawn contemptuously:

> I'm thinking you're too fine for the like of me, Shawn Keogh of Killakeen, and let you go off till you'd find a radiant lady with droves of bullocks on the plains of Meath, and herself bedizened in the diamond jewelleries of Pharoah's ma. (*Plays* II p. 155)

It is the inconsistency of Pegeen's imagination which makes this speech funny. 'Shawn Keogh of Killakeen' is completely local and familiar – giving him his full title is an ironic mark of respect. The 'radiant lady' is out of a folk-story, but she is juxtaposed with the thoroughly mundane 'droves of bullocks', and the 'plains of Meath', which we may assume are the actual limits of Pegeen's horizon. Finally the vague and fantastic 'diamond jewelleries' are associated with the Biblical memory of the grandeur of the Pharoahs, and the whole phrase is deflated by the colloquial 'ma'. The full comedy is available only to an audience who are capable of realising this pattern of incongruity, of which Pegeen herself is unaware.

'The people have a gentle laudable habit of mixing up sacred names and pious phrases with their ordinary conversation, in a purely reverential spirit', P. W. Joyce tells us.[19] Synge clearly exploited this habit for purposes which were not purely reverential. There is, notoriously, Christy's confession in *The Playboy*:

> Pegeen (with blank amazement).   Is it killed your father?
> Christy.   With the help of God I did surely, and that the Holy Immaculate Mother may intercede for his soul. (*Plays* II p. 73)

The effect is less explicit in *The Shadow* when Nora tells the Tramp, 'He's after dying on me, God forgive him, and there I am now with a hundred sheep beyond on the hills, and no turf drawn for the winter.' (*Plays* I p. 33) The phrase 'on me', which is borrowed from Irish, is like an English dative of disadvantage. Juxtaposed with the automatic 'God forgive him', it gives a suggestion of accusation to the sentence – the crime for which Dan needs God's forgiveness is dying at such an inconvenient time. A deeper irony is involved in Martin Doul's exclamation in *The Well of the Saints* when he hears the Saint returning to cure him and Mary for the second time: 'The Lord protect us from the saints of God!' (*Plays* I p. 133) In a sense, this one comic line represents Synge's most serious critique of Christianity. Martin feels threatened by the Saint who will not allow him his own kind of life and happiness, and yet in the monotheistic world in which he lives, there is no authority to turn to for protection save only that which the Saint represents.

Synge was supposed to have shouted once, on reviving from an anaesthetic, 'Damn the bloody Anglo-Saxon language that a man can't swear in without being vulgar!'[20] One of the attractive features of the Anglo-Irish dialect for him was its wealth of fantastic terms of abuse. It used to be said of someone particularly adept in swearing that 'he could quench a candle at the other side of the kitchen with a curse'.[21] Synge may well have heard this expression, for he develops it in *The Tinker's Wedding* where Mary Byrne threatens Sarah Casey with exposure:

> I'll be telling old and young you're a weathered heathen savage, Sarah Casey, the one did put down a head of the parson's cabbage to boil in the pot with your clothes (the priest comes in behind her on the left, and listens), and quenched the flaming candles on the throne of God the time your shadow fell within the pillars of the chapel door. (*Plays* II p. 33)

Instead of the plain domestic candle of the original, Synge makes them the holy candles on the church altar, and thus they become explicitly an image of the force of blasphemy. The denunciation is, of course, given dramatic point by the entrance of the priest who is supposed to marry Michael and Sarah.

This sort of fantastic abuse is common in the plays, where the characters are often at their most imaginative when pouring out invective. In *The Well of the Saints*, Mary Doul, cured of her blindness, sees her husband for the first time:

> It's many a woman is married with finer than yourself should be praising God if she's no child, and isn't loading the earth with things would make the heavens lonesome above, and they scaring the larks, and the crows, and the angels passing in the sky. (*Plays* I p. 99)

Or in the same vein, Christy tells how he refused to marry the Widow Casey:

> I won't wed her . . . when all know she did suckle me for six weeks when I came into the world, and she a hag this day with a tongue on her has the crows and seabirds scattered, the way

they wouldn't cast a shadow on her garden with the dread of her curse. (*Plays* II p. 103)

The ugliness is so terrible that it is an offence to the natural creation and to the Creator. The abuse is not merely an attempt to find superlatives in vituperation, but is given a definite imaginative pattern, in which the element of Satanic deformity is deliberately developed. We can see this in Pegeen's famous denunciation of the Widow Quin:

> Doesn't the world know you reared a black ram at your breast, so that the Lord Bishop of Connaught felt the elements of a Christian, and he eating it after in a kidney stew? (*Plays* II p. 89)

We find the source of this in one of the Kerry notebooks, where Synge jotted down 'woman suckles lamb in which doctor detects the elements of a Christian in Cahirciveen' (*Plays* II p. 88). Here the 'detection' is purely medical – there is no special significance in 'Christian' which is used in the Irish countryside to mean simply 'human'. But with the introduction of the Lord Bishop, and the suggestive 'black ram', the accusation is given a decidedly diabolic cast. What is aimless fantasy in the speech of the people, under Synge's hand takes on the dimension of a grotesque vision of the world.

Where he used the dialect for lyrical, comic or fantastic effects Synge was developing specific imaginative tendencies within the popular speech. Occasionally, however, he exploits single words or phrases which have almost accidentally come to have a multiple significance. In the plays these are made to bear a weight of importance beyond their immediate context; they are key-words around which the meaning of the action crystallises. 'Queer', for example, has a whole range of values. It is sometimes used perfectly normally to mean eccentric – 'He was always queer, stranger', Nora says to the Tramp of Dan. Occasionally it stands for madness as when Michael Dara asks about Patch Darcy, 'Is it the man went queer in his head'. It can have overtones of admiration – Brendan Behan's play *The Quare Fellow* – but Synge seldom uses it in this sense, and more often it suggests contempt and dislike. Molly Byrne's comment to Martin Doul in *The Well of the Saints* is somewhere between surprise and a grudging interest: 'It's queer talk you have if it's a little, old, shabby stump of a man you are itself.' (*Plays* I p. 115) In certain contexts, Synge makes use of the word to evoke a universal uneasiness in the human situation:

Martin Doul.   It's a queer thing maybe for all things is queer in the world. (*Plays* I p. 115)

Nora.   It's a pitiful thing to be getting old, but it's a queer thing surely . . . It's a queer thing to see an old man sitting up there in his bed, with no teeth in him, and a rough word in his mouth . . . (*Plays* I pp. 51–3)

Those who are 'queer', those who see the 'queerness' of things have a special importance in Synge's world.

The archaic word 'lonesome' was a great favourite with Synge – he used it repeatedly not only in his plays but in his letters to Molly Algood. Often it is no more than a poetic synonym for 'lonely', but it is also used to mean 'deserted' or 'desolate': 'Oh there's sainted glory this day in the lonesome west' (*Plays* II p. 65), 'Bravery's a treasure in a lonesome place' (*Plays* II p. 75). In some cases, it seems to function as a combination of 'lonely' and 'alone'. Nora remarks about the death of Patch Darcy:

it's very lonesome I was after him a long while and then I got happy again – stranger – if it's ever happy we are – for I got used to being lonesome. (*Plays* I p. 39)

This hints at something brought out in *The Playboy*, that to be 'lonesome' may not be merely a particular mood, but an enduring state of being. Pegeen cannot see why a 'coaxing fellow' like Christy should be lonesome: 'It's only letting on you are to be lonesome, the way you'd get around me now.' Christy replies:

I wish to God I was letting on; but I was lonesome all times and born lonesome, I'm thinking, as the moon of dawn. (*Plays* II p. 111)

The line is significant in defining Christy's distinction from the Mayo men.

Perhaps the most striking example of this sort of multiple meaning is the title itself – 'the playboy of the western world'. A 'playboy', a literal borrowing from Irish, is an admiring word for a tricky rascal, but throughout the play it varies in significance. Christy is first called a playboy by the Widow Quin with ironic respect, when she has just discovered that the father he claimed he had 'split to the breeches belt' is alive and well. In Act III, where he becomes the 'champion playboy of the western world', the title is no more than his due as an athlete. The champion is deflated by old Mahon's reappearance, but finally after he has left, Pegeen laments her lost heroic ideal: 'Oh my grief, I've lost him surely. I've lost the only playboy of the western world.' (*Plays* II p. 173) As often with the use of 'world' – which is commonplace in Irish – Synge achieves a universal amplification. 'Western world' may mean no more than the western coast of Ireland, but obviously it lends to the play's title an ambiguous suggestion of the whole of Western Europe. Yet the original meaning of the 'playboy' stands, and to the end Christy may be seen as a liar, making up stories to impress the girls. In somewhat the same way Ibsen's Master-builder is both the ideal hero of Hilde Wangel and the man painfully conscious that he is not a trained architect. In both cases the ambiguity is at the centre of the play's meaning.

'Synge wrote plays about characters whose originals in life talked poetically, so that he could make them talk poetry and remain real people.'[22] This is, in a sense, a fair point of Eliot's, in that it was important to Synge that his audience should believe in the reality of his speakers of dialect. It is also true that he used what he found, the energy and vitality of popular speech, and he was no doubt right to acknowledge the people as his collaborators. But Eliot's statement, which represents a widespread view of Synge's language, can be misleading in so far as it suggests that the poetic effects of the plays were inherent in the dialect itself. Synge gave direction and form to the peasant speech, at times, as we have seen, a direction and form which were by no means those of the original. He was aware that because of its unfamiliarity, and its exoticism, he could expect from his audience that attention to words for their own sake normally accorded to poetry. Where in prose drama language tends to be transparent, allowing us direct access to the meaning of the speaker, or by small distortions suggesting his character, in poetry meaning is expressed through the very colour and tone of the medium itself. It is in this sense, ultimately, that Synge's language is poetic and his own creation. For the effect of his drama depends not on the representation of peasant characters speaking realistic 'poetic' dialect, but on the total structure of the language, artistically controlled.

The understanding of the difference between the poetic qualities of the dialect and Synge's poetic handling of it, is frequently further confused by the identification of certain of his characters as 'poetic'. Everyone in the plays talks in much the same way, almost equally 'poetically', even those like Timmy the smith, or the Widow Quin, from whom we would not expect 'poetry talk'. Synge does not, like so many prose dramatists, differentiate his various characters by obvious tricks of speech, favourite expressions, or distinct linguistic mannerisms. The rhythmic patterns in his plays, for example, are surprisingly consistent. P. L. Henry, in his excellent analysis of the speech-rhythms of *The Playboy*, concludes:

> To a certain extent, then, the primary cadence may be said to relate to the mood (and manner) of the drama(tist) rather than to immediate exigencies of context and character. So too we find a tendency towards regular metre not only in Christy's speeches, where we might expect it, but also in utterances by characters such as the Widow, Michael and Shawn.[23]

There is undoubtedly a danger of monotony here, and when read aloud Synge's lines sometimes can seem monotonous. But in the theatre the variation in the voices of the speakers and the substance of their speech removes the impression of mechanical regularity, and the underlying cadences provide a norm like that of blank verse. To this extent the traditional comparison of Synge's rhythms to those of the Elizabethan dramatists holds good. The essential poetic structure is the consistent medium for his work, in itself as neutral as the Elizabethan blank-verse line.

However, there are very different attitudes towards language in Synge's plays, and though the standard of expression may be consistently high, yet there are characters – Christy Mahon, Martin Doul, to a lesser extent the Tramp and Mary Byrne – who may be differentiated from those around them by their feeling for language. These, what we might call the 'poetic' characters, are to be distinguished not so much by the manner of their speech, but by the emotions they express, and by their self-consciousness in the expression. This will be discussed in more detail when we look at the comedies in turn. Here it is worth considering the range of different attitudes to language in the plays and how they relate to the ordinary experience of the people.

The vividness of popular speech has often been explained by the restrictions of a rural community, where the majority of people are barely literate and the news media do not penetrate, and where, therefore, the ability to talk is at a premium. People who lead a narrow monotonous sort of life with a minimum of social contact and little or no mobility, have a special need for the entertainment of stories and conversation. We see this at its simplest in *The Tinker's Wedding*, where Mary Byrne, who is evidently renowned for her story-telling, invites Sarah to listen:

> so let you sit down there by the big bough, and I'll be telling you the finest story you'd hear any place from Dundalk to Ballin-acree, with great queens in it, making themselves matches from the start to the end, and they with shiny silks on them the length of the day, and white shifts for the night. (*Plays* II p. 23)

Such stories represent more than a temporary escape to a fantastic never-never land. They are part of the living present. 'I've a grand story of the great queens of Ireland with white necks on them the like of Sarah Casey, and fine arms would hit you a slap the way Sarah Casey would hit you.' (*Plays* II p. 25) This is not simply bathetic – the fabulous enhances the conscious splendour of present vitality. Yet when deprived of an audience, Mary loses her confidence, and dismisses her stories as no more than a meaningless anodyne:

> What good are the grand stories I have when it's few would listen to an old woman, few but a girl maybe would be in great fear the time her hour was come, or a little child wouldn't be sleeping with the hunger on a cold night? (*Plays* II p. 27)

In *The Playboy*, of course, the joy of story-telling is one of the mainsprings of the comic action, and part of the delight of the play is to watch Christy's story grow. His audience listens with approval as he tells how he killed his father – 'That's a grand story', 'He tells it lovely'. Such comments do not suggest that they disbelieve him, but they make it clear that he is valued as much for his 'fine words' as his 'savagery'. 'There's a great gap between a gallous story and a dirty deed', not just because the 'gallous story' is a fable, but because the 'dirty deed' is so bare and unadorned. We are used to hearing a great deal about the Irishman's love for 'blarney', as though it were a taste for uncontrolled fantasy or baroque lies. This is to misunderstand the function of such story-telling as we find in *The Playboy*. Language is used to make the actual pheno-mena of life more categorical, more interesting and more wonderful.

Admiration for the powers of language, however, is not uniform or universal in Synge's comedies. In *The Shadow*, for example, a significant opposition is set up between 'talk' and its derogatory alternative 'blather'. 'Blather' is Dan Burke's word – 'It's near dead I was wanting to sneeze, and you blathering about the rain, and Darcy – the devil choke him – and the towering church.' (*Plays* I p. 43) Obviously Dan, who has had to lie motionless under the sheet throughout, is in no mood to appreciate the Tramp and Nora's conversation, especially when they talk about Patch Darcy, his wife's suspected lover. Throughout the play, indeed, the Tramp's sort of talk is no more to him than a senseless and irrelevant intrusion on his privacy. When he turns Nora out, he sends the Tramp along with her to do his 'blathering' below in the glen. The Tramp picks up the word:

> Come along with me now, lady of the house, and it's not my blather you'll be hearing only, but you'll be hearing the herons crying out over the black lakes, and you'll be hearing the grouse, and the owls with them, and the larks and the big thrushes when the days are warm (*Plays* I p. 57).

It is not just this promise of natural beauty which consoles Nora, but the Tramp's ability to describe it: 'you've a fine bit of talk, stranger, and it's with yourself I'll go.' (*Plays* I p. 57) This rhymes with the Tramp's earlier praise of Nora, 'Is it herself, master of the house, and she a grand woman to talk?' (*Plays* I p. 43) 'Talk' is what they have in common.

We see something of the nature of the Tramp's talk when he imagines a future life with Nora:

> You'll be saying one time, 'It's a grand evening, by the grace of God,' and another time, 'It's a wild night, God help us, but it'll pass surely.' (*Plays* I p. 57)

He has a formula for each occasion, a conventional response which will be shared with his companion, phrases which are like spell-words against disaster. By interpreting the natural world we may go some way towards controlling it. A barrier is needed against the possibility of madness like Patch Darcy's, or bitterness like Dan's, and language here becomes the means of defence. Talk is not only a form of communication bringing comfort in shared thoughts and emotions, it is a method of reassurance, a way of reaffirming our existence and our relation to the universe. This sort of feeling for language, however, is rare, and those who have it, like the Tramp, are sharply distinguished from those who do not, those to whom such talk is meaningless blather.

Michael Dara is uneasily aware that there is something odd about Nora:

> What is it ails you this night, Nora Burke? I've heard tell it's the like of that talk you do hear from men, and they after being a great while on the back hills. (*Plays* I p. 49)

Michael's attitude is the conventional one. We find it again in Molly Byrne's reaction to Martin's love-making in *The Well of the Saints*: 'It's the like of that talk you'd hear from a man would be losing his mind.' (*Plays* I p. 117) What is incomprehensible is dismissed as madness. But when the incomprehensible words suggest deep emotion, there is an element of uneasiness in the dismissal. The braggart hero wins respect – Christy's proud boasting of his deed is received with admiration and awe; even lyricism can be attractive – Molly Byrne is 'half-mesmerised' by the wooing of Martin Doul. But ultimately the people regard with a contempt which is close to fear those who can give them a glimpse of an inner world of the imagination. It is unknown and mysterious territory which they are inclined to think of as madness. They hate emotion which is deeply felt and which is uncontrolled. Christy and Martin, at their worst moments of pain, when they are at their most eloquent, are for the people an open invitation to mockery.

Language in its highest forms in Synge's plays is an attempt to articulate the extremes of emotion. Loneliness, hatred and joy are the strongest feelings for Synge, and it is these which the central characters express most powerfully. Associated with loneliness is the dread of old age, and the obsession with time; hatred is most frequently caused by intense humiliation; joy comes with the fulfilment of love, or love is brought about by the need for joy. These are the basic emotions of Nora, the Tramp, the tinkers, Martin Doul and Christy Mahon, and to express them they enlist the fullest powers of their imagination. The great moments of Synge's comedies – Nora recalling the desolation of her past life, Martin rejected by Molly Byrne, Christy wooing Pegeen – involve the passionate articulation of loneliness, hatred and joy. These characters are the 'temperaments of distinction', and the badge of their distinction is the power of self-expression.

The prolonged controversies over the nature of Synge's language have not been caused merely by a misunderstanding of his intention, a mistaken belief that his object was to represent accurately the speech of the people. The fact is that Synge's use of dialect is very unusual indeed, virtually unparalleled, and such analogies as have been drawn tend only to confuse the issue. The often quoted preface to *The Playboy* is perhaps most misleading of all, for in stressing his 'collaboration' with the people, Synge makes it sound a far less complicated matter than it actually was. The process we have considered, by which the dialect which he heard was elaborated into the language of the plays, was not a simple selection but a radical reshaping. It was a method of creation which suited Synge temperamentally. He needed to work with a plastic medium which required meticulous, laborious craftsmanship, where his tireless patience and tenacity, his slow methodical cast of mind, became an enormous advantage. In working upon material so wholly unimagined, he liberated his own creative imagination. At the same time he prepared for himself a medium which, in its potential range of lyrical, comic and grotesque powers of language, exactly suited the comedies which he was engaged in writing, the plays in which the attitude to language is itself a major theme.

5

In Wicklow: *The Shadow of the Glen, The Tinker's Wedding*

The Wicklow essays are intimately related to the plays. Again and again, when reading through them, we come across anecdotes and phrases which reappear in *The Shadow* or *The Tinker's Wedding*. But even more interesting than such source material is the social background which the essays provide, Synge's view of the whole Wicklow community. Three different groups can be distinguished. In the remote mountain areas live the sheep-farmers who graze their stock on the common land of the hills; down in the valleys are the villages which supply agricultural labour, and the arable farms – Michael Dara is 'a kind of a farmer has come up from the sea'; a shifting third estate is made up by the vagrants, the tramps, tinkers and 'travelling people'. The range of the Wicklow essays allows us to look at each group in turn, and see where they stand in Synge's perspective.

Two essays are principally concerned with the people of the mountains – 'An Autumn Night in the Hills' and 'The Oppression of the Hills'. In 'An Autumn Night in the Hills', Synge describes a visit he made to a 'wild glen on the western slope of County Wicklow', to pick up a dog which had been wounded out shooting and left to recover at a mountain cottage. From the details given the glen may be identified as Glenmalure, the setting of *The Shadow*.[1] 'The road which led up to the cottage' is now tarred most of the way, and so it cannot be swept 'as smooth as a fine beach by the rain', like the dirt road of Synge's time. The granite of the mountains can no longer be seen on one side of the glen, which has been planted with firs. But the bridge and the 'range of slippery stones' at Baravore Ford are still the alternative means of crossing the river Avonbeg. And the final description of the dusk is

a vivid evocation of the desolation and sombre splendour of Glenmalure on a rainy night in autumn.

Not only the setting but the atmosphere of the essay is that of
The Shadow. The men of the household have all gone out to meet
the cortège of Mary Kinsella – 'a fine young woman with two
children [who] went wrong in the head' and died in the Richmond
Asylum. The women are left alone, a loneliness to which they are
accustomed. The young girl who has looked after the wounded dog
hands Synge a glass of milk:

> 'I'm afraid it's a lot of trouble I'm giving you,' I said as I took it,
> 'and you busy, with no men in the place.' 'No trouble at all in
> the world,' said the girl, 'and if it was itself, wouldn't any one be
> glad of it in the lonesome place we're in?' (*Prose* p. 188)

This becomes in the mouth of Nora Burke, 'It's in a lonesome place
you do have to be talking with someone, and looking for someone,
in the evening of the day' (*Plays* I p. 49). The emotions of the girl
in the essay are the emotions of Nora. The depth of her feeling for
the pointer dog which she has nursed, suggests her intense loneliness and her capacity for love. 'It's herself will be lonesome when
that dog is gone', says the woman. Nora recalls the dead Patch
Darcy, 'it's very lonesome I was after him a long while'. The slight
pathos of the girl who is so starved for love and companionship that
she must lavish it on a dog, becomes in the play the moving predicament of the woman who defends herself to Dan Burke: 'What way
would a woman live in a lonesome place the like of this place, and
she not making a talk with the men passing?' (*Plays* I p. 57)

In 'The Oppression of the Hills' Synge is concerned with various
instances of the 'tendency to nervous depression' among the people
of the hills caused by the desolate loneliness of their situation. These
range from a hysterical girl whom he had to conduct through a bog
one night to assure her that her sisters had not been drowned, to
the original of Patch Darcy in *The Shadow*:[2]

> there was a poor fellow below reaping in the glen, and in the
> evening he had two glasses of whiskey with some other lads.
> Then some excitement took him, and he threw off his clothes
> and ran away into the hills. There was great rain that night, and
> I suppose the poor creature lost his way, and was the whole
> night perishing in the rain and darkness. In the morning they
> found his naked footmarks on some mud half a mile above the

road, and again where you go up by a big stone. Then there was nothing known of him till last night, when they found his body on the mountain, and it near eaten by the crows. (*Prose* pp 209–210)

The 'oppression of the hills' is virtually another name for 'the shadow of the glen'. The essay gives us the generalised and discursive picture of which the play's title is emblematic. The hills are to the Wicklow men what the sea is to the Aran islanders, at once their source of livelihood and a potentially terrible enemy. In the empty spaces of the Wicklow mountains, as on the bare rocks of Aran, nature seems at best indifferent, at worst malevolent and destructive. The shadow of the glen is more than the shadow of old age and death; it is that force in nature which crushes man's consciousness and denies his being, which annihilates him with the sense of his insignificance.

Synge had relatively little interest or sympathy for the people of the villages and the valleys. Comparing 'The People of the Glens' and 'At a Wicklow Fair' with the other essays, it is easy to distinguish those areas of peasant life which are lit up by his imagination. His distaste for the villagers comes through in the description of a small town in 'The People of the Glens':

As soon as I came near Rathnew I passed many bands of girls and men making rather ruffianly flirtation on the pathway, and women who surged up to stare at me, as I passed in the middle of the road. . . . Half-drunken men and women stand about, wrangling and disputing in the dull light from the windows, which is only strong enough to show the wretchedness of the figures which pass continually across them. (*Prose* pp. 217–218)[3]

The censorious tone of disapproval sounds suspiciously like simple class prejudice. Again, we can just see Michael Dara in the atmosphere evoked in 'At a Wicklow Fair' – bustling, canny, self-satisfied: 'they were saying in the fair my lambs were the best lambs, and I got a grand price, for I'm no fool now at making a bargain when my lambs are good.' (*Plays* I p. 51) The original of Michael Dara might well be the farmer Synge meets 'standing before a public-house, looking radiant with delight', who explains, 'it's a fine fair, Mister, and I'm after selling the lambs I had here a month ago and no-one would look at them.' (*Prose* p. 226) Synge is scarcely very interested in such smug success. His attention is caught rather by the eccentrics of the community, the 'characters' he describes in 'The People of the Glens' – the returned emigrant with his stories of his life abroad, or the old man Cavanagh, who prided himself on his knowledge of local history. The ordinary local people often regard these eccentrics with dislike. ' "That's the greatest old rogue in the village," said the publican, as soon as [Cavanagh] was out of hearing; "he's always making up to all who pass through the place, and trying what he can get out of them." ' (*Prose* p. 224) Synge, however, delights in their oddity, and by comparison the solider citizens look tame and uninteresting.

Obviously, the tramps and tinkers were, for Synge, the most interesting group of all, and 'The Vagrants of Wicklow' is like a notebook of themes and incidents for the plays. There is the tramp who claimed to be over a hundred, who had spent many years at sea in his youth, and returned to Wicklow 'when he was too old to wander in the world'. The extraordinary story of his marriage at ninety and his fierce quarrel with his wife, his lament for his long white hair which was cut off in prison, must have been in Synge's mind when he imagined Martin Doul. Then Synge comments on 'the tramps and tinkers who wander round the West [and who] have a curious reputation for witchery and unnatural powers.' (*Prose* p. 203) A man in Aughavanna told him a story of the tinkers' powers of clairvoyance, and went on to describe a tinker gathering, which was to be used in *The Tinker's Wedding*:

> One time I seen fifty of them above on the road to Rathdangan, and they all match-making and marrying themselves for the year that was to come. One man would take such a woman, and say he was going such roads and places, stopping at this fair and another fair, till he'd meet them again at such a place, when the spring was coming on. Another, maybe, would swap the woman he had with another man, with as much talk as if you'd be selling a cow. . . . Sometimes when a party would be gone a bit down over the hill, a girl would begin crying out and wanting to go back to her ma. Then the man would say: 'Black hell to your soul, you've come with me now, and you'll go the whole way.'
> (*Prose* p. 204)

The vagrants, Synge points out, 'are nearly always at war with the police, and are often harshly treated.' He tells of a drunken flower-seller he once saw in a battle with the police, who wanted to force her out of a village. The woman refused to go quietly, and in the end, got the best of the struggle.

> 'Let this be the barrack's yard if you wish it,' she cried, tearing off the rags that still clung about her, 'Let this be the barrack's yard, and come on now, the lot of you.' Then she rushed at them with extraordinary fury; but the police, to avoid scandal, withdrew into the town, and left her to be quieted by her friends. (*Prose* p. 207)

The vagrants, with whom violence is habitual and unthinking, are not intimidated by the official representatives of law and order. They have no concept of social sanctions, no fear of 'scandal', and the flower-seller here can confront the police without shame, as the tinkers in *The Tinker's Wedding* stand unawed by the Priest. The last of the vagrants in the essay is a young ballad-singer, who was reprimanded by the police for his refusal to work for his living. His reply was to sing a ballad, pass round the hat, and insist on payment for what he had earned. Like all the vagrants in Synge's plays, he asserts his right to dispense with the conventional claims of society.

Synge is a little inclined to blur distinctions between one type of vagrants and another. Tramps and tinkers, for example, have always been quite distinct. The tramp is a solitary; the union implied between the Tramp and Nora at the end of *The Shadow* would, in fact, be rather uncommon. A tramp, as Synge suggests, is most often a single dropout from an ordinary rural family who chooses to take to the roads for personal reasons of temperament or circumstance. The tinkers, on the other hand, although they are not, like the Romanies, a different race, belong to large clans or tribes. Within the tinker world there is a considerable hierarchy, ranging from families who are all but respectable horse-dealers, to those who are permanently in and out of jail. In *The Tinker's Wedding*, 'Jaunting Jim' with his 'fine eye for a horse', and the 'rich tinkers of Meath', were obviously a cut above Michael Byrne who is only a tinker by trade.[4]

The relations of the two sorts of vagrants with the rest of the community is also different. The tramp could be virtually a free-lance agricultural labourer. When the Tramp in *The Shadow* says that he knows all the ways a man can put food in his mouth, these would include working short spells at harvest-time or potato-picking. Other tramps were professional drovers, and earned their living by driving sheep and cattle to the fairs. The tramp was an accepted part of the farming community; he would reappear in particular houses in a neighbourhood once or twice a year, where he was welcome to a night's board and lodgings in exchange for news of other parts of the country, and perhaps a little light work. Tinkers, on the other hand, were always genuine outcasts. The begging of the tinker women was often resented by small farmers, who suspected that the tinkers were better off than themselves. They had an age-old reputation for dishonesty, which made all the country people wary of having any dealings with them. The mutual suspicion and dislike between the tinkers and the 'rural people' could, on occasion, ignite into open conflict. In Ballinaclash, the setting of *The Tinker's Wedding*, the tale is still told of the great tinker fight, when the tinkers took over the village. The men were all away working in the mines of Avoca, but they were quickly summoned, and with the aid of red-hot iron bars heated by the smith (original of Timmy in *The Well of the Saints*), they drove the tinkers out.[5]

Although Synge neglects the distinction between tramp and tinker in his essay, it is clear from *The Shadow* and *The Tinker's Wedding* that he was aware of it. The Tramp, for example, is ushered into the house by Nora without undue hesitation, invited to the wake, and left alone in the cottage with the 'dead' man. He is familiar with the neighbourhood – he knew Patch Darcy, he had noticed the situation of the Burkes' house. He is closely related to the hill-folk and easily accepted, even though he is a 'stranger'. The tinkers, however, have no ties with the village people. The priest regards them as intruders in his parish, and distinguishes Sarah and Michael from one of his 'own couples'. (Synge cut out scenes from an earlier draft in which the tinker children gape with amazement at the village children going to First Communion.) Although Mary can buy porter from Jemmy Neill the publican, she does not drink it on the premises. It is obviously convenient for Synge to have Mary enter clutching the jug of porter, so we should not make too much of this, but it is true that many public-houses until recently would not serve itinerants drink except to take away.

Such a 'who's who in Wicklow' is not undertaken in defence of Synge's realism in the comedies. In the essays he does try to present, concisely and clearly, accurate social observations, and there is generally a discursive argument tying together the various passages of description. However, it is necessary to take in this Wicklow background, not principally in order to establish the authenticity of the plays, but to understand the precise social distinctions which are involved. 'There's a fine Union below in Rathdrum', suggests Michael Dara, when Nora is about to be turned out by her husband, but Dan knows that 'the like of her would never go there'. (*Plays* I p. 55) Nora would never go to the Union – the 'County Home' as it is now called – because for a farmer's wife like her it would be an impossible social degradation. If we are not in a position to pick up such details, our focus will always be softened, our view of the plays liable to the minute distortions which add up to misunderstanding.

The Shadow of the Glen

In 'The Oppression of the Hills' and 'An Autumn Night in the Hills' we saw the atmosphere and setting of *The Shadow*, but we must look beyond the Wicklow essays for the play's origins. The theme of *The Shadow* bears a curious resemblance to *When the Moon Has Set* – curious in that the one-act peasant comedy seems an odd metamorphosis for Synge's pseudo-Ibsenian country-house drama. Under the obvious differences, however, the essential movement of the plays is similar: the intellectually 'enlightened' Colum wins Sister Eileen away from a house of death and a conventional religion, as the Tramp gives Nora a definite alternative to the misery of the loveless marriage. The union with which both plays end is celebrated with a lyrical vision of natural harmony. Synge's concern with freedom was prior to his discovery of a means to express it artistically. That the vehicle which he did find to express the theme of *When the Moon Has Set* should have been the Aran folk-tale of Pat Dirane, is even more surprising. The story of the husband who pretends to be dead is non-moral and non-emotional, a swift and sparse action on which the narrator makes no comment, and needs to make none.[6] The story has no specific or inherent moral. It is a version of the January/May situation, to which the audience reaction is necessarily ambiguous: old husbands are jealous, young wives give them reason, such is the way of the world in fabliaux and folk-tale. It depends entirely on the particular instance which of the two triumphs – on which side we are supposed to be cheering.

The essential disparity between form and meaning, which is

emphasised by this identification of origins, necessarily entailed the play's failure according to some critics. 'If Synge had succeeded in harmonising a fine and sensitive creature [Yeats's description of Nora] with a story so integrally rough and comic, he would indeed have achieved a miracle.'[7] Perhaps he did achieve such a miracle. If we look at the play with an idea of harmony involving balance and contrast, rather than homogeneity, we may find that it does have its own form of unity. The 'sensitive creature' and the rough comedy are both there, and their apparent incompatibility is accepted. We can best see Synge's dramatic use of the play's contrasted modes if we make our way through it scene by scene, watching the way he exploits the varying expectations of his audience. (Even with the tiny dimensions of *The Shadow*, it is worth dividing into scenes, on the basis of Synge's own later practice, a new scene for each change of characters on stage.) After following through the linear movement of the action as audience, we may stand back, as readers, and consider the pattern made by the whole play.

Scene i   Nora + Tramp   (*Plays* I pp. 33–41)
In the opening dialogue between Nora and the Tramp, we are provided with all the essentials of atmosphere and situation. A formal relationship is presented in the social terms of address the Tramp and Nora use – 'stranger' and 'lady of the house'. We learn of Dan's death, and just possibly the Tramp's remark, 'It's a queer look on him for a man that's dead', may alert a faint suspicion. Nora's reaction to his death is certainly not quite normal. She can joke about him, 'he was always queer, stranger, and I suppose them that's queer and they living men will be queer bodies after', and speak almost as though he were a casual acquaintance. A great deal depends on the way this scene is directed, and no doubt Nora's indifference to her husband's death may be presented as callousness. Yet there is no sign of any great emotion, neither exultation nor grief, and she seems simply unaffected, moving about her household work in a perfectly normal manner. As she says to the Tramp: 'It doesn't matter, any way'.

Having settled in and been provided with whiskey and tobacco as required by the custom of the wake, the Tramp strikes up conversation with Nora. From a general discussion of the hills and their terrors, they move on to what is still in some sort the local news – the death of Patch Darcy. Synge deliberately quickens the pace of his language as the Tramp tells the story of his last encounter with Darcy:

> I was passing below on a dark night the like of this night, and the sheep were lying under the ditch and every one of them coughing, and choking, like an old man, with the great rain and the fog. . . . Then I heard a thing talking – queer talk, you wouldn't believe at all, and you out of your dreams, – and 'Merciful God,' says I, 'if I begin hearing the like of that voice out of the thick mist, I'm destroyed surely.' Then I run, and I run, and I run, till I was below in Rathvanna. I got drunk that night, I got drunk in the morning, and drunk the day after, – I was coming from the races beyond – and the third day they found Darcy . . . Then I knew it was himself I was after hearing, and I wasn't afeard any more.

It is the vivid narrative, the circumstantial recollection of the expert story-teller, who can even find time to explain how he had the cash to get drunk three days in a row. Nora's reaction is significant.

> *Nora* (speaking sorrowfully and slowly).   God spare Darcy, he'd always look in here and he passing up or passing down, and it's very lonesome I was after him a long while (she looks over at the bed and lowers her voice, speaking very clearly), and then I got happy again – if it's ever happy we are, stranger – for I got used to being lonesome.

The slow reflective melancholy of Nora's speech contrasts sharply with the excitement of the Tramp's story. It is obvious that she had a special feeling for Darcy, the glance over at the bed suggests that Dan was jealous, but Synge does not intend us to know whether he had cause to be.

Nora's mind runs from Patch to Michael Dara – because Michael Dara supplied Darcy's place? She certainly feels some constraint in speaking of him to the Tramp. Although the Tramp remarks jocularly (and of course ironically) 'A man that's dead can do not hurt', he is uneasy at being left alone in the cottage, while Nora goes out to look for Michael, and he asks for a needle to stitch up his coat and to provide him with talismanic protection – 'there's great safety in a needle, lady of the house'. Nora's reply is hardly cheering: 'isn't a dead man itself more company than to be sitting alone, and hearing the winds crying and you not knowing on what thing your mind would stay'. Again, as in the Tramp's description of crossing the mountains, there are hints of the uncanny and an uneasy awareness of 'the oppression of the hills'.

Scene ii   Dan + Tramp   (*Plays* I pp. 41–5)
When the dead man rises from his bed, the audience may share the Tramp's bewilderment: is this a ghost or not? The Tramp's comic confusion is our own: 'I meant no harm, your honour; and won't you leave me easy to be saying a little prayer for your soul?' But Synge quickly removes all doubts as to Dan's materiality by playing up his thirst – 'How would I be dead, and I as dry as a baked bone?' – and there is nothing unearthly about the old man as he complains, 'I've a cramp in my back, and my hip's asleep on me, and there's been the devil's own fly itching my nose'. All the suggestion of mystery and the macabre are apparently blown away by the mock resurrection. This is straightforward boisterous comedy, and Dan Burke is the typical choleric old husband of comic stock, crude, cantankerous and suspicious. We laugh at him, but true to the ignoble ethics of comedy, we are placed on his side – the side of the deceiver against the deceived. This, the simplest sort of comic irony, involves a sense of superiority over the less informed, which we share with those as well informed as ourselves. The Tramp, as Dan's passive ally, is our representative: 'What is it that I know of the like of you that I'd be saying a word or putting out my hand to stay you at all?'

Scene iii   Nora + Michael + Tramp; Nora + Michael
                                                          (*Plays* I pp. 45–53)
At the beginning of this scene we are in an assured world of comedy, waiting for Nora and Michael to betray themselves to the listening husband. The Tramp plays his part – 'There was no sign from himself? – No sign at all, lady of the house' – and sits back to watch what will happen. The efforts of Nora to get rid of the Tramp are in the vein of ironic comedy we would expect:

> Will you drink a sup of tea with myself and the young man, stranger, or (speaking more persuasively) will you go into the little room and stretch yourself a short while on the bed. I'm thinking it's destroyed you are walking the length of that way in the great rain.

The Tramp, of course, will not budge. However, the interchange between the Tramp and Michael which follows while Nora is busy with the tea things, is not quite what we would expect, and it is at this point that the unusual quality of the play begins to emerge. Michael sneers at the Tramp's old coat, the Tramp sneers at Michael's inability to drive sheep; Michael comes off worst in the argument. Nora seems to be on the side of the Tramp rather than Michael, and both of them praise Patch Darcy at Michael's expense. The action does not appear to be running along the regular comic lines. Mike, who was cast for the role of lover, turns out to be a poor-spirited creature, and there is already a closer understanding between Nora and the Tramp who have only just met. The recurrence of Patch Darcy's name makes it clear that the figure of the dead shepherd is somehow significant, but we cannot as yet see in what way.

The Tramp retires to his corner, and the stage is effectively left to Nora and Michael. This is where the 'goings-on' for which Dan is waiting might be expected to begin:

Michael (looking at her with a queer look).   I heard tell this day, Nora Burke, that it was on the path below Patch Darcy would be passing up and passing down, and I heard them say he'd never pass it night or morning without speaking with yourself.

Michael has only just heard the gossip about Nora, and a reference to his predecessor is perhaps as appropriate an opening for courtship as any other. For a moment – and it is the only moment in the play – there is a suggestion of the coquette in Nora's speech:

if it's a power of men I'm after knowing they were fine men, for I was a hard child to please, and a hard girl to please (she looks at him a little sternly), and it's a hard woman I am to please this day, Michael Dara, and it's no lie, I'm telling you.

Michael's retort, however, kills the flirtation dead: 'Was it a hard woman to please you were when you took himself for your man?' Michael moves on to the immediate business in hand, finding out what money the old man left, but Nora is led off into a reflection on her past life with Dan. Her marriage with him was a mistake, not because she did not love him – she never even thinks of that – but because the monotonous constriction, the desolate loneliness of her life in that cottage has been intolerable. Her meditation is wholly serious, and she is given all the audience's respectful attention. She is infinitely remote from Michael Dara, whose part remains essentially comic. Absorbed in counting out the supposed dowry, he has no ears for Nora's 'queer talk'. He carries all the comic interest of the basic situation: it is Dan's money he is appropriating, and we know that Dan is listening to him count it.

The scene between Nora and Michael is scarcely a love-scene. Presumably Dan could feel that he is given evidence that there was an understanding between them, and Michael's haste in planning marriage is certainly unseemly. But what Dan rises from his bed to hear, is by no means love-making. There can be no trace of flirtatiousness in Nora's voice as she says:

> Why would I marry you, Mike Dara? You'll be getting old, and I'll be getting old, and in a little while, I'm telling you, you'll be sitting up in your bed – the way himself was sitting – with a shake in your face, and your teeth falling, and the white hair sticking out round you like an old bush where sheep do be leaping a gap.

It is hard to know which way the laugh goes as Dan re-enacts this description, '(Dan Burke sits up noiselessly from under the sheet, with his hand to his face. His white hair is sticking out round his head.)' Nora's ignorance that her husband is listening may be comic, but what he overhears is an analytic and objective account of his physical repulsiveness. This is not the comedy we might expect – the unfaithful wife caught maligning the supposedly dead husband – for there is no malice here, no gloating joy to be reversed or deflated. The bitterness of Nora's reflection is generalised: 'God forgive me, Michael Dara, we'll all be getting old, but it's a queer thing surely.'

Scene iv   Omnes   (Plays I pp. 53–7)

The vigorous éclat of Dan's leap from the bed, like the eruption of Old Mahon into Act III of *The Playboy*, is wholly comic. (It is introduced by what must be one of the oldest gags of farce – the violent sneeze of the eavesdropper.) The moment where Dan threatens Michael with the stick and Michael cowers in the corner, 'Get me out of it, Nora, for the love of God. He always did what you bid him, and I'm thinking he would do it now', is the broadest comedy. Dan facing his wife, however, turns gradually from the comic stock figure into a very real and terrible old man. The hatred we hear in his voice cannot be softened with the solvent of laughter:

It's lonesome roads she'll be going, and hiding herself away till the end will come, and they find her stretched like a dead sheep with the frost on her, or the big spiders, maybe, and they putting their webs on her, in the butt of a ditch.

The confrontation between them is in deadly earnest.

Nora (angrily).   What way will yourself be that day, Daniel Burke? What way will you be that day and you lying down a long while in your grave? For it's bad you are living, and it's bad you'll be when you're dead. (She looks at him a moment fiercely, then half turns away and speaks plaintively again.) Yet, if it is itself, Daniel Burke, who can help it at all, and let you be getting up into your bed, and not be taking your death with the wind blowing on you, and the rain with it, and you half in your skin.

The flaring anger followed by the tone of tired pity was, no doubt, habitual with Nora in her fights with Dan. We are given a terrifying glimpse of the married life of the Burkes.

The Tramp, who has been more or less forgotten in the chimney corner, comes forward to take Nora's side, and his protest signals the moment at which the jealous old husband stops being funny: 'It's a hard thing you're saying, for an old man, master of the house, and what would the like of her do if you put her out on the roads?' The dialogue between the Tramp and Nora in the first scene established links between them, so it is not altogether surprising that they should go off together now. But Synge is careful to make the dénouement itself dramatically plausible. The Tramp tries to reconcile her to Dan, asks whether Michael Dara will take her, and clearly regards the life of the roads as a last resort. It is by Dan's order that they leave together. 'Let her walk out of that door, and let you go along with her stranger – if it's raining itself – for it's too much talk you have surely.' It is only when they find themselves in company, that the Tramp attempts to console Nora. The two speeches in which he imagines the pleasures Nora will meet on the roads tend to look like a lyrical set-piece, and the play for a moment seems dominated by an idealised vagrant/poet. But the speeches are broken up theatrically by Nora's movements on stage as she gathers up her belongings, and the Tramp's rhetoric is qualified by the grumbling reply, 'I'm thinking it's myself will be wheezing that time with lying down under the Heavens when the night is cold'. Where the romantic ending of *When the Moon Has*

Set is impossibly sentimental and unconvincing, the hard realism of *The Shadow* can carry the alliance between the Tramp and Nora. They are not lovers making their exit into the rosy glow of sunset and happy-ever-after, but a couple thrown together by chance going out into a wild rainy night, taking the only road they can.

Scene v   Dan + Michael   (*Plays* I pp. 57–9)
Dan may have won, but Nora's is, in a sense, the last word:

> what way will yourself live from this day, with none to care you? What is it you'll have now but a black life, Daniel Burke, and it's not long, I'm telling you, till you'll be lying under that sheet, and you dead surely.

We see in this scene what way he will live – he will spend his time drinking whiskey with Michael Dara. The little epilogue is a splendid ironic touch, with outraged husband and putative adulterer sitting down for a peaceful drink together. Michael, true to form, is not put out by the embarrassing situation, nor offended by the contempt of Dan's tone: 'I was thinking to strike you, Michael Dara, but you're a quiet man, God help you, and I don't mind you at all.' Nora was right. 'It's in a lonesome place you do have to be talking to someone, and looking for someone, in the evening of the day.' Nora's crime was talking to Patch Darcy, or to Michael Dara, but Dan too will talk to Michael Dara, *faute de mieux*, and it is indeed a 'black life' which is now before him.

After watching *The Shadow*, an audience might well be doubtful of their reactions. Within the compass of some twenty minutes, they will have passed through a variety of attitudes towards the characters on stage, and the result may be a blurred sense of what they have seen. Although several moments are theatrically striking, the after-image may be confused and discordant. But *The Shadow* repays re-reading. The strength of the play only appears when it is considered with the view of the relationship of its parts which is never possible for an audience, who are always attending to an unfinished structure. The varying configurations of character, which may be bewildering at first sight in the theatre, with detailed consideration resolve themselves into complex and subtle patterns. These are patterns which can be traced in the texture of the language, in the recurring words, names and phrases which run through the play.

When Dan appears from under the bed-clothes for the first time, he ridicules the idiotic chatter he has overheard: 'It's near dead I was wanting to sneeze, and you blathering about the rain, and Darcy (bitterly) – the devil choke him – and the towering church.' (*Plays* I p. 43) The repetition of the Tramp and Nora's conversation adds to the basic comedy – the eavesdropper, supposed dead, listening in to the conversation of the 'survivors'. Michael's plan for marriage with Nora is the most incriminating part of the singularly innocent 'love-scene':

> We'd do right to wait now till himself will be quiet a while in the Seven Churches, and then you'll marry me in the chapel of Rathvanna, and I'll bring the sheep up on the bit of a hill you have on the back mountain, and we won't have anything we'd be afeard to let our minds on when the mist is down. (*Plays* I p. 51)

When Dan makes his second resurrection, therefore, brandishing his stick, he naturally throws Michael's words in his teeth.

> Now you'll not marry her the time I'm rotting below in the Seven Churches, and you'll see the thing I'll give you will follow you on the back mountain when the wind is high. (*Plays* I p. 53)

The eavesdropper has his moment of triumph, and it is his special delight to show those overheard how completely they have been caught out.

Dan, however, does not repeat Michael's words quite unchanged. 'Quiet' – Michael is afraid of the old man's ghost – becomes 'rotting'. The substitution is itself comic, but in the context it is suggestive of Dan's frame of mind. He turns on Nora, and repeats words she has spoken earlier. 'There'll be an end now of your fine times, and all the talk you have of young men and old men, and of the mist coming up or going down.' (*Plays* I p. 53) He recalls here the speeches in which Nora expressed the monotonous desolation of her life,

> seeing nothing but the mists rolling down the bog, and the mists again, and they rolling up the bog, and hearing nothing but the wind crying out in the bits of broken trees were left in the great storm, and the streams roaring with the rain . . .

and her feeling of the meaningless approach of old age, 'the young growing behind me and the old passing' (*Plays* I p. 49). Dan completely distorts her words; these were anything but 'fine times'. It is the measure of his obsessiveness that he can transform Nora's lament on the passing generations into evidence of a swarm of lovers. We are made to realise that Nora's infidelity is not the issue. To Dan, morosely absorbed with his own old age and coming death, the very fact of her youth is an insult, a constant humiliation.

All through the play the characters talk about sheep. What else would sheep-farmers talk about? Michael Dara's inability to drive mountain ewes, Patch Darcy's expertise are, no doubt, everyday topics of conversation. With such natural allusions, however, Synge deliberately creates a motif running through the play. Dan, for instance, is associated with sick or dying sheep. 'When the sun set on the bog beyond, he made a great lep, and let a great cry out of him, and stiffened himself out the like of a dead sheep.' (*Plays* I p. 35) As the Tramp prepares to leave with Nora, he assures her that for the future 'there'll be no old fellow wheezing the like of a sick sheep close to your ear'. In his description of the hills earlier, the terms were reversed: 'the sheep were lying under the ditch and every one of them coughing, and choking, like an old man, with the great rain and the fog' (*Plays* I p. 39). The owner grows like his animals, and Dan Burke becomes a grotesque figure of sheep/man. The animal association heightens our sense of the imminent corruption of the flesh. Elsewhere sheep may be associated with pastoral bliss – Phyllis and Strephon and love in the spring – but not in *The Shadow*.

The names of certain off-stage figures which are mentioned in *The Shadow* help to suggest the community of the glen. There is Mary Brien, who is a younger contemporary of Nora's and presumably a close neighbour. Peggy Cavanagh is an old woman, who was once a prosperous farmer's wife, but is now homeless and reduced to begging at the cross-roads. The madness and death of the shepherd Patch Darcy in the previous year, is still a subject which comes up naturally in the conversation. With allusions to these people, Synge extends the dimensions of the little society presented, and gives it a familiar reality. It is not necessary to know much about the characters whose names are mentioned; the fact that they recur in the conversation establishes a context beyond that of the cottage room and the four characters we see on stage.

The names, however, are not merely picked at random. Together the three off-stage figures illustrate the plight of Nora Burke. Mary Brien is one of the 'young growing behind' Nora, and her life is for

Nora a reminder of the meaningless passing of her own. On the other hand, the fate of Peggy Cavanagh, the homeless woman of the roads, is the alternative to the monotonous career of the farmer's wife:

> there she is now walking round on the roads, or sitting in a dirty old house, with no teeth in her mouth, and no sense, and no more hair than you'd see on a bit of a hill and they after burning the furze from it. (*Plays* I p. 51)

Maybe, in future, as the Tramp says, she will not be 'hearing a talk of getting old like Peggy Cavanagh', but there is no guarantee that she will not find herself in the same situation. Patch Darcy's end is even more terrifying, a byword for the destructive power of the hills:

> If myself was easy afeard, I'm telling you, it's long ago I'd have been locked into the Richmond Asylum, or maybe have run up into the back hills with nothing on me but an old shirt, and been eaten with crows the like of Patch Darcy – the Lord have mercy on him – in the year that's gone. (*Plays* I p. 37)

His death, and the manner of his death, so cows the people of the glen, that Nora is surprised to hear the Tramp praise him – 'isn't it a grand thing when you hear a living man saying a good word of a dead man, and he mad dying?' (*Plays* I p. 47) If Nora, as she comes to see her life in the course of the play, is caught between the thought of Mary Brien and Peggy Cavanagh, it is perhaps the fate of Patch Darcy which is the ultimate terror.

And yet Darcy is more than a particularly horrifying *memento mori*, for the characters in *The Shadow* are divided and distinguished by the attitude they express towards his memory. Nora remembers him with affection and regret, in tones which suggest a lost companion and friend rather than a dead lover. Dan quite obviously hated him, and curses bitterly at the mention of his name. Michael Dara, who, it must be remembered, has only recently come to live in the glen, enquires casually, 'Is it the man went queer in his head the year that's gone?' (*Plays* I p. 47) It is the Tramp who speaks of him at length, and it is his attitude which gives significance to that of the others. He praises Patch in words which Synge records hearing in the essay on Aughrim fair:

> That was a great man, young fellow, a great man I'm telling you. There was never a lamb from his own ewes he wouldn't

know before it was marked, and he'd run from this to the city of Dublin, and never catch for his breath. (*Plays* I p. 47)

This eulogy, the emphasis on the word 'great', together with his spectacular death, make us think of Patch in terms of an heroic ideal of the past. It is appropriate that Nora and the Tramp should find common ground in their admiration for the dead shepherd. As Dan and Michael both in different ways reject his image, so the other two characters in their feeling for Patch Darcy proclaim their identification with what is extraordinary and strange in life.

When we stand back, finally, to consider the play in its entirety, it is the shadow of the glen itself which is central.[8] There is a network of allusions running through the play, which suggests the effect the shadow of the glen has upon the lives of the characters. Dan 'dies', appropriately enough, 'the time the shadow was going up through the glen'. More often, the shadow is the mountain mist rather than the darkness – 'the mists rolling down the bog, and the mists again and they rolling up the bog'. Michael Dara, who is out of his natural territory in the glen, is uneasily aware that there are things 'we'd be afeard to let our minds on when the mist is down'. Nora describes Dan to the Tramp: 'He was an old man, and an odd man, and it's always up on the hills he was, thinking thoughts in the dark mist.' (*Plays* I p. 35) The whole of Dan's behaviour, his obsessive jealousy, his hatred of his wife, the trick of assumed death itself, seems more plausible when we think of his solitary life, herding sheep in the darkness of the hills. For Nora herself, from within the security of the cottage, the shadow is not so much an object of fear as a figure for boredom and loneliness. It is just that banal quality of repetition in the mists going up and going down, which Synge's parodists have ridiculed, that is typical of her situation. The Tramp, although he protests that he is not 'easy afeard', has a healthy respect for the shadow. It is, however, supernatural rather than natural forces which he fears. He was terrified by the 'voice out of the dark mist', but when he learned that it had been the mad Patch Darcy, he 'wasn't afeard any more'. The Tramp's world is one peopled with uncanny powers, which it would be foolhardy to disregard, but in so far as natural phenomena are concerned, he has the sane realism of the human being who knows his own limitations. 'It's a wild night, God help us, but it'll pass surely.'

*   *   *

There are only four characters in *The Shadow*, but as with any play, the reader or audience instinctively groups them in the dynamic relations of the theatre: 'them' and 'us', heroes and villains, principals and subordinates. Synge's technique, as it emerges from a combined theatrical and literary reading of *The Shadow*, is to make us constantly re-group his characters, and to revise the criteria by which they had been grouped before. What he found in Pat Dirane's folk-tale were the three characters of the love-triangle and a narrator. For much of *The Shadow* the Tramp keeps the neutral role of the observer, equally polite to the 'lady of the house' and the 'master of the house', uncommitted in the battle between them. It is only when he is included with the audience in Dan's secret, that he seems to be on the old husband's side, as the narrator in the story is. The Tramp is the outsider who happens into the drama. And yet in some ways Michael Dara, the 'kind of farmer has come up from the sea', the man who cannot drive mountain eyes, is more like the odd man out in the group. Although the Tramp is the 'stranger', by his knowledge of the mountains he is more closely related to the hill men than Michael. In so far as they all belong in the glen, the Tramp, Nora and Dan all share an experience which Michael Dara scarcely understands. The ultimate development by which the Tramp and Nora find themselves together in opposition to Dan and Michael is, of course, Synge's special twist to the story.

The different groupings of the characters may be isolated to illustrate the different levels of dramatic experience which Synge worked into the play. The Tramp is set against the other three as in the folk-tale structure, in which we are given action at its simplest and least individualised. The story dramatised develops into the ironic comedy of the eavesdropper, where the division is Dan + Tramp versus Nora + Michael. At the same time we are asked to recognise the social distinction between shepherd and lowland farmer which divides Michael from the rest. The play is given the detailed setting of actuality, and so demands the attention to social differentiation proper to naturalism. At this level *The Shadow* may be called a 'peasant play'. But within this realistic context, the language is often used with the oblique effect of symbolism. It is by poetic indirection that we are made aware of the differences which set the imaginative Tramp and Nora against the unimaginative Dan and Michael. Folk-tale and farce, peasant naturalism and poetic drama all coexist within *The Shadow*, and it is the balance and ironic contrast between these several modes which go to make up the play's meaning.

The Tinker's Wedding

The Tinker's Wedding is the least distinguished of Synge's plays, a play to forget about, many of his critics have felt. 'One is sorry Synge ever wrote so poor a thing, and one fails to understand why it should have been staged anywhere.'[9] 'Why he decided to publish *The Tinker's Wedding* is difficult to fathom.'[10] The only recent attempt to defend it is not very convincing. Robin Skelton detects hidden mythological motifs in the play, largely on the basis of discarded draft material. He stresses 'the Movements of May', a title Synge considered for the play, and argues that 'the awakening of the year is given mythic overtones, and linked with the emotional excitement of Sarah Casey'.[11] Synge, we are told, 'was struggling to present a vision of humanity trapped by the "movements of May"'.[12] This is certainly too solemn and too pretentious an interpretation of *The Tinker's Wedding*.

However, the play is not as bad as its critics claim, and it does not deserve the neglect it has met. When the Abbey theatre finally 'risked' producing it – some sixty-four years after its publication – it played very well. If it seems poorer than it actually is, it is perhaps because when we compare it with Synge's other plays, it appears light-weight. One of the questions which *The Tinker's Wedding* raises, indeed, is why it should have been so much less successful than the other plays. It was started in the very productive summer of 1902, at the same time as *Riders* and *The Shadow*, and it was repeatedly re-worked before being published in 1907. The process of its development was the same as with most of Synge's plays: he dramatised a story he had heard, first very literally, then gradually working beyond his source through several drafts towards a fully elaborated dramatic structure. It is closely related in form and content to the more successful comedies, *The Shadow*, *The Well of the Saints* and *The Playboy*. And yet it seems very unsatisfactory by comparison with these other three. We should try to do justice to the neglected merits of *The Tinker's Wedding*, but it may also be valuable for our understanding of Synge to define the sources of its failure.

The comic mainspring of *The Tinker's Wedding* is an ironic situation, the clash between two mutually uncomprehending worlds. Literally speaking, there is a double irony in the dealings between the Priest and the tinkers, for both are ignorant of the other's style of life and way of thinking. With the audience in a position to understand both, the result is something like the delight of a cross-talk act. Two moments are outstanding. In Act I Mary innocently asks the Priest to say a prayer for her to hear:

Mary . . . I often heard the rural people making a queer noise and they going to rest; but who'd mind the like of them? And I'm thinking it should be great game to hear a scholar, the like of you, speaking Latin to the saints above.

Priest (scandalised). Stop your talking, Mary Byrne; you're an old flagrant heathen, and I'll stay no more with the lot of you. (He rises.)

Mary (catching hold of him). Stop till you say a prayer, your reverence; stop till you say a little prayer, I'm telling you, and I'll give you my blessing and the last sup from the jug. (*Plays* II p. 21)

Mary can see no harm in her request for a private prayer-show; it is for her only like asking a foreigner to say a few words in his own tongue to see what it sounds like. The drunken old tinker woman offering the priest her 'blessing' is a specially funny twist.

The high-point of the play is the moment of confrontation between the tinkers and the Priest in the second act:

Priest (losing his temper finally). Go on, now, or I'll send the Lords of Justice a dated story of your villainies – burning, stealing, robbing, raping to this mortal day. Go on now, I'm saying, if you'd run from Kilmainham or the rope itself.

Michael (taking off his coat). Is it run from the like of you, holy father? Go up to your own shanty, or I'll beat you with the ass's reins till the world would hear you roaring from this place to the coast of Clare.

Priest. Is it lift your hand upon myself when the Lord would blight your members if you'd touch me now? Go on from this. (He gives him a shove.)

Michael. Blight me is it? Take it then, your reverence, and God help you so. (*Plays* II p. 45)

The Priest has lived so long among people who hold his cloth in awe, that he really believes that his person is sacred, but to his opponents he is no more than a weedy physical specimen. Sarah's tone is contemptuous: 'I've bet a power of strong lads east and west through the world, and are you thinking I'd turn back from a priest?' (*Plays* II p. 43)

The physical vitality of the tinkers, which is always on the edge of violence, is one of the play's strongest features in the theatre. Mary Byrne tells of the 'great queens of Ireland with white necks on them the like of Sarah Casey, and fine arms would hit you a slap the way Sarah Casey would hit you.' (*Plays* II p. 25) In the second act we are made to realise that Mary has good reason to be frightened of Sarah's 'fine arms', for when she learns that Mary has sold the can which was to pay for her marriage, she picks up a bottle and tries to break her head. It is the Priest's interference in this quarrel, as much as his refusal to marry the tinkers, which leads to the attack on him. Synge allows his audience to revel in the comic violence of the assault, and the situation which follows with the Priest tied up in a sack and Mary Byrne sitting on his head. Yet there is a moment at which it seems as if the play will leave the rails of farcical comedy altogether. There is something genuinely terrifying in Michael's casual suggestion of murder: 'I have a mind to run him in a bog-hole the way he'll not be tattling to the peelers of our games today.' (*Plays* II p. 47) If Synge is perhaps inclined to idealise the tinkers' way of life, he does not let us forget that the corollary of their freedom is their total lack of restraint. This sort of moment of uncertainty, in which the comically acceptable form of violence seems to be turning into a horrifying reality, was to be extended into a basic technique in *The Well of the Saints* and *The Playboy*.

The star part of *The Tinker's Wedding*, the only really effective character, is Mary Byrne. She is a splendid comic mixture of *naïveté* and cunning, wisdom and ignorance. She sincerely pities the Priest his hard life, and quite unselfconsciously tries to cheer him up:

> It'd break my heart to hear you talking and sighing the like of that, your reverence. (She pats him on the knee.) Let you rouse up, now, if it's a poor single man you are itself, and I'll be singing you songs unto the dawn of day. (*Plays* II p. 19)

'The Night before Larry was Stretched' is her theme tune, but she has the tact to realise that she should not sing 'a bad wicked song' in the presence of the Priest. Mary is the only character in the play who has the range of tone and mood which makes possible a rounded stage impersonation. She is jovial, maternal and benign with the Priest, but a minute later she is screaming down the road at Sarah, 'Let you be walking back here, Sarah Casey, and not be making whisper-talk with the like of him in the face of the Almighty God' (*Plays* II p. 21). She has nothing but good-humoured contempt for the sulky and weak-willed Michael:

> You'll breed asses, I've heard them say, and poaching dogs, and horses'd go licking the wind, but it's a hard thing, God help me, to breed sense in a son. (*Plays* II p. 35)

When she is left alone at the end of Act I, she has a moment of pathos before her comic buoyancy reappears:

> What good am I this night, God help me? What good are the grand stories I have when it's few would listen to an old woman, few but a girl maybe would be in great fear the time her hour was come, or a little child wouldn't be sleeping with the hunger on a cold night? (*Plays* II p. 27)

Mary Byrne stands out from her surroundings as a comic character to compare with the Widow Quin or Michael James in *The Playboy*.

What then is wrong with *The Tinker's Wedding*? Even though we laugh at it, and enjoy its farcical moments, the situation seems somehow spurious, and the whole play leaves an uncomfortable impression of falsity. This may be partly because Synge had no first-hand knowledge of the tinker's life. His nephew Edward Stephens tells us,

> The material of the play was derived from the lore of the country people, not from any direct association with the tinkers them-selves. They were so dirty and in their mode of life so disreput-able that it would have been impossible for John to mix with them at his ease. He warned me against dropping into conversa-tion with them on the road.[13]

This may not be entirely accurate, but certainly Synge was less familiar with the tinkers than with the tramps, with whom he often stopped to talk. As a result, the assumptions on which *The Tinker's Wedding* was based were largely mistaken. The *Report of the Commission on Itinerancy* (1963) reveals that virtually all itinerants are Catholics, and although they do not regularly attend Mass, they 'see to it that their children receive the Sacraments of

Baptism, Penance, Holy Communion and Confirmation'.[14] The marriage tie, it seems, 'is not any weaker than it is in other Catholic marriages . . . itinerants have a high standard of sexual morality and there is no evidence of promiscuity'.[15] The evidence in a government report may perhaps have an element of window-dressing, and, of course, the situation may have changed since Synge's day. But it seems likely that the story of the tinker wife-swapping told in 'The Vagrants of Wicklow' is a malicious invention of the peasant community. The tradition of free love which is implied in *The Tinker's Wedding* with marriage regarded as an absurd innovation – this Synge surely invented.

Logically, in a farcical comedy where implausibility is of the essence, such inaccuracy should not matter, but in *The Tinker's Wedding* it makes for inconsistency in the comic situation itself. The tinkers, supposedly, have no experience of orthodox institutional religion, their knowledge of Catholicism is hearsay only.

> *Mary.*   If it's prayers I want, you'd have a right to say one yourself, holy father; for we don't have them at all, and I've heard tell a power of times it's that you're for. (*Plays* II p. 21)

Why, then, at the end of the play, should they be frightened from the stage by a Latin malediction? Their talk suggests that they are not wholly ignorant of the Church. Sarah says of Mary, 'She's no shame the time she's a drop taken; and if it was the Holy Father from Rome was in it, she'd give him a little sup out of the mug' (*Plays* II p. 19). The Priest himself is addressed throughout as 'holy father' or 'your reverence'. The candles on the altar are the 'flaming candles on the Throne of God'. The fact is that the tinkers' language in the play is the language of the ordinary Catholic peasants, for Synge knew no other speech to give them. Although for the purposes of the situation they are seen as a pagan 'natural tribe', as separate from the country people as the true gipsies, it was not possible to make them convincingly different in words and behaviour.

The tinker's life which he imagines, free and unfettered by convention, is very obviously an ideal for Synge – too obviously, we may feel. The ironic comedy of misunderstanding depends for its effectiveness on a dispassionate neutrality between the two sides. What is funny is that tinkers should not understand priests, or priests tinkers, and if we are disposed to favour one or the other, the good humour of the laughter is tainted. The trouble is that in

The Tinker's Wedding it is plain where Synge's allegiance lies. Even though he tried to restore the ironic balance by giving the final triumph to the Priest, the ideological weight of the play is with the tinkers, or at least with Mary Byrne. Mary quite clearly has her creator's sympathy and is intended to win ours. We can sense the authorial approval in her words, as she decries marriage: 'what good will it do? Is it putting that ring on your finger will keep you from getting an aged woman and losing the fine face you have?' (*Plays* II p. 37) Her speech, as she holds down the Priest, has a didactic ring which picks it out as the 'moral' of the story:

> It's sick and sorry we are to tease you; but what did you want meddling with the like of us, when it's a long time we are going our own ways – father and son, and his son after, or mother and daughter, and her own daughter again – and it's little need we ever had of going up into a church and swearing . . . (*Plays* II p. 47)

(The smug tone of self-righteousness is hardly justifiable; after all, it was the tinkers that meddled with the Priest, not the other way round.) In the debate between the conventional religion of the Priest and the 'natural' religion of the tinkers as expressed by Mary, it was impossible for Synge to remain neutral. The Priest is perhaps too farcical a figure to make the play in any serious sense anti-clerical. But if Synge did not create a fully realised representative of orthodoxy, he could not hold back his reaction against it, and as a result the drunken old tinker Mary Byrne seems to take on the uncomfortable role of doctrinaire apologist.

Perhaps the main reason for the failure of *The Tinker's Wedding* is that the story on which it was based was not suitable for Synge's purposes. It is, like the other three comedies, concerned with the clash between conventional and unconventional, with the relation of the eccentric individual to the ordinary community. Yet it could not engage Synge's most serious concerns. We can see this if we compare the situations of Nora Burke and Sarah Casey. Both are caught between the possibility of security and respectability on the one hand, and freedom and fulfilment on the other. Nora is forced to forsake the shelter of the farm, and to accept the life of the roads, more or less against her will. Sarah's main object in marrying seems to be to become an 'honest woman': 'I'll be married now in a short while; and from this day there will no one have a right to call me a dirty name and I selling cans in Wicklow or Wexford or the city of Dublin itself.' (*Plays* II p. 35) But why should she care? She is not conventionally squeamish about anything else. Her desire for marriage is ironically attributed to the change of the moon: May, the traditional month of romance, absurdly, makes Sarah long for matrimony. 'The spring-time is a queer time, and it's queer thoughts maybe I do think at whiles'. In fact, Synge could hardly conceive a plausible motive for Sarah, for he did not see why someone in her position should want to change it. The story of Sarah Casey remains at the level of whimsical incident, where the figure of Nora Burke illustrates a major truth.

Synge's comedies are concerned with the struggle of the individual to achieve freedom. In *The Shadow, The Well of the Saints* and *The Playboy*, the central character is brought to the point of realising a new life in which conventional restrictions will be withdrawn. Central to each of the plays is the process by which Nora Burke, Martin Doul and Christy Mahon come to recognise their difference from other people, to detach themselves from their society. Throughout most of the action we are watching their ambiguous relations with the ordinary community. It was only in *The Tinker's Wedding* that Synge tried to show the lives of people who were already liberated. The result was a failure of the imagination. It was the tramp rather than the tinker that was, in his own phrase, of 'peculiar value' to him, the tramp who is still on the fringes of the community, apart but related, rather than the outcast and outlawed tinkers.

We have traced here some of the strands that went into the making of *The Shadow* and *The Tinker's Wedding*, the way in which the varied experience of Wicklow was woven into the plays. Where the coincidence of different elements was happiest, it became possible to make the imaginative identification which is something more than self-expression. Synge understood Nora Burke; he did not merely substitute his emotions for hers. In *The Shadow* the balanced and contrasted levels of dramatic play make up a significant pattern, and none of the ironies are trivial. But Synge always worked blind, feeling his way towards meaning through the plastic medium of his materials. He could spend months of effort on an unlikely project, revising and reshaping a light farce like *The Tinker's Wedding* with nothing but a pious hope that what resulted would be important. Fortunately with his two three-act comedies all the necessary prerequisites were to be satisfied, and he could create major works.

6

The Dramatic Structure of
The Well of the Saints

The Well of the Saints is unusual among Synge's works in that a fable is what he started with, the parable-like story of the beggars who prefer blindness to sight. Where other plays were based on anecdotes or tales which he had heard, the plot of *The Well of the Saints* was invented, though the idea may have been suggested by the fifteenth-century *Moralité de L'Aveugle et du Boiteux* of Andrieu de la Vigne. The stories used for *The Shadow* or *The Tinker's Wedding* attracted his attention initially simply as narrative, striking in their peculiarity rather than for any obvious meaning. But the fable of the couple who choose a 'wilful blindness' seems to cry out for a moral, or at least to demand an interpretation. As Synge developed the play through numerous manuscript drafts, he moved away from the diagrammatic lucidity of the parable. He rooted it in a definite setting, fleshed the simple outline of the plot, and overlayed it with ironic moments of comedy, thwarting the audience's expectations of a clear-cut and obvious pattern of meaning.

The Well of the Saints has not been particularly popular, perhaps partly because of this equivocal quality. It has been relatively rarely produced, and some critics have gone so far as to dismiss it as an apprentice-piece – Synge's first attempt at a full-length play. Other features may have contributed to its neglect: Willie Fay, the play's first director, complained to Synge that all the characters were bad-tempered, and the harsh, melancholy atmosphere is certainly in contrast with the exuberance of *The Playboy*. For whatever reasons, the complexity and subtlety of *The Well of the Saints* has never been fully appreciated. To do it justice we need to look in detail at the way in which the dramatic structure is developed. Synge's own plan for the play (MS 4338 f. ii, *Plays* I p. 264), which is reproduced below (p. 112), provides us with a convenient scene-division, and an illuminating commentary; each scene is given its specific tone or mood, and its 'current' or line of interest which an audience is expected to follow. With this plan as a guide we can follow through the action in slow motion, and watch the effect of its continual dramatic modulation.

The opening scene of the play gives us the situation of the blind couple, ugly and weather-beaten, living happily in the illusion of beauty. Synge is careful not to overplay Martin and Mary's happiness; their contentment is displayed in continual marital wrangling and a flow of teasing insults exchanged without offence:

> Martin Doul. If I didn't talk I'd be destroyed in a short while listening to the clack you do be making, for you've a queer cracked voice, the Lord have mercy on us, if it's fine to look on you are itself. (*Plays* I p. 71)

In the course of such continuing repartee Synge manages his 'exposition of characters', and the differences between the blind couple emerge. Mary is conventionally vain and there is a comic preening in her words:

> there isn't anything like the wet south wind does be blowing upon us, for keeping a white beautiful skin – the like of my skin – on your neck and brows, and there isn't anything at all like a fine skin for putting splendour on a woman. (*Plays* I p. 71)

It is her beauty which is most important to both of them: Martin is the lover, she is the beloved. She is self-sufficient, determined where possible to shut out the ordinary world – 'they're a bad lot, those that have their sight'. Martin, however, is more dependent on the opinion of others than Mary. He listens to what the seeing people say, and is worried by it, for the security of his illusion is disturbed:

> I do be thinking in the long nights it'd be a grand thing if we could see ourselves for one hour, or a minute itself, the way we'd know surely we were the finest man, and the finest woman, of the seven counties of the east . . . (bitterly) and then the seeing rabble below might be destroying their souls telling bad lies, and we'd never heed a thing they'd say. (*Plays* I p. 73)

From the first Martin wants reassurance; he feels the need for absolute certainty on which to found his sense of distinction.

Analysis Well of Saints

Act I			
	1	Martin and Mary	Exposition of characters and psychics

	2	+ Timmy
		                    narrative
		        crescendo [*climactic*]
			comedy

	3	+ girls current more Martin excitement	
	4	+ Saint	
	5	minus Saints	
	6	quarrel	tragic
II		Timmy and Martin no current	comic
	2	Martin and Molly Love current	traPoetical
III		Martin and Mary current of reawakened interest	

	2	plus crowd
		   current
		      to make Martin
		      recured	

Synge marks for this scene 'psychics' as well as 'exposition of characters'. We can only guess at which he means by this, but it may be the psychological situation of the beggars as blind people, the peculiar features of the blind world. The other senses do duty for sight, and Martin's sensuality is all the more vivid for being expressed in terms of touch and hearing alone: Molly Byrne has

> a sweet beautiful voice you'd never tire to be hearing, if it was only the pig she'd be calling, or crying out in the long grass, maybe, after her hens . . . It should be a fine, soft, rounded woman, I'm thinking, would have a voice the like of that. (*Plays* I p. 73)

The isolation of the blind is striking. The phrase, 'the seeing rabble below' conveys both the feeling of separation, and the sense of contempt which is Martin's attitude towards those with sight. The sighted are stupid, capricious and untrustworthy. The comic irony of the situation is that the blind think of blindness as the mark of sense, almost of clear sight.

Just as in *The Shadow* the neutral opening scene was followed by the comedy of Dan and the whiskey bottle, so the second scene of *The Well of the Saints* is in a more definitely comic vein. The 'narrative crescendo', as Synge calls it, of Timmy the smith's news involves an ironic exposition of the meaning of the word 'wonder'. When Martin and Mary are told that a 'wonder' is about to be done, their guesses are comically suggestive. Martin recalls the last wonder which was done in that place, when 'they killed the old fellow going home with his gold'. He becomes interested when he thinks that they may be 'putting up a still behind in the rocks'. Mary is hopeful that 'they're hanging a thief, above at the bit of a tree', but then reflects sadly, 'what joy would that be to ourselves, and we not seeing it at all?' This is grim humour. Strange that the audiences who resented the implications of national infamy in *The Shadow* and *The Playboy* should not have seen this passage as a caricature of Ireland as a land of ghouls and drunkards. This harsh laughter, however, moves towards something more delicate when the blind couple learn that they may be cured. They are then genuinely excited, and though an audience may smile at their *naïveté* as they enquire how they can obtain the miraculous holy water, we begin to feel some uneasiness at their approaching disillusionment.

The third scene, in which Molly Byrne and Bride come in and

fool around with the Saint's cloak, bell and holy water, has occasionally been criticised as a piece of unnecessary padding. It has, however, an important preparatory function in the play, for Molly's character, her vulgarity and her vacant insensitivity, is deftly established. The orthodox Timmy is made uneasy by her irreverence as she tries the cloak on Martin:

> *Timmy.*   You'd have a right to be leaving him alone, Molly. What would the saint say if he seen you making game with his cloak?
> *Molly Byrne* (recklessly).   How would he see us, and he saying prayers in the wood? (She turns Martin Doul round.) Isn't that a fine holy-looking saint, Timmy the smith? (Laughing foolishly.) There's a grand handsome fellow, Mary Doul, and if you seen him now, you'd be as proud, I'm thinking, as the archangels below, fell out with the Almighty God. (*Plays* I p. 85)

By contrast with this jeering tone the beggars gain dignity.

> *Mary Doul* (with quiet confidence going to Martin Doul and feeling his cloak).   It's proud we'll be this day surely. (*Plays* I p. 87)

Martin's gathering excitement (the 'current' of the scene) makes his imminent disappointment so pathetic that even Timmy is moved to pity. As we see more of the emotions of the beggars, as the cruelty of the basic joke is brought home to us by the silly heartless girls, we move steadily away from the detachment of comedy towards an uncomfortable region where pain and suffering are no longer anaesthetised.

With the entrance of the Saint the level of the drama is suddenly lifted, and the problems of the beggars are temporarily forgotten. For the duration of the short fourth scene, the Saint is in complete command of the stage, and we are made to feel the authority of his presence. The parody figure of Martin dressed as one of the 'Saints of God' in the previous scene, makes the Saint all the more impressive when he puts on the tokens of his office. His austere Christianity stands out by contrast with the profane fooling we have just been watching.

> *Saint* (to Martin Doul and Mary Doul).[1]   It's a hard life you've had not seeing sun or moon, or the holy priests itself praying to the Lord, but it's the like of you who are brave in a bad time will

make a fine use of the gift of sight the Almighty God will bring
to you to-day. (He takes his cloak and puts it about him.) It's on
a bare starving rock that there's the four beauties of God, the
way it's little wonder, I'm thinking, if it's with bare starving
people the water should be used. (He takes the water and bell and
slings them round his shoulders.) (*Plays* I p. 89)

In this solemn atmosphere, our impulse, with Timmy the smith, is
to hush Martin Doul when he tries to interrupt:

Martin Doul (moving uneasily).   When they look on herself
who is a fine woman —
Timmy (shaking him).   Whisht now and be listening to the
saint. (*Plays* I p. 89)

But in Scene v, when Martin has been taken up to the church,
we are given an ironic comment on the impressive appearance of
the Saint. Molly Byrne reveals how completely his audience have
failed to understand the Saint's creed.

It'd be a fine thing if some one in this place could pray the like of
him, for I'm thinking the water from our own blessed well would
do rightly if a man knew the way to be saying prayers, and then
there'd be no call to be bringing water from that wild place,
where, I'm told, there are no decent houses, or fine-looking
people (*Plays* I p. 91)

'Saying prayers' is for Molly a magical abracadabra which anyone
could learn. She can see no reason why the water should be brought
from a 'bare starving rock'; from her point of view, the home of the
four beauties of God, so far from being a sacred shrine mysteriously
blessed by the divine presence, is a 'wild place' where civilisation
has never penetrated.

The dramatic low-point of this scene – Molly is in the middle of a
characteristic squabble with Mat Simon – is interrupted by Martin's
cry of joy and the Saint's Latin benediction. With this we are
prepared for Martin's entry and the beginning of the final scene of
the act. Martin's exultation in his sight, and his lyrical rhapsody to
the woman he supposes to be Mary, are witnessed awkwardly by
the crowd, who are already uneasy about their deception of the
blind couple. Even Molly 'lowers her head, a little confused', as
Martin marvels at her grand hair, and her soft skin, and her eyes
'would make the saints, if they were dark awhile and seeing again,

fall down out of the sky'. (*Plays* I p. 95) Molly's retort, 'let you keep away from me, and not be soiling my chin', arouses the worst instincts of the crowd. 'The people laugh loudly.' After the first open attack, like the first blow at a defenceless animal, the embarrassment of the crowd turns to cruel mockery. Synge has marked this scene as 'tragic' in his plan, but it is a peculiar form of tragedy. What we see on stage is a psychological reaction which is like the reverse of the Aristotelian 'catharsis'. Instead of being purged by pity and fear of the like emotions, the crowd recoils in revulsion and dread. The people jeer at Martin and his blatant grotesque suffering in order to escape the intolerable burden of sympathy.

With the entry of Mary, the public humiliation of the couple is complete. As the two face each other in their disillusionment, the power of the language increases with the emotional stress:

> *Mary Doul* (beginning to realise herself).   If I'm not so fine as some of them said, I have my hair, and my big eyes, and my white skin —
> *Martin Doul* (breaking out with a passionate cry).   Your hair, and your big eyes, is it? ... I'm telling you there isn't a wisp on any grey mare on the ridge of the world isn't finer than the dirty twist on your head. There isn't two eyes in any starving sow, isn't finer than the eyes you were calling blue like the sea. (*Plays* I p. 97)

As in many scenes of comic 'flyting' Mary and Martin try to outgo one another in abuse. But as they look for images commensurate with their feeling of loss, the comic nature of their quarrel is transmuted. It is impossible to laugh at them, not only because we pity their suffering, but because we are impressed by its seriousness and intensity. They take their tragedy tragically. Any person can be hurt and humiliated, but only a few can make of that humiliation a significant betrayal.

The Saint puts an end to the fight, and brings the act to a close, in control of the situation, dominating the stage:

> May the Lord who has given you sight send a little sense into your heads, the way it won't be on your own two selves you'll be looking – on two pitiful sinners of the earth – but on the splendour of the Spirit of God, you'll see an odd time shining out through the big hills, and steep streams falling to the sea. For if it's on the like of that you do be thinking, you'll not be minding

the faces of men, but you'll be saying prayers and great praises, till you'll be living the way the great saints do be living, with little but old sacks and skin covering their bones . . . let the lot of you, who have seen the power of the Lord, be thinking on it in the dark night, and be saying to yourselves it's great pity, and love he has, for the poor, starving people of Ireland. (*Plays* I p. 101)

It is a fine speech and we notice that Synge gives to the Saint his own pantheistic belief, the only form of the 'Spirit of God' which he himself recognised. Yet we can see that it will hardly reach the Saint's listeners. No one on stage, least of all Mary and Martin, is likely to respond to the ascetic ideal of saintliness, for they are all irretrievably secular. The Saint is shut up in his own vision, and does not understand the people he works among; he does not understand, for instance, that they would not think of themselves in this disparaging way as the 'poor starving people of Ireland'. The last word is his, but the play has already exposed problems to which he offers no answer.

Synge allows his audience to relax after the climax of the final scene in Act I, and the second act opens with 'no current'. The first scene is static comedy. Martin appears as the traditional comic beggar, lazy, cowardly and vindictive, contrasted with the hard-working energetic Timmy:

> *Martin Doul.* . . . it's more I got a while since, and I sitting blinded in Grianan, than I get in this place, working hard, and destroying myself, the length of the day.
> *Timmy* (stopping with amazement).   Working hard? (He goes over to him.) I'll teach you to work hard, Martin Doul. (*Plays* I p. 103)

Timmy and Martin are on terms of mutual misunderstanding, here suggested by their different standards of hard work. Throughout the scene, the smith bustles about the forge, hardly paying any attention to Martin's gloomy complaints. He talks merely to pass the time at his work, whereas for Martin talk has been a substitute for work for years. Typical of the beggar, both real and fictional, is the turn for invective:

> I've heard tell you stripped the sheet from your wife and you putting her down into the grave, and there isn't the like of you for plucking your living ducks, the short days, and leaving them

running round in their skins, in the great rains and the cold. (*Plays* I p. 105)

If the beggar is a professional liar who needs the art of flattery to make his living, he is equally adept at cursing for his private solace.

The scene is preparatory, with discreet indications that Martin's cure is wearing off:

> *Martin Doul*. . . . if it's a dark day itself it's too well I see every wicked wrinkle you have round by your eye.
> *Timmy* (looking at him sharply).   Dark day is it? The day's not dark since the clouds broke in the east. (*Plays* I p. 107)

We see too Martin's dissatisfaction with the sight he has been given:

> it's a raw beastly day we do have each day, till I do be thinking it's well for the blind don't be seeing the like of them grey clouds driving on the hill, and don't be looking on people with their noses red, the like of your nose, and their eyes weeping, and watering, the like of your eyes, God help you, Timmy the smith. (*Plays* I p. 105)

If in the first joy of sight he marvelled at the wonders of nature, he has come by this stage to see the ugliness around him. His comic grumbles, his abuse of Timmy merge into a general feeling of revulsion from the world which the Saint has permitted him to see. Even the insensitive Timmy is disturbed and upset by the lucid force of novelty in Martin's vision, which reveals what habituation enables people normally to ignore:

> it's a queer thing the way yourself and Mary Doul are after setting every person in this place, and up beyond to Rathvanna, talking of nothing, and thinking of nothing, but the way they do be looking in the face. (Going towards forge.) It's the devil's work you're after doing with your talk of fine looks, and I'd do right, maybe, to step in and wash the blackness from my face. (*Plays* I p. 111)[2]

All Martin's delight in seeing is now concentrated on Molly Byrne:

> there's one fine thing we have, to be looking on a grand, white, handsome girl the like of you . . . and every time I set my eyes on you, I do be blessing the saints, and the holy water, and the

power of the Lord Almighty in the heavens above. (*Plays* I
p. 111)

The scene between Molly and Martin is more sexual than anything
else in Synge. Molly's attractiveness was made obvious from the
beginning, in her own attitude, and in the reaction of the men
around her. 'You'll hear Timmy himself, the time he does be sitting
in his forge, getting mighty fussy if she'll come walking from
Grianan, the way you'll hear his breath going, and he wringing his
hands.' (*Plays* I p. 75) Here the stage directions suggest the dynamic
of the scene. Molly's tone – 'half invitingly' – indicates her
ambivalent flirtatiousness. We see Martin after a rebuff, 'drawing
back a little, hurt but indignant', but then when Molly is 'interested, off her guard', 'seizing the moment he has her attention'.
The sexual content is no less vivid for being underplayed.

Molly's response has the deliberate dishonesty of the coquette.
She affects not to understand Martin's meaning, taunts him with
his ugliness, threatens to tell his wife, but all the time she is flirting
with him:

> Molly Byrne (half invitingly).   It's a fine way you're wanting to
> pay Timmy the smith . . . And it's not his *lies* you're making
> love to this day, Martin Doul. (*Plays* I p. 115)

She plays Martin along automatically, without thinking, and only
becomes alarmed when the situation seems to get out of control. Of
course she would never take the beggar Martin Doul as a lover. His
ugliness and the difference in ages quite apart – they are, after all,
no bars to marriage with Timmy the smith – she is horrified that
someone of Martin's class should make such a proposition to her:

> Go off now after your wife, and if she beats you again, let you go
> after the tinker girls is above running the hills, or down among
> the sluts of the town, and you'll learn one day, maybe, the way
> a man should speak with a well-reared civil girl the like of me.
> (*Plays* I p. 123)

Here we have the basic discrepancy between Martin's view of himself, and that of those around him, the discrepancy exploited for its
comic effect in the scene with the hard-working Timmy. The
poignancy of the situation is that Martin is making love to a girl
who would never regard him as a social equal, scarcely as a fellow
human being. Small wonder that Synge 'would not budge' when

Willie Fay suggested that 'Molly Byrne might be made a loveable young girl'.

The 'love current' of this scene, Synge notes is 'traPoetical' – tragic/poetic. Martin's vision of Molly is expressed with the metaphysical imagery of love-poetry:

> I'm thinking by the mercy of God it's few sees anything but them is blind for a space. It's few sees the old women rotting for the grave, and it's few sees the like of yourself, though it's shining you are, like a high lamp, would drag in the ships out of the sea. (*Plays* I p. 117)

This is not mere hyperbole, or ornamental conceit, but a real vision of the world in which the object of love is the centre of the universe. The poet is not only an impassioned lover, but consciously a poet as well. 'I'm seeing you this day, seeing you, maybe, the way no man has seen you in the world.' Martin expresses the self-consciousness of the poet in his sense of difference from the people who have never been blind – he is the only one with 'fit eyes' to look at Molly. She is not only the object of his love, but the source of his inspiration, the light which illumines the world and allows him to see, as only he can.

The light is swiftly put out. Molly, though she may be momentarily 'half mesmerised' by Martin's words, has little time for the ravings of the 'lunatic, the lover and the poet'. 'It's the like of that talk you'd hear from a man would be losing his mind.' (*Plays* I p. 117) She calls for Timmy the smith, turns on Martin Doul and castigates his presumption. This is Martin's second humiliation, as terrible as the first, and his anguished speech is the most moving moment in the play:

> *Martin Doul* (turns round, sees Mary Doul, whispers to Molly Byrne with imploring agony). Let you not put shame on me, Molly, before herself and the smith. Let you not put shame on me and I after saying fine words to you, and dreaming . . . dreams . . . in the night. (He hesitates, and looks round the sky.) Is it a storm of thunder is coming, or the last end of the world? (He staggers towards Mary Doul, tripping slightly over tin can.) The heavens is closing, I'm thinking with darkness and great trouble passing in the sky. (*Plays* I p. 119)

The loss of sight is a complex dramatic image. The Biblical echo – 'and your young men shall see visions, and your old men shall dream dreams' – may be accidental, but the apocalyptic overtones of the passage are intentional. As Martin physically goes blind, the 'high lamp' is quenched, and his world is annihilated. The gathering darkness is the appropriate expression of his total humiliation.

The scene rises to a climax of pathos with the torture of Martin Doul, but as his bitterness turns to curses against his enemies, there is a new comic strain in the language. Mary joins in, and the voices of the beggars are temporarily reunited in a chorus of abuse. She says of Molly Byrne,

> It's them that's fat and flabby do be wrinkled young, and the whitish yellowy hair she has does be soon turning the like of a handful of thin grass you'd see rotting, where the wet lies, at the north of a sty. (*Plays* I p. 121)

Under this onslaught we almost see Molly change before our eyes; we expect the process of physical decay to set in directly. 'Oh, God protect us, Molly, from the words of the blind', says Timmy, with some reason. Throughout this scene we have a comic double vision of Timmy and Molly. In Martin's imagination, Timmy is a sort of grotesque Titan, grunting and groaning at his diabolic trade:

> Look on him, Molly, look on him, I'm saying, for I'm seeing him still, and let you raise your voice, for the time is come, and bid him go up into his forge and be sitting there by himself, sneezing, and sweating, and he beating pot-hooks till the judgement day. (*Plays* I p. 121)

He looks forward to seeing Molly and Timmy 'the two of them on a high bed, and they screeching in hell'. But Martin's arch-villains are here, as throughout, very ordinary, very conventional people:

> *Timmy* (pointing to Molly Byrne . . . It's well you know a decent girl, I'm thinking to wed, has no right to have her heart scalded with hearing talk – and queer, bad talk, I'm thinking – from a raggy-looking fool the like of you. (*Plays* I p. 121)

Timmy's prim sense of decorum cannot but make us laugh. Yet Martin's extravagant execration of 'the villainy of a woman and the bloody strength of a man' does not seem inappropriate, for the humiliation he has suffered at their hands warrants the vivid infernal picture of his final speech.

All three acts of *The Well of the Saints* have a similar movement: beginning on the level of detached ironic comedy the action

develops to a point of all but complete identification with the
protagonists. At the start of Act III, as with the opening scenes of
the other acts, the angle of vision is widened, and we are back in a
predominantly comic world. In Martin's 'soliloquy', which is, of
course, overheard by Mary Doul, what had been the rhetorical
damnation of his enemies at the end of Act II becomes a comic
crescendo of curses:

> The devil mend Mary Doul for putting lies on me, and letting on
> she was grand. The devil mend the old Saint for letting me see it
> was lies. The devil mend Timmy the smith for killing me with
> hard work, and keeping me with an empty windy stomach in me,
> in the day and in the night. (*Plays* I p. 125)

Mary nods approvingly as he curses Molly Byrne, and no doubt
relishes the tone in which he says that 'Mary Doul herself, and she
a dirty, wrinkled-looking hag, was better maybe to be sitting along
with than no one at all.' Yet the soliloquy is complicated by a
moment of real pathos emerging from the comic self-pity:

> I'll be getting my death now, I'm thinking, sitting alone in the
> cold air, hearing the night coming, and the blackbirds flying
> round in the briars crying to themselves, the time you'll hear one
> cart getting off a long way in the east, and another cart getting
> off a long way in the west, and a dog barking maybe, and a little
> wind turning the sticks. (*Plays* I pp. 125–7)

It is a difficult speech for an actor to control, moving from the
broad comedy of the beginning through this moment of lyricism to
the equally broad comedy of the recognition.

Martin and Mary begin to find each other again – the 'current'
of the scene is 'reawakened interest'. They spar for dominance in a
sequence of delicate and gentle comedy. Mary, because she has overheard Martin, has a temporary advantage. 'There's a sweet tone in
your voice I've not heard for a space. You're taking me for Molly
Byrne, I'm thinking' – and she has his cowardice to taunt him
with:

> I'm bearing in mind I'm married to a little dark stump of a fellow
> looks the fool of the world, and I'll be bearing in mind from this
> day the great hullabaloo he's after making from hearing a poor
> woman breathing quiet in her place. (*Plays* I p. 127)

The abuse goes on, but it has the friendly tones of the opening scene of the play. When Mary reveals the great discovery of her long white hair, there is a warm response.

> *Martin Doul* (with real admiration).   You're a cute thinking woman, Mary Doul, and it's no lie. (*Plays* I p. 129)

Martin's line suggests the ambiguity of the beggar's illusion. They are both professional liars, and if Martin admires Mary, it is partly for her ingenuity, as though she had spun a really convincing story for the gentry. But at the same time he allows the validity of the fiction, congratulating her on discovering a fact which had previously escaped attention.

Mary is now on top, and she pushes home her advantage. She rejects contemptuously the idea that Martin might have a 'whiteness the like of that coming'.

> In a short while you'll have a head on you as bald as an old turnip you'd see rolling round in the muck. . . . I can't help your looks, Martin Doul. It wasn't myself made you with your rat's eyes, and your big ears, and your griseldy chin. (*Plays* I pp. 129–131)

Even at this moment of *rapprochement*, the beggars never turn soft and Synge is careful to avoid sentimentality. It is only when Martin has made his 'discovery', when he has his own claim to beauty, that they can recover terms of equality. When each separately has had their self-confidence restored, they can relax together and listen to the sounds of spring in the single moment of serene happiness which is granted them in the play.

Their serenity is soon disturbed by the Saint's bell heard in the distance, and the beggars immediately feel their danger. Their anxious attempts to avoid being cured again and their confused theology – 'who'd know rightly if it's good words or bad words would save us this day from himself' – are grotesquely comic. But if their fear of sight seems absurd, their growing panic as they try to escape and cannot find their way is pathetic.

> It's hard set I am to know what would be right. And isn't it a poor thing to be blind when you can't run off itself, and you fearing to see? (*Plays* I p. 133)

They do not even bother to keep up their illusions, or rather they face the fact that they are illusions – 'what good'll our grey hairs be itself, if we have our sight, the way we'll see them falling each day, and turning dirty in the rain?' (*Plays* I p. 135) When they crawl in under a bush, and lie like ostriches confident that they are out of sight, we are conscious of the terrible physical humiliation of being blind.

The terror of the blind couple has made the Saint and his attendant crowd of villagers seem like a pack of hounds or a band of hunters on their trail. But when they come in, they are ironically unlike persecutors. The Saint is in a hurry to get away and, so far from dogging the footsteps of the beggars, he regards curing them as rather a nuisance. Timmy has asked the Saint to do it as a special favour because, as he says himself, he has a kind heart and pities Mary and Martin 'sitting dark again, and you after seeing a while, and working for your bread.' (*Plays* I p. 137) Here, as so often in the play, Synge insists on the very ordinariness of Timmy the smith – humane after his own lights, hot-tempered but forgiving, a decent man whose worst fault is his stupidity. The crowd are equally kind. When Martin tries to escape they lead him back, 'You're going wrong. It's this way Martin Doul.' (*Plays* I p. 137) Martin is finally goaded into speaking out:

> We're not asking our sight, holy father, and let you be walking on and leaving us in our peace at the crossing roads, for it's best we are this way, and we're not asking to see. (*Plays* I p. 139)

This is beyond the comprehension of the Saint or the others. 'Is his mind gone that he's no wish to be cured this day, and looking out on the wonders of the world?' (*Plays* I p. 139)

In Act I Martin was silenced by the Saint, but by this point he is no longer intimidated. He expresses boldly his own vision, the ugliness of the visible world, the beauty of the picture which he imagines. When the Saint tells him of the joys of sight he retorts, 'What was it I seen my first day, but your own bleeding feet and they cut with the stones, and my last day, but the villainy of herself that you're wedding, God forgive you, with Timmy the smith.' (*Plays* I p. 141) The Saint urges the wonders of natural beauty:

> Did you never set eyes on the summer and the fine spring in the places where the holy men of Ireland have built up churches to the Lord, that you'd wish to be closed up and seeing no sight of the glittering seas, and the furze is opening above, will soon have the hills shining as if it was fine creels of gold they were, rising to the sky. (*Plays* I p. 141)

Martin's reply is equally impressive:

> Isn't it finer sights ourselves had a while since and we sitting
> dark smelling the sweet beautiful smells do be rising in the warm
> nights and hearing the swift flying things racing in the air, till
> we'd be looking up in our own minds into a grand sky, and see-
> ing lakes, and broadening rivers, and hills are waiting for the
> spade and plough. (*Plays* I p. 141)

The crowd mark points, watching the clash with spectators' delight
in the sport, but directed always by the malice of Molly Byrne
towards hostility to Martin and support for the orthodoxy of the
Saint.

Martin can at least hold his own in debate with the Saint, but he
is at the mercy of his opponents once they resort to force. He is
attacked first through his wife whom the Saint threatens to cure.
Although Mary is inclined to stay blind with her husband, Timmy
applies the pressure of sanctions – 'if it's choosing a wilful blindness
you are there isn't any one will give you a hap'worth of meal or be
doing the little things you need to keep you at all living in the
world' – and Mat Simon throws out a persuasive suggestion: 'If
you had your sight you could be keeping a watch that no other
woman came near him at all'. She gives in, and there is nothing
Martin can do about it. He is dragged off bodily when he tries to
prevent her being cured.

The ruse by which he eventually manages to save them both is
particularly plausible because he reverts to the servile beggar's
whine which we heard briefly in Act I. The Saint is prepared to
accept his apparent change of heart, and preaches with unconscious
irony. 'Men who are dark a long while and thinking over queer
thoughts in their heads, aren't the like of simple men, who do be
working every day' (*Plays* I p. 147). He soon sees how unlike
simple men the blind can be, when Martin knocks the can of holy
water out of his hands. 'If I'm a poor dark sinner I've sharp ears,
God help me, and it's well I heard the little splash of the water you
had there in the can.'

The crowd are deeply shocked, by the outrageousness, as much
as the impiety, of Martin's action, and they turn with angry
violence on the beggars. But Martin justifies what he has done:

> We're going surely, for if it's a right some of you have to be
> working and sweating the like of Timmy the smith, and a right

some of you have to be fasting and praying and talking holy talk the like of yourself, I'm thinking it's a good right ourselves have to be sitting blind, hearing a soft wind turning round the little leaves of the spring and feeling the sun, and we not tormenting our souls with the sight of the grey days, and the holy men, and the dirty feet is trampling the world. (*Plays* I p. 149)

Martin has found the confidence in himself which he lacked in the opening scene of the play. After three successive humiliations, he has learned to fight to defend his right to be different. But the ending of the play is not an unequivocal triumph for Martin. Mary has doubts about the journey to the south on which he pins his hopes:

we'd have a right to be gone, if it's a long way itself, where you do have to be walking with a slough of wet on the one side and a slough of wet on the other, and you going a stony path with a north wind blowing behind. (*Plays* I pp. 149–51)

We are reminded of Nora's hesitant acceptance of the Tramp's offer of a new life at the end of *The Shadow*.

Even more disquieting is Timmy's casual remark:

There's a power of deep rivers with floods in them where you do have to be lepping the stones and you going to the south, so I'm thinking the two of them will be drowned together in a short while, surely. (*Plays* I p. 151)

Do the beggars go out to meet an almost certain death, or is this merely a callous parting shot from Timmy, a brutal dismissal? The whole issue is ambiguous. The 'south' is the centre of Martin's ideals, the beautiful country to which he earlier wanted to take Molly, and it has something of the insubstantial quality of a 'never-never' land. It seems difficult, therefore, to think of it as a real geographical location, to imagine the beggars trying to cross flooded rivers in their efforts to reach it. The quality of Synge's drama is not such that we have any very strong sense of the continued existence of his characters after they leave the stage. What we are left with, at the end of *The Well of the Saints*, is an impression that, in some way, Martin's defiant apologia is qualified both by Mary's fears of danger, and by Timmy's hints of death.

The Well of the Saints was disliked by the audiences which watched it for the first time. When the play closed after a week's run, Joseph Holloway recorded what was, most likely, the majority view in his journal:

> Saturday February 11 [1905]. Probably the curtains have closed in on *The Well of the Saints*, Mr. Synge's harsh, irreverent, sensual representation of Irish peasant life, with its strange mixture of lyric and dirt, for the last time as far as Dublin is concerned . . . and I for one am not at all sorry.[3]

However Holloway was wrong, and when the play was revived three years later, he found it improved by a change of cast.

> The wild beast nature of 'Martin Doul' was artistically kept in check, and it made him a far more agreeable personage. W. G. Fay made him a very repulsive old man overwhelmed in sensuality. Arthur Sinclair made him more of a dreamer with a longing for the beautiful . . . In fact, the play was lifted out of reality into the realm of fancy where it should have been from the first . . .[4]

As so often Holloway's testimony is like a clear photographic negative: hold it up to the light and the true picture can be seen. There can be little doubt that Fay's Martin Doul was as Synge intended the part to be played, while Arthur Sinclair's sounds like a sentimentalised, emasculated version. (The revival was produced in May 1908 when Synge was critically ill and could not be in the theatre, whereas he worked closely with Fay in directing the first production.) *The Well of the Saints* is indeed, if we accept Holloway's terms, 'a strange mixture of lyric and dirt'. Its greatest strength is that it cannot be lifted wholly 'out of reality into the realm of fancy'. The play is obviously concerned with abstract ideas, the story is not realistic in origin, but the action has a dramatic reality which cannot be reduced to intellectual paraphrase, nor summed up by a single moral. Martin Doul is 'a dreamer with a longing for the beautiful', but he is also a dirty old man, literally and metaphorically. If his illusion in the play stands for an ideal, it is also seen as the ridiculous self-esteem of a comic beggarman.

The peculiar quality of *The Well of the Saints* emerges by comparison with three other modern plays concerned with the same theme, *The Wild Duck*, *The Lower Depths* and *The Iceman Cometh*. All three are probably more widely known than *The Well of the Saints*, but Synge's play is not the least successful of the four, nor the least profound. The concept of the life-lie, the sustained illusion, originates with Ibsen. In *The Wild Duck*, Hjalmer Ekdal lives on his belief that he will be a great inventor; the whole Ekdal family have a fantasy world to which they retreat, in which the wild duck itself is the central symbol of their imaginary lives. When Gregers Werle presents his 'claim of the ideal' and insists on exposing the truth, the results are catastrophic. In Gorki's *The Lower Depths*, the deliberate fostering of illusion is equally disastrous. Luka, the mysterious visitor to the doss-house, encourages all the fantasies of the down-and-outs, but when he disappears they are even more despairing than before. O'Neill's play is very like Gorki's, with a similar collection of drop-outs living on 'pipe dreams'. *The Iceman Cometh* focuses on the defence mechanism by which the day-dreamers protect their illusions. At the end of the play they can label Hickey, the man who has tried to destroy their fantasies, as a madman and return with relief to their dream-world. Hickey's only success is with Larry, the 'foolosopher', who is forced to drop his mask of disenchanted dispassionate observer, accept responsibility for his actions, and face the tragic reality of his life.

Synge's first critics complained of the cynicism and perversity of *The Well of the Saints*: according to Padraig Pearse, the play 'railed obscenely against light, and sweetness, and knowledge, and charity'.[5] But it is by no means as pessimistic, as deeply destructive as *The Wild Duck*. There is an element almost of self-hatred in Ibsen's portrait of Gregers Werle. The man who postures as the lone idealist is like a caricature of Ibsen, dogmatically dedicated to his concept of truth, the self-exiled, rejected prophet. As we come to see the mixed motives of Gregers' mission, his weakness and pomposity, his pretensions as truth-teller are devastatingly exposed. Hjalmer Ekdal, on the other hand, is an equally satiric figure. Ibsen's acid scorn runs everywhere in *The Wild Duck*, and we are allowed sympathy only with the victims, Gina and Hedwig. The last word is with the bitterly cynical Relling, who can see that even Hedwig's death will soon be assimilated into the melodramatic imaginings of Hjalmer.

By contrast *The Well of the Saints* is concerned with the conflict of genuine ideals, and both the Saint and Martin Doul represent positives which we can respect. The Saint's integrity is never questioned; though he is inflexible and narrow-minded, the strength of his conviction and the eloquence of his words are impressive. Where Hjalmer Ekdal's illusion testifies only to his capacity for self-deception, Martin Doul's image of himself is extended into a vision which is imaginative rather than simply imaginary. The illusion of beauty is necessary to him not merely to protect his ego. Against the ugliness and mediocrity of the actual, he opposes his sense of a world where superlatives are possible.

Both *The Lower Depths* and *The Iceman Cometh* illustrate the difficulty of writing plays of ideas with a naturalistic setting. Gorki and O'Neill go to considerable lengths to establish the reality of the dead-end cellars where their characters congregate. Both plays, for example, have elaborately detailed sets. The whole of the first act of *The Lower Depths* is taken up with setting the scene, sketching in the numerous different people who live in the flop-house, and showing the relations between them. As the play develops, the abstract issues with which Gorki is concerned tend to stick out uncomfortably from their naturalistic context. Luka telling fables or repeating proverbs, offering soothing folk-philosophy to his fellows, clearly represents the Tolstoyan Christianity which Gorki wants us finally to reject. Against Luka, Satin is given lines which carry the unmistakable doctrinal approval of the author:

> Lies are the religion of slaves and masters. Truth is the God of the free man.

> Everything is in man, all things are for man. Only man exists – all the rest is the work of his hands and his mind. . . . We must respect man! not pity him – not denigrate him with our pity . . .[6]

In *The Iceman Cometh*, again, the meaning is constantly piercing the fabric of the play's action. The private illusion of character after character is displayed, only to be as systematically destroyed. Overstatement was always O'Neill's weakness, but in *The Iceman Cometh* the mechanical repetition of a single formula (the words 'pipe dream' recur nearly fifty times) makes for intolerable artificiality.

Gorki was his own best critic. Expressing his dissatisfaction with his plays, he explained why he thought they failed. 'The reason for this is probably the fact that, before sitting down to write a play, I first construct its ideological framework, and combine beforehand the course and connection of the various comical and tragical events.' He contrasted his own work with that of other playwrights, including Synge, whose plays are 'penetrated with an inner harmony. The artificiality in such plays is not discernible – it is replaced by art.'[7] This is indeed the achievement of *The Well of the Saints.* In it, the naturalistic detail blends with the peculiar form of the fable, so that the meaning is an inherent part of the dramatic texture. The play grew out of an idea but it took on substance as a whole within Synge's imagination. With Gorki and O'Neill, the attempt to create the effect of reality is constantly at odds with the author's desire to say something. There is no such fissure in *The Well of the Saints.* One sort of dramatic experience moves imperceptibly into another, and the constantly shifting focus of the play makes the thematic development complex and elusive.

Looking at *The Well of the Saints* in the context of Ibsen, Gorki and O'Neill, what is most striking of all is Synge's attitude towards truth and illusion. All three of the others have an absolute respect for the concept of truth. Those who try to destroy the illusions of others, like Gregers Werle in *The Wild Duck,* or Hickey in *The Iceman Cometh,* are suspect only in so far as they prove to be even more deeply dishonest themselves; honesty remains a principal criterion of value. The three plays leave very different impressions, but they have certain basic assumptions in common. It is the weakness of humanity which makes necessary illusion and self-deception. 'Human kind cannot bear very much reality' – Ibsen, Gorki, O'Neill all hammer home the point. It is only Synge who questions whether there may not be more than one kind of reality, one kind of truth. The dramatic form of the play makes it possible for him to give a multiple view of the beggars' illusion of beauty. The ideal world of the beggars is an absurd one in the comic mood in which the play starts. In the farcical figures of Mary and Martin, the lazy and cunning beggars, we laugh at universal human traits: the infinite capacity for self-deception, the buoyancy of the ego. The attitude is that of the comedian, where a moralist's condemnation of the 'life-lie' would seem ridiculously solemn and pretentious. And yet, as Synge takes us inside the situation and develops the emotional life of the protagonists, we are made aware that their need for a sense of distinction is neither superficial nor wholly comic. The figures around them insist that they should share the common view of reality, deny them their individual vision. Martin's choice of blindness, therefore, comes to represent a deliberate attempt to retain an inner feeling of dignity and freedom. His eloquent plea for his right to 'be sitting blind' cannot be dismissed as escapism or perversity; if nothing else, the violence of the crowd's reaction convinces us of the seriousness of his claim. Martin's vision is at once delusion, and imaginative truth. The distinction and originality of *The Well of the Saints* is that it presents instead of the ordinary dualism of truth and illusion, appearance and reality, a serio-comic view of the world which is deeply committed and yet austerely detached.

7

Approaches to *The Playboy*

The Playboy is not a play with a 'purpose' in the modern sense of the word, but, although parts of it are or are meant to be extravagant comedy, still a great deal that is in it and a great deal more that is behind it is perfectly serious when looked at in a certain light. This is often the case, I think, with comedy, and no one is quite sure today whether Shylock or Alceste should be played seriously or not. There are, it may be hinted, several sides to *The Playboy*.[1]

Synge's cautiously worded letter to the *Irish Times*, following the 'Playboy riots', is well known. To critics of the play, it reads like a challenge to understand the complexities of a work which the Dublin audiences had so completely failed to comprehend. Synge's 'hint' has not been neglected; several sides of *The Playboy* have been thoroughly investigated, and it has been looked at in a number of different lights. The letter, however, still illustrates the peculiar critical problems which the play raises. It is accepted that there are 'several sides' to *The Playboy*, but it is hard to avoid stressing one side at the expense of another, difficult to find a critical view which will adequately represent the play's multiplicity. *The Playboy* is accepted as 'serious'. There it is in all the anthologies of modern drama – no one is likely to dismiss it as a slight extravaganza. The problem indeed is how to handle its seriousness lightly enough, how to interpret a serious play which includes scenes of extravagant comedy. There are moments in *The Playboy* which are extremely funny, outbursts of real hilarious laughter. In the critical search for meaning, there is always a danger that such moments will be 'solemnised' or neglected, and that the life of the play will vanish. Looking over a range of the various critical approaches to *The Playboy*, we can see the difficulty in finding an approach sufficiently flexible to do justice to Synge's constantly changing technique.

One of the most inflexible and unhelpful critical attitudes involves the detection of concealed analogies. Christy Mahon, it has been claimed, is a parody version of Cuchullain – or at least 'has done a deed equivalent to Cuchullain's in modern peasant terms'.[2] Or Christy the parricide is a mock Oedipus, and the structure of *The Playboy* is matched point for point with *Oedipus Rex*.[3] Even more often the playboy has been seen as a Christ figure. Beginning with the argument that Christy's progress is an analogue for Christ's, a scapegoat who can, however, only save himself and not the world,[4] the theory is elaborated to the point where one critic claims that 'it is through his exploitation in *Playboy* of the ministry and crucifixion of Jesus that Synge crystallised the elements of his play into a coherent masterpiece'.[5]

What is wrong with this sort of criticism is that it is quite unrelated to the actual experience of *The Playboy*. The action of the play is rooted in a substantial and immediate reality, without mythical or literary *arrière-pensées*. There is no evidence to support the idea that Synge intended to parody any of the figures suggested, Cuchullain, Christ or Oedipus, and this is an argument that needs evidence to support it. It is not a matter of unconscious or semi-conscious echoes, where the degree of authorial awareness may be left uncertain. The mock-heroic style implies a deliberate imitation of another structure, in which the consciousness of disparity is all-important. Synge was no Joyce or Eliot. He had not the mind which could see and delight in endless ironic correspondences. The reader of modern literature, his appetite whetted for parody, must be careful not to look for mock-heroics everywhere.

'Synge intended that the play should run its course between antinomies. It is, for all its apparent simplicity of plot, a delicately balanced system of ironies, ambivalences, both of words and situation.'[6] It is difficult for critics to avoid upsetting this delicate balance, by leaning on one side or another. For instance, in the attitude which we are supposed to adopt towards the playboy himself, there are two basically opposed views which make up an axis of critical debate. Alan Price remarks that *The Playboy* might be taken as an illustration of Keats's dictum: 'The Imagination may be compared to Adam's dream – he awoke and found it truth.'[7] He traces the way dream is transformed into actuality and sees the ending of the play as the triumphant vindication of the creative imagination. Una Ellis-Fermor argues that the central movement of the play is the 'growth, like a Japanese flower dropped into a bowl of water, of Christopher Mahon's new self'.[8] According to Patricia Spacks, Christy through a series of fantasy adventures reaches a peak of real achievement in the dominance of his father and the crowd.[9] For all these critics, Christy is like the romantic poet, a self-created myth-maker.

Such romantic conceptions of *The Playboy*, however, have not gone unchallenged. Howard D. Pearce, for example, questions whether the ending is a real triumph for Christy, and stresses the importance of the Widow Quin's part in the play: 'If Widow Quin lacks the sparkle and romance of Christy, nevertheless her actions, grounded in actuality, in such sharp contrast to Christy's, which are irremediably floating in the dream vision, point up Synge's ironic detachment.'[10] Ronald Peacock sees another sort of irony at work in the play. He comments on what he calls 'Synge's delicate self-mockery' and implies that in *The Playboy* the author is parodying his own attraction to gaudy and outrageous language.[11] R. R. Sanderlin holds that the play is in fact a direct satire on Irish romanticism – on blather and blarney. As the 'poetry talk' of all the characters is uniform, and the Mayo men are as poetic as Christy, he argues that they are all equally satirised and that it is unreal to distinguish between the imaginative playboy and the prosaic 'fools of earth'.[12]

The critical controversy here represents a real ambiguity in the play. Price's analysis, for example, of the peaks and troughs of Christy's self-confidence, his progress to hero-status, is very illuminating. On the other hand, there are scenes which he neglects almost completely, or remarks of them vaguely that they illustrate Synge's capacity for amusing comedy. The emphatic focus on Christy tends to reduce the importance of other characters and other views in the play. For the romantic vision is indeed qualified by irony, and Synge does make us aware of the poetic extravagance of Christy:

> *Christy.*   Amn't I after seeing the love-light of the star of knowledge shining from her brow, and hearing words would put you thinking on the holy Brigid speaking to the infant saints, and now she'll be turning again, and speaking hard words to me, like an old woman with a spavindy ass she'd have, urging on a hill.
> *Widow Quin.*   There's poetry talk for a girl you'd see itching

and scratching, and she with a stale stink of poteen on her from selling in the shop. (*Plays* II pp. 125–7)

The widow's speech reveals the ironic disparity between the image and the reality, and exposes the hyperbolic nature of Christy's language. But irony is not simply corrosive, it is a controlled and measured effect. We do not dismiss the poetry as 'blather and blarney' because it is undercut by the widow's cynical realism. The Widow Quin sees Pegeen by the harsh light of day, in a sense more clearly than Christy can, yet Christy's description of his emotion is vivid and genuine, and in no way denied by the incongruity of object. Negative does not cancel out positive, but between the two an electric current is set flowing.

Those who emphasise the progress of Christy through the play, often press home an identification of the playboy as poet. It has been argued by J. F. Kilroy that '*The Playboy of the Western World* dramatises the gradual development of the poet's craft from its first uncertain expression to the full display of mature art'.[13] The prizes presented to Christy after the sports, according to Arthur Ganz, 'suggest consecration of a bard rather than triumph as an athlete'.[14] Edward Stephens considers that it was his own growth as an artist which Synge symbolised in the play.[15]

It seems likely that Stephens is right, and that *The Playboy* did have its origins in personal experience; it may well be that the unexpected blossoming of the shy and inarticulate Christy somehow represented Synge's own surprising success as a dramatist. But tracing back to the emotional sources of a work does not always supply us with significant truths about it, and to see in *The Playboy* a detailed allegory of the development of the artist is to restrict rather than to enrich its meaning. Christy Mahon is not a poet, in the literal sense, nor can he be said to symbolise the artist as such. There may well be poets like Christy, but there are many Christys who are not poets. He is rather, like the tramps of Wicklow, a 'temperament of distinction', a man capable of imaginative reflection. Synge did once attempt an artistic self-portrait in *When the Moon Has Set*, and the result was the effete and pretentious Colum. One of the sources of Christy's lasting attraction is that he is not a writer of prose poems, but a far more basic and complete representative of the imagination.

Literary criticism of drama is always in danger of becoming too exclusively literary, not to say academic. The 'portrait of the artist as playboy' is the sort of ingrowing interpretation to which we are prone, transferring the apprehension of the play to a familiar world of intellectual analysis. It is all too easy to reduce a play to the sum of its themes, and lose the sense of its dramatic dimension. Particularly with *The Playboy*, where so much of the effect depends upon variation in dramatic mode, where 'several sides' alternate, we must not let ourselves be drawn away from the substance of the play by attractive literary interpretations. Perhaps the best way to approach *The Playboy*, therefore, is to establish the simple theatrical forms on which it is based, and then to look at the way Synge develops them towards something more complex. The technique is similar to that which we have already seen in *The Shadow* and *The Well of the Saints*, but with *The Playboy* it is still more elaborate than in the other two.

The first extant record of *The Playboy* is a scenario entitled 'The Murderer: A Farce' in which the action was to begin with the fight between father and son in the potato garden, and to end with Christy's exposure just as he has been elected County Councillor in Mayo. (See *Plays* II p. 295.) It was farce which provided Synge with the basic structure for his play. Its central device is what Bergson called the 'snowball' – the preposterous growth of a misconception which we find also in Lady Gregory's little one-act plays, *Spreading the News* and *Hyacinth Halvey*. As so often with farce, it depends on a simple mechanism for the creation of misunderstanding. Indeed, Bergson's theory of comedy, although he ingeniously extends it to the comedy of character and wit, belongs most properly to farce, for there the source of laughter is, as he claims, the substitution of mechanical for vital process. Instead of seeing people behaving normally, that is with an autonomous will subject only to social custom and necessity, we watch them enslaved by an artificial system the operation of which only we, the audience, understand. A comic Providence brings all the lovers to the same place of assignation, or contrives that letters should be switched, or brings long-separated identical twins on the scene at the same moment. It is such a mechanism, a mechanism which gathers speed and momentum as the action progresses, that we find in *The Playboy*. The lie expands to such monstrous size that it becomes inevitable that it should be exploded. In early versions of the play, the device was more obviously mechanical, with Christy's steps to glory taking the tangible form of election as County Councillor, marriage with Pegeen, appointment to a government sinecure. Synge's instinct, also, was to preserve the circular movement commended by Bergson as the finest type of the 'snowball', and in all the first drafts Christy ends up as the snivelling weakling – the 'Fool of Farnham' – once again.

The farcical substratum remained in the completed text, where Christy is led on by easy stages to claim that he 'cleft his father with one blow to the breeches belt'. We watch with delight as the blow, through successive versions of the story, travels down the old man's anatomy. Each new outrage against our sense of truth adds to our feeling that the author is testing the limits of Christy's powers of fantasy and the stage audience's capacity for credulity. As in *Henry IV Part I* where Falstaff creates eleven adversaries out of two in the space of some five minutes, we wait expectantly for the balloon to be burst. Christy, in fact, is deflated again and again. In the first act, when he is just beginning to swell with his new sense of pride – 'and I a seemly fellow with great strength in me and bravery of . . .' – a knock at the door sends him running to Pegeen in terror: 'Oh, glory! it's late for knocking, and this last while I'm in terror of the peelers, and the walking dead' (*Plays* II p. 85). Or again just before the actual arrival of his father, he is boasting of his deed to the Widow Quin.

Christy and Falstaff share as common ancestor the *miles gloriosus* of Roman comedy, and yet Christy is very different from the traditional comic boaster. He is not a knowing, a conscious liar like Falstaff. His lies are not 'gross as a mountain, open, palpable', but unconscious fantasies which delicately mark his own growing sense of self-esteem. If much of the comic momentum of the play derives from the successive deflations of Christy the boaster, yet this pattern also expresses a real development in his character. Although in the earliest drafts Synge kept the more usual comic denouement, with the return to *status quo ante*, the final text shows a definitive change in Christy by the end of the play. There is here a duality which is central to Synge's vision: the playboy as a comic type is by definition incurable, the daydreamer whose fantasies are constantly exposed by reality; and yet the 'likely gaffer' of the end has learned by his mistakes, has achieved that development which the dimensions of the comic stock-character seem to preclude.

We can readily believe in Christy's growth. From the beginning he is extremely naïve, and when asked the motive of his crime, he replies disarmingly: 'He was a dirty man, God forgive him, and he getting old and crusty, the way I couldn't put up with him at all.' (*Plays* II p. 73) Which is no more than the truth, after all. Here, as so often in the play, even the most obviously comic passages help us to establish the reality of Christy's past life with his father. When he is telling the fully elaborated story of the murder in Act II, some of the dialogue he recounts has the unmistakable ring of truth: ' "You squinting idiot," says he, "let you walk down and tell the priest you'll wed the Widow Casey in a score of days" ' (*Plays* II p. 101). We are to see very shortly that this is indeed Old Mahon's peremptory style of conversation. The father's account of his son, when he does appear, is comically biased, but it too contributes to our understanding of Christy. Christy, he says, is 'a lier on walls, a talker of folly, a man you'd see stretched the half of the day in the brown ferns with his belly to the sun' (*Plays* II p. 121). Mahon intends this as a description of a lazy good-for-nothing, but we may guess that Christy's talk may have had more to it than idle foolishness. Again 'he'd be fooling over little birds he had – finches and felts – or making mugs at his own self in the bit of a glass we had hung on the wall' (*Plays* II pp. 121–3). We have already heard from Christy of the 'divil's own mirror we had beyond, would twist a squint across an angel's brow', and the corroboration is amusing. But the bird fancying is almost certainly intended to be a mark in Christy's favour. A love for natural things is a sure touchstone of value in Synge. Our sympathy for Christy is engaged even as his pretensions to glory are debunked.

While the myth of the playboy remains static, and Christy tries desperately to live up to it, a real and organic change is taking place in his personality. At the end of Act I Christy sums up his position: 'it's great luck and company I've won me in the end of time – two fine women fighting for the likes of me –, till I'm thinking this night wasn't I a foolish fellow not to kill my father in the years gone by.' (*Plays* II p. 93) This is purely comic, the direct address to the audience has the knowingness of farce. But in the second act Pegeen's admiration for Christy becomes more to him than merely an instance of his 'great luck and company'. Partly because she was the first girl to take an interest in him, partly because he senses in her a special response to his fine words, Pegeen occupies the centre of his mind. The 'two fine women' were of more or less equal value, but by the end of Act II Christy is pleading with Widow Quin: 'Aid me for to win Pegeen. It's her only that I'm seeking now.' (*Plays* II p. 127) He is in love for the first time, and though his love is still part of the image of the admired playboy, it now has priority over everything else. It earns him our admiration and sympathy, narrows our comic distance from him.

In the final act Christy reaches a new peak of self-assurance as playboy in his triumph at the sports. The 'crowning prize', however, is still Pegeen, and when he is discomfited by the appearance of his father, it is her love only which he wishes to regain. He no longer cares for general adulation, but commits the 'second murder' so that 'Pegeen'll be giving me praises the same as in the hours gone by'. The braggart has completely disappeared, and Christy is a young lover like any other desperate to win the approval of his mistress. It is the terrible shock of her betrayal of him which awakes him from his dream. His belief in Pegeen is shattered but this ultimately only strengthens his belief in himself. Where before he had thought his love, and the words he used to express it, originated with her, his inspiration, he can now see that it had springs within himself. The play traces Christy's development from dependence on his father, through dependence on his first love, to a healthy and mature self-sufficiency.

The Playboy is at once an extravagant comedy of situation, and a dramatic *Bildungsroman* in little. We witness the metamorphosis of a figure of farce into a dynamic character. A single moment in *All's Well that Ends Well*, after the exposure of Parolles, is similar to the ending of *The Playboy*.

> Yet I am thankful: if my heart were great
> 'Twould burst at this. Captain I'll be no more
> But I will eat and drink, and sleep as soft
> As captain shall: simply the thing I am
> Shall make me live.[16]

The deflated boaster is suddenly human. Synge, however, goes beyond this affirmation of continued existence, and gives Christy a triumphant defiance of his persecutors. Where Shakespeare complicates the comic pattern by a moment of human reality, Synge turns it inside out, so that the scorned butt of laughter becomes the hero. Perhaps this is what Synge had in mind when he referred to the ambiguity of Shylock and Alceste in his letter defending *The Playboy*.

In a different way Synge manipulates the balance between comedy and realism in the figure of the Widow Quin. She originated in the earliest drafts of the play as the boldest of the hero-worshipping girls, appearing only in Act II. Changed from Sally Quin, when she was presumably Pegeen's contemporary, to the older and more experienced widow, she developed into one of Synge's favourite characters, and her part was expanded until for a time she looked like dominating the play. She seems at one point to be closer to Christy than Pegeen could ever be, with a feeling of loneliness very like Christy's:

> I'm above many's the day, odd times in great spirits, abroad in the sunshine, darning a stocking or stitching a shift, and odd times again looking out on the schooners, hookers, trawlers is sailing the sea, and I thinking on the gallant hairy fellows are drifting beyond, and myself long years living alone. (*Plays* II p. 127)

But Synge deliberately limited the Widow's attractiveness and gave her only this one moment of seriousness. Once Christy decides definitely for Pegeen, she returns to her role as the cynical comic widow, bargaining for what she can get as she had done earlier with Shawn Keogh:

> *Christy* (with agitation). . . . Will you swear to aid and save me for the love of Christ?
> *Widow Quin* (looks at him for a moment).   If I aid you, will you swear to give me a right of way I want, and a mountainy ram, and a load of dung at Michaelmas, the time you'll be master here? (*Plays* II p. 131)

She is completely reinstated as a figure of farce by the tag ending of the scene:

> Well if the worst comes in the end of all, it'll be great game to see there's none to pity him but a widow woman, the like of me has buried her children and destroyed her man. (*Plays* II p. 131)

Synge seems to have been in doubt whether or not to include these lines, and it was only in rehearsal that he decided to leave them in. (See *Plays* II p. 130.) They help to keep the Widow well back from the edge of pathos.

The Widow Quin has a very functional part in the play; she is the stage-manager of the piece, contriving action, supplying information, providing links between one scene and another. She is also something like the comic *raisonneur*, giving us a clear-sighted and realistic commentary on the action. Her view of Christy, for example, from the start is nearer the truth than that of the others: 'it'd soften my heart to see you sitting so simple with your cup and cake, and you fitter to be saying your catechism than slaying your da' (*Plays* II p. 87). Her reactions are, on the whole, ordinary and normal, in so far as anyone is normal in *The Playboy*. Although she like the rest is impressed with the myth of the father-killer, she is 'scandalised' at the depth of hatred she sees in Christy after Old Mahon has actually appeared. Her basic good nature is revealed again when all the others turn against him, and she tries to save him from the lynch-mob. And yet, although we can recognise the Widow's humanity, there seems to be something sordid and grotesque about her struggles to pin petticoats on the recalcitrant Christy. Her commonsensical decency and compassion is no longer relevant in the intensified emotional atmosphere of the concluding scenes, and in fact Synge allows her to vanish from the play without a final appearance. Like the Fool in *King Lear*, she is no longer needed. She can be no further help to Christy, for he has to lose all his allies in order to win through by himself. In the final series of confrontations between Christy and the crowd, Christy and Pegeen, Christy and his father, the shrewd and genial comic widow can have no part.

Comic convention throughout grows into a different sort of dramatic reality. Take, for example, the use of violence in the play. We can laugh at the story of Christy's deed in the opening scenes, by virtue of the comic immunity which dissociates violence from pain. 'I just riz the loy and let fall the edge of it on the ridge of his skull, and he went down at my feet like an empty sack, and never let a grunt or groan from him at all.' (*Plays* II p. 73) Our moral self-respect is protected by the comic guarantee of painlessness. It is a straightforward comic attitude which Synge encourages us to adopt to the story of the parricide, not 'black' or 'sick' comedy, where the laughter has an undercurrent of guilt. It is not even a satire on the specifically Irish sympathy for criminals. In spite of Synge's own professions and the instance of the Lynchehaun case which he said suggested the idea for the play, he does not focus directly on the rural Irish opposition to law. The comic convention established is basically independent of the local setting, and the unusual attitude to violence in Ireland is only of incidental relevance.

We can see this if we compare *The Playboy* with its 'source' in

The Aran Islands. Synge tells the story of the parricide whom the people sheltered, and then comments on the islanders' attitude:

> If a man has killed his father, and is already sick and broken with remorse, they see no reason why he should be dragged away and killed by the law.
>
> Such a man, they say, will be quiet all the rest of his life, and if you suggest that punishment is needed as an example, they ask, 'Would any one kill his father if he was able to help it?' (*Prose* p. 95)

This is a profoundly moral response to a crime of violence: it implies both an appreciation of the dreadfulness of the action, and the deep remorse it must necessarily bring to the criminal. Synge also comments on the fact that the islanders dispatch a man judged guilty of a crime, alone, to present himself at the jail in Galway where he is to serve his sentence. This is not a lawless people, but one whose attitude to law is more sensitive than that of ordinary society.

Nowhere in *The Playboy* is the tone anything like that of the simple unanswerable question, 'Would any one kill his father if he was able to help it?' Instead we have the interrogation of Christy leading up to the splendid interchange:

> *Pegeen.*   Is it killed your father?
> *Christy.*   With the help of God I did surely, and that the Holy Immaculate Mother may intercede for his soul. (*Plays* II p. 73)

Of course Synge is putting to ironic effect the Irish custom of the promiscuous invocation of the deity. But just as surely he is signalling from the start that this is comedy, that we are not to consider Christy's deed in its full moral implication. The inversion of values indicated by Michael James's 'great respect' for the parricide is part of the comic convention. It is neither a direct nor a satiric portrayal of the Irish peasants, in so far as they may be characterised as condoning violence. Nobody outside a comedy, however anarchic, would say as Pegeen does of a man who has killed his father – 'That'd be a lad with the sense of Solomon to have for a pot-boy' (*Plays* II p. 75). The very absurdity of the logic makes it impossible to take this seriously.

The Playboy starts with a comic hypothesis: a man who thinks himself a parricide finds that he is not regarded with horror but with respect, that he has come by means of his deed to a brave new world of glory. What happens to the man as a result? Synge undoubtedly took his cue for this hypothesis from the abnormal attitude to crime among the Irish country people, but it remains essentially a hypothesis, agreed between author and audience, as remote from ordinary reality as the absurd *malentendus* of farce. We can shamelessly enjoy Christy's full-scale account of the murder in Act II:

> *Christy* . . . Then I turned around with my back to the north, and I hit a blow on the ridge of his skull, laid him stretched out, and he split to the knob of his gullet. (He raises the chicken bone to his Adam's apple.) (*Plays* II p. 103)

At this climactic moment, any tendency we might have to consider the implications of splitting a man's head open is subverted by the gesture with the chicken bone. Long before Old Mahon appears on stage, we have realised that there is something unreal about Christy's deed, or at least attention has been comically arrested, so that we do not fully examine the reality of the murder.

Yet there is more than mock violence in *The Playboy*. Incidental remarks disturb the audience's attitude of comic anaesthesia. 'Where now will you meet the like of Daneen Sullivan knocked the eye from a peeler, or Marcus Quin, God rest him, got six months for maiming ewes', says Pegeen complaining of the degeneracy of the times. Or again from Pegeen:

> You never hanged him, the way Jimmy Farrell hanged his dog from the licence and had it screeching and wriggling three hours at the butt of a string, and himself swearing it was a dead dog, and the peelers swearing it had life? (*Plays* II p. 73)

The same image is picked up when she frightens Christy with hanging in Act II: 'it'd make the green stones cry itself to think of you swaying and swiggling at the butt of a rope' (*Plays* II p. 109) These lines are comic but it is a sardonic humour, for the description is rather too vivid for comfortable laughter. Where the fantastic absurdity of the playboy/parricide ensures a comic reaction, the hanging of the dog and the savagery of the 'patriots' is closer to truth, less simply funny. Even more upsetting, because quite casual, is Widow Quin's warning to Old Mahon on the dangers of madness: 'them lads caught a maniac one time and pelted the poor creature till he ran out raving and foaming and was drowned in the sea.' (*Plays* II p. 145) We are given a horrifying glimpse of a community where madness is still laughable and cruelty commonplace.

Our comic attitude is unsettled by such passages, but it is only in the final act that violence suddenly becomes immediate and real. With the reappearance of Old Mahon and the exposure of Christy the emotional level of the play rises. Christy's humiliation is initially comic, but as Peegen and the crowd turn on him, their cruelty becomes apparent. The climax comes as the taunted victim 'swings round with a sudden rapid movement and picks up a loy'. This loy has been used several times in the earlier scenes, when it needed only one look at it to start Christy off: 'It was with a loy the like of that I killed my father'. The comic prop now becomes a real instrument of violence, and the effect of Christy's movement on the audience is that of complete bewilderment. With the scene of the burning of Christy's leg, we are a long way from the comic security with which we received the news of his deed. Synge leads us across the 'great gap between a gallous story and a dirty deed', from mock murder to real violence.

There is some evidence to suggest that it was this shattering of comic convention which provoked the reaction of the first-night audience. 'The first act went well,' according to Maire Nic Shiublaigh, 'there was laughter at the right places and the correct degree of solemnity was maintained when it was demanded.' The audience evidently accepted the fantastic plot – in this act as much as anywhere Irish men and women are shown hero-worshipping a parricide – and Lady Gregory was able to send a telegram to Yeats after the first act, announcing the play's success. But, Maire Nic Shiublaigh continues, 'during the second act I began to feel a tenseness in the air around me'.[17] Padraic Colum, who was also present, thought that the audience started 'growing hostile to the play from the point where Christy's father enters. That scene was too representational. There stood a man with horribly-bloodied bandage upon his head, making a figure that took the whole thing out of the atmosphere of high comedy.'[18] The line which actually started the row is well known (though it was apparently slightly altered on the night):

what'd I care if you brought me a drift of chosen females, standing in their shifts itself maybe, from this place to the Eastern world. (*Plays* II p. 167)

It has been generally assumed that the puritanical Dubliners objected instantly to this vision of a nation-wide harem, but it is worth noticing where the line comes in the play. Christy has just returned to the stage, apparently having murdered his father. It may well be that, after a few moments of stunned amazement, the audience reacted against this display of violence, and that it was all but accidental that the delayed response came at the word 'shifts'.

When the Abbey revived the play after Synge's death, they took care to avoid similar reactions:

> Originally that excellent actor W. G. Fay was in the part of the Playboy. He made the role a little sardonic, and this . . . took from the extravagance of the comedy. Afterwards the Playboy's father was made a less bloody object, and the part of the Playboy in the hands of another actor was given more charm and gaiety, and there was no trouble with the audience.[19]

(A photograph of Fred O'Donovan as the playboy in 1910 makes clear the sort of conventional juvenile lead the part became.) In later productions *The Playboy* was played fast as a comedy, whereas 'when it was given for the first time it was played seriously, almost sombrely'.[20] These remain the basic alternatives for directing the play. Both extravagant comedy and a more realistic form of drama are there and the central effect of the play depends upon the relation between the two.

*   *   *

The dramatic substance of *The Playboy* is so diverse that we cannot afford to abstract a theme and say – this is what the play is about. As soon as we formulate some such theme, the relation between fantasy and reality, the nature of role-playing, the growth of personality, it distorts the play's vision. The various levels of meaning which stand in relation like the terms of a fraction are then divided out into a false decimal finality. The play is puzzling, and a common reaction to seeing or reading it for the first time is complete bewilderment. This bewilderment, however, is perfectly appropriate. In *The Playboy*, as in the other comedies, Synge is deliberately exploiting a pattern of unstable and fluctuating convention, so that uncertainty and confusion is built into his dramatic strategy. There are no short-cuts to the play's meaning. The success of *The Playboy* is that the precisely achieved structure holds together the different modes of action in a complex and resonant whole.

8

Unhappy Comedies

We have looked in turn at *The Shadow*, *The Tinker's Wedding*, *The Well of the Saints* and *The Playboy*, without finally placing them in a specific genre. Are they correctly called comedies, or should we try to find a more appropriate name for them? T. R. Henn considers that *The Playboy* is a 'deliberately distorted tragedy, all the joints wrenched out of place by a comic vision that Synge imposed upon it, a comic vision in the manner of Molière'.[1] According to Alan Price, *The Well of the Saints* belongs to

> that kind of play – so far without a name – of which *The Wild Duck* and *The Three Sisters* are examples: the kind that, barely tickled by the comic spirit and mainly unpurged by purely tragic exaltation, deals searchingly with serious issues, and, unblurred by morbidity, reflects, with some compassion, a melancholy vision of the human condition.[2]

Another critic has identified the mixed dramatic form which is so common in the modern period as 'dark comedy'.[3] Among the formulations which suggest the discordant character of such plays we find Ionesco's 'tragic farce' (*Les Chaises*), or Beckett's ambiguous 'tragicomedy' (*Waiting for Godot*). Synge's own title-pages are non-committal: *The Tinker's Wedding* and *The Playboy* are both 'comedies', but *The Shadow* and *The Well of the Saints* are merely 'plays'. If a comedy is, by the crudest definition possible, a play with a happy ending, then perhaps it would be simplest to call these four plays of Synge unhappy comedies.

In one of the early drafts of *The Wells of the Saints* Timmy the smith was to end the play by inviting all the people to come dance at his wedding (*Plays* 1 p. 150). It is a traditional ending for a comedy, the marriage feast which re-establishes order, harmony and good humour. But the wedding which is celebrated at the end of *The Well of the Saints* is strikingly different from the usual comic union, for it is a *mariage de convenance* rather than a love-match. It was, of course, inconceivable that Molly Byrne should elope with Martin Doul, but that would have been the 'happy ending' in the traditional terms of comedy, at least in so far as it is the alternative to the socially safe marriage with a middle-aged man which is so often the fate which the heroine has to avoid. The comic marriage generally brings us back to normality, to a sane and healthy situation where the law of nature and the social law are at one. The marriage between Timmy and Molly also represents a return to normal reality, but it is hardly a norm which we regard as desirable. Far from being a festive celebration of the continuing pattern of life, it is a sour recognition of an entrenched *status quo*. By deliberately withholding the traditional pattern, it acts as an ironic parody image. Synge knew what he was doing; when asked why *The Wells of the Saints* was attacked at its first production, 'he said that people accustomed to the commercial stage wanted plays with plots and happy endings'.[4] The bleak atmosphere of *The Well of the Saints* came as a shock.

If we wanted a single phrase to suggest the pattern of Synge's comedy we might call it *le mariage echoué* – the marriage that doesn't come off. In *The Shadow* it is a marriage which was never likely to succeed and has in fact failed. Such a situation is common enough in comedy, with the restless young wife married to the jealous old man, but what makes *The Shadow* unusual is that the couple actually separate at the end. It is relatively seldom that the unfaithful wife of comedy leaves her husband; the comedy of infidelity is normally conceived as a perennially recurring situation which cannot be radically altered. *The Shadow*, by contrast, shows the definitive break-up of a marriage. It takes us inside the stock comic household and investigates the emotions of January and May. In *The Tinker's Wedding* the very idea of marriage is an absurdity – a 'notion' which Sarah takes, a capricious feminine whimsy. It has nothing to do with the normal tinker's life and the whole action goes to show the farcical results of their attempt to adopt the ridiculous shibboleths and ceremonies of society. In *The Playboy* once again, as in *The Well of the Saints*, the play ends with the wrong wedding in prospect. Shawn congratulates himself that all's well that ends well, 'It's a miracle Father Reilly can wed us in the end of all', and though Pegeen's immediate response may be to hit him a box on the ear, she will probably end up marrying him, given the local conditions. Whether she does or not, the natural marriage, the romantic union which might have been, has fallen through and for Pegeen at least it is a very unhappy ending.

In other ways, also, Synge twists the received pattern of comedy. The usual comic relation between fantasy and reality is inverted. The period of anarchic licence in which fantasies are allowed to grow and blossom, is strictly limited in most comedy. The extra-ordinary world of misrule is framed by the ordinary world with which the comedy starts and to which it returns. The characters and audience are purged at least temporarily of unreason, and contentedly resume their working-day lives. For the midsummer madness of lovers, the end of comedy brings the stability of mar-riage; those who are incurably disposed to fantasy suffer a ritual humiliation. In the general laughter of the final scene, anyone who remains out of humour or who cannot accept the return to nor-mality, must leave the stage or be mocked into conformity with the prevailing mood.

Christy Mahon and Martin Doul, who continue to believe in the inverted images of make-believe long after the jokes are over, are odd men out – like Arnolphe at the end of *L'Ecole des Femmes*, or Jacques in *As You Like It*. But our sympathy and our respect go with Christy and Martin when they leave. We are certainly not asked to stay in spirit to attend the wedding of Timmy and Molly Byrne, or join in the drinking at Michael James's shebeen. The characters whose foolish delusions are the butt of the comedy, whom we laugh at for their absurd fantasies of beauty or daring, are finally far preferable to those who mock and banish them. This is partly because the society which expels them remains itself un-changed. There is none of the feeling which is common particularly in romantic comedy, that the lives of the characters will be better and more reasonable for their temporary immersion in the absurd abnormalities of comic confusion. The community at the end of *The Playboy* and at the end of *The Well of the Saints* is the same community that played the initial trick on the beggars, or hero-worshipped the parricide. They are unrepentant and unrecon-structed. The main incident of the play in each case was for them an incident merely, an idle diversion in their otherwise dreary lives. It is the central characters who make something of what happens to them in the comedy. Their comic fantasies are trans-formed into an imaginative reality, which is at odds with the ordinary reality of the other characters.

In the great comedians, in Jonson, Shakespeare or Molière, there is an underpinning security of viewpoint. Jonson presents formally in the Induction to *Bartholomew Fair* what is the underlying convention of comedy:

> the author promiseth to present them, by us [the actors], with a new sufficient Play called *Bartholomew Fayre*, merry, and as full of noise, as sport: made to delight all, and to offend none. Provided they have either, the wit, or the honesty to think well of themselves.[5]

Jonson is here as pugnacious as usual, but he indicates the attitude which he expects his audience to adopt: to watch the fair as reasonable people, to laugh at the absurdity of the fools and the roguery of the knaves, without taking them so seriously as to imagine they themselves are being attacked. We are asked, in comedy, to watch the absurdities of human beings from the secure vantage-point of a reasonable sense of proportion – to smile with Puck, 'Lord, what fools these mortals be!' We can view the childish antics of the monomaniacs in Molière, with the detachment of adults. Our security depends ultimately on our sense of the strength and sanity of the social order which can withstand a great deal of comic lawlessness and even convert it to advantage. In the plays which are closer to satire, in *Volpone*, *Measure for Measure* or *Le Misanthrope*, where this belief in the enduring value of society seems to be questioned, we are left much less sure of the attitude we are supposed to take towards the comic action.

In Synge, as we have seen, there is no secure convention at all. In one scene we are invited to laugh at a comic situation – say an old man pretending to be dead to catch his wife making love to a neighbour – but before the play is over we have been through several different sorts of reaction, which make the straightforward response impossible. The basic structure in Synge often corresponds to the usual pattern of comedy, and we are encouraged to view with detached amusement Dan Burke's trick, the beggars' vanity or the inflated pride of Christy. For a time at least we can, as in Jonson's injunction, 'have the honesty or wit to think well of our-selves', maintaining our distance from those whom the play mocks. But Synge leads us to wonder whether the eccentricities of his central characters are not of some value; he takes us away from the decorous belief in moderation which makes so many comedies a celebration of the ordinary. As the stable comic convention rests ultimately on a confident belief in the organisation of society, so

Synge's deliberate manipulation of audience response results in a sceptical and ironic attitude towards the laws society imposes upon the individual.

An example from Aristophanes will illustrate the difference between Synge and the traditional comedian. There is a character in *The Birds* who comes to Cloudcuckooland in the hope that it will sanction his impulse to kill his father. Cloudcuckooland, he thinks, is the permissive country where anything goes. But he discovers finally that beneath the appearance of comic anarchy, the orthodox moral standards hold good. In the fantasy world of Mayo, however, the 'fools of earth' are firmly in charge, and we are given no alternative to their crazy upside-down view of the parricide. True when Christy repeats his deed in front of them they try to hale him off to justice, but it is for the worst possible self-interested reasons: 'It is the will of God that all should guard their little cabins from the treachery of law and what would my daughter be doing if I was ruined or was hanged itself?' (*Plays* II p. 173) There is nothing in the community which rejects Christy with which we can decently identify.

Synge is writing in what Northrop Frye has called the ironic mode of literature, presenting 'an ironic deadlock in which the hero is regarded as a fool or worse by the fictional society, and yet impresses the real audience as having something more valuable than his society has'.[6] It is a valuable definition to describe the structure of Synge's comedies, in which a post-Romantic individualist vision is controlled by an ironic formal setting. We are given two views of man in society: the majority opinion which holds that all deviation from the norm is laughable or ridiculous, and that of a vociferous minority who insist on a personal set of values.

Frye's classification would seem to suggest that this ironic mode is especially characteristic of the modern period, and Synge's 'unhappy comedies' have been tentatively linked with the general twentieth-century trend towards the redefinition of dramatic genre.[7] How far can this comparison be pursued? Synge has always been a difficult writer to place in any context. As Thomas Kilroy puts it, in an excellent article:

> The position of Synge . . . is rather a special one, he cannot be simply accommodated within the early Abbey Theatre Movement and left there. There is a similar discomfort for those who

try to associate him with the standard anthology of modern drama, however much his stature as an artist may be recognised.[8]

One possible way to escape this critical dilemma is to set Synge in turn beside other twentieth-century writers of 'tragicomedy', both Irish and European. Such an approach may provide us with a view of Synge which relates him to the main tendencies in modern drama, so that he is no longer left in that secluded corner where he is a 'minor classic' who wrote peasant plays. At the same time, it may help us to define more clearly our sense of his distinctive success.

There is no writer from whom Synge needs more distinguishing than Sean O'Casey. The two are all but interchangeable to many people who have only an idea that they both wrote Irish plays. Most histories of modern drama give them a chapter together as the two most important playwrights to emerge from the Irish dramatic movement. The riots which greeted O'Casey's *The Plough and the Stars*, paralleling the Playboy riots, add to the feeling of congruity between the two. The general impression is that O'Casey did for the people of the Dublin tenements what Synge had done for the peasants of Aran, that each 'expressed a life that had never found expression'. Thus it is inevitable that comparisons should be drawn between the dramatic techniques of the two, and that O'Casey's tragicomedies should be related to Synge's work. If, therefore, we can make some basic distinctions between the intentions and effects of the two playwrights, both may perhaps be rescued from this rather misleading Siamese twinship.

The Shadow of a Gunman, Juno and the Paycock and *The Plough and the Stars*, the plays sometimes known as the Dublin trilogy, are all called tragedies by O'Casey himself. He may be justified in the use of the term, but they are certainly tragedies in which the comic relief has taken over a large part of the play. The basic pattern is established already in the first of them, *The Shadow of a Gunman*, which consists of a melodramatic plot with a series of very funny character-sketches loosely attached. There is in O'Casey very clearly a high and a low level – the level at which Johnny Boyle is shot and his sister seduced, and the level of the Captain and Joxer, of Fluther, Peter Flynn and the Covey. O'Casey's technique throughout involves the juxtaposition of high and low to ironic effect. As the Speaker in *The Plough and the Stars* declaims the rhetoric of Padraig Pearse off-stage, we watch the mock-heroic battle of Fluther and the Covey over the whore Rosie Redmond. After the moving final speech of Juno lamenting her son's death, comes the drunken sententiousness of the Captain – 'Th' whole worl's in a terrible state o' chassis'. What O'Casey has to say is never in doubt; like Wilfred Owen, his subject is war and the pity of war, and by the bathetic comments of the Dubliners he satirises the 'old lie, dulce et decorum est pro patria mori'.

Synge also mixes the comic and the serious, but in different proportions and to quite different effect. Comedy is what Synge starts with and it provides the essential structure of the plays; his plots are comic where O'Casey's are tragic. The situations, as we have seen, derive from the stylised forms of folk-tale, fable or farce. Although he gives them a meticulously naturalistic setting, Synge's are not, at bottom, naturalistic plays. They are governed by the conventions of comedy, and it is through the delicate manipulation of these conventions that Synge brings us towards serious drama. By contrast in O'Casey the balance between comic and tragic is a seesawing effect which is not always satisfactory. At times O'Casey seems to be trying to save himself from sentimentality by the harshness of his contrasts. In the first three acts of *The Plough and the Stars* the consumptive child Mollser wanders pathetically in and out of the tenement; in the final act her death is only an incidental, and the men sit and play cards by her coffin. At the end of *Juno and the Paycock* O'Casey plans a shock effect. But it is doubtful if an audience will be able to control the automatic laughter which always greets the appearance of the Captain and Joxer, and the scene may be mistaken for just one more comic turn. At his very best, in the last scene of *The Plough and the Stars* for example, O'Casey's irony is devastating, with Bessie's hymn and the soldiers' 'Keep the Home Fire Burning' providing a genuinely tragicomic climax. But it is not always possible thus to qualify the melodrama with ironic comedy, or to prevent some of the central scenes – Nora the bereaved wife, or Johnny Boyle the traitor – from looking like the stock situations they are.

O'Casey's plays are always in danger of coming unstitched. In *The Shadow of a Gunman* some of the gloriously comic set-pieces such as Mr Gallogher and Mrs Henderson, do not advance the plot in the slightest. They are there largely because they were there in the tenements O'Casey knew. Even in *Juno and the Paycock*, a company must always be aware that if the magnificent first act is played in too genial a spirit of comedy, Juno herself, who is to be the heroine of the action, will scarcely recover from the role of nagging termagant in which she is cast *vis-à-vis* Captain Boyle and Joxer. Synge never writes tragicomedy like this, where the comedy threatens to pull apart from the serious drama which surrounds it. The plays are perfectly unified and perfectly controlled, with hardly a spare line or a spare scene throughout. There are no comic extras and every character has a functional role in the play. Synge has the form of his work always in mind, and the meaning is deeply embedded in the form. The ambiguity of the mixed genre remains ambiguous to the end and it does not work towards a single conclusion. There is no moment in *The Playboy* or *The Well of the Saints* at which we can say that the point of the play becomes obvious, as it does when Juno repeats Mrs Tancred's cry: 'Sacred Heart o' Jesus take away our hearts o' stone, and give us hearts o' flesh! Take away this murdherin' hate, an' give us Thine own eternal love!'[9] There are instants of illumination in *The Playboy*, lines where we are conscious of a meaning going beyond the immediate context: 'if it's a poor thing to be lonesome, it's worse maybe go mixing with the fools of earth', 'there's a great gap between a gallous story and a dirty deed'. But they are assimilated into the action and are used as keypoints in the development of a complicated pattern of meaning, in which one statement is counterpointed with another.

The formal organisation of material in Synge and O'Casey, in spite of superficial similarities, is radically different, partly because their attitude towards the people in their plays is different. O'Casey came from the community he describes, and his commitments within it can be seen in the plays. The figures he satirises, Jerry Devine the union leader, the Covey the half-educated socialist, the men of the Citizen Army, are people he knew at first-hand, often in fact colleagues whom he had outgrown. The women he admires, Juno, Bessie, Minnie Powell, he admires for their courage, gaiety and stamina, the qualities of his own mother. He can give us an inside view of the tenements, and the great merit of his plays, for all the critical attempts to turn them into heavily-disguised expressionist experiments, is the atmosphere of the Dublin slums which he evokes so vividly. Synge is distanced from his characters by the social gap between him and them. There is a deliberate self-consciousness in the way in which he handles his material which originates partly in his detachment from it. He can concentrate on the form of his play, adjusting and readjusting effects with an eye to the shape of the action, because he is not trying to render a whole reality in which he is involved. He works into his composition the fragments which he has collected, the phrases, incidents and anecdotes he has heard among the country people, but these are always subordinate to the discipline of his artistic purpose. All this is not merely to say that Synge is a greater writer than O'Casey, though that may well be true. It is important rather to establish that they were writing different sorts of play, and that if we want to find parallels for Synge's comedies, O'Casey, though he is the most obvious, is not the most instructive playwright with whom to compare him.

Further from home, less immediately comparable, are the absurdist dramatists, Beckett, Ionesco and Pinter, whose breaches of theatrical convention are far more sensational than Synge's. In the unexpected use of violence, for example, *The Playboy* now looks tame and decorous in comparison with what we have seen on the stage since. Every form of violence previously considered obscene has now been displayed, and is often designed as an essential part of dramatic strategy. Pinter is certainly not alone in wanting to show the 'weasel under the cocktail-cabinet'. A characteristic theme of the theatre of the absurd is the concealed aggression which is always present under the civilised veneer of ordinary human interaction. In *The Caretaker*, Mick enters and suddenly, without explanation, attacks the old tramp Davies; seconds later he is launched into a stream of bland introductory remarks. The conversation of the phrase-book families in Ionesco's *La Cantatrice Chauve* turns into angry dispute and back to the polite formulae without any apparent cause. The unexpected burst of violence disturbing the exchange of 'polite meaningless words' is a characteristic shock tactic of the absurdists. We are unnerved by the abrupt dislocation of normality, and forced to re-examine the social restraint which we take to be normal in order to account for the aberration.

In spite of the obvious differences in scale, Synge's use of violence can be compared with that of Pinter or Ionesco. The moment at which Christy drives at his father with the loy is as unsettling to an audience as the more spectacular outbreaks of violence in the theatre of the absurd. The burning of Christy's leg has long been outgone in brutality, yet within its context it is a frightening action. The main difference here between Synge and the absurdists, is in his alternation between real and comic violence. The cruelty and aggression in Pinter and Ionesco comes as a shock because it is what we least expect from the situation. The 'second murder' of Old Mahon, obviously, cannot be unexpected in this way; from the beginning of the play violence has been accepted not only as normal but as admirable. We are surprised at the event, because we have been lulled into a sense of comic security in which assault is painless. The technique of the absurdists is, in a way, a didactic one, to make their audience aware of the violence which they would prefer to ignore, to insist, often dogmatically, that man is naturally violent. It has been argued that Synge has a similar object in *The Playboy*, that 'the greatest shock of recognition for the audience comes precisely at the moment of realising that we who have laughed are also guilty'.[10] But Synge is hardly as tendentious as this would imply. He does make us feel the disparity between our (and the Mayo men's) attitude to the story of the murder and the real event, but it is not just to shake our complacency. We are not required to sacrifice our enjoyment of the fantasy violence to the sobering realisation of the actuality. The two are held in play by the whole conception of the situation.

We are accustomed to think of Beckett, Ionesco or Pinter as experimental dramatists, working with new forms, and by comparison Synge's plays seem transparent, old-fashioned, conceived in the straightforward terms of naturalistic theatre. Beneath a carefully cultivated naturalistic surface, however, the dramatic structure of the comedies is as complicated, as far from simple realism as later more overtly unconventional plays. Synge also manages to avoid some of the problems of the self-consciously 'experimental' playwright. A basic objection to many of the plays of the absurdists is that they are impossibly obscure when first encountered. Beckett, Pinter, Ionesco all met with blank incomprehension in the fifties. The simple fact that the situations which they represent do not resemble any recognisable reality, makes it hard for us to assess what goes on. An audience is constantly preoccupied with the whys and wherefores which the dramatist deliberately suppresses: why is Stanley in *The Birthday Party* persecuted by two strange men? or why does everyone turn into rhinoceroses in Ionesco's play? why, above all, do Vladimir and Estragon stand on a country road and wait for Godot? However, paradoxically, this initial obscurity can come to seem childishly easy to penetrate. We are encouraged to find a solution, an inner interpretation of the action, and soon what at first appeared incredibly opaque, virtually nonsense, looks almost embarrassingly obvious. Stanley's nightmare paranoia stands for the tyrannies, real and imagined, which we all fear; *Rhinocéros* is an allegory of pre-war Rumania, and Godot = God, it's as simple as that. This is, of course, a parody of audience reaction, but it does represent something like the change which has taken Beckett and Ionesco from the fringe *avant-garde* to the Nobel prize or the Academie Française.

Waiting for Godot is the best instance of the revolutionary experiment turned classic-masterpiece-of-our-times. Didi and Gogo, the tramps who stand around exchanging the cross-talk of the music hall, come from nowhere, belong nowhere. The names do not help to place them – Vladimir might perhaps be thought to be Russian, Estragon French, but there are some indications, at least in the English text, that they are Irish. Pozzo and Lucky are even more mysterious, and we are given no clues at all as to where they are going, or in what sort of fair Lucky is to be sold. They must mean something, we feel, the artificiality of the whole situation can only be justified if the author is trying to say something which could be said in no other way. So we go in search of interpretations. Didi and Gogo are perhaps the mind and the body which can find no adequate relationship since the severance of the Cartesian dualism. (Beckett himself has given some warrant for this supposition.) Pozzo and Lucky possibly figure the degenerate master/slave situation of a materialistic society. Or *Waiting for Godot* exposes the predicament of a world in which God is dead but still needed. Whichever explanation we accept, the more we discuss the play in terms of general philosophic issues, the more pretentious it seems. The integrity of Beckett's images is always in danger of being destroyed by the profundities which must be posited behind them.

Unlike Didi and Gogo, Synge's tramps and beggars are recognisably what they claim to be, the outcasts of a specific community. In *The Shadow* it is clear that the Tramp speaks for Synge in his celebration of the natural world, in his tolerance and open-mindedness. But he is convincingly a Wicklow tramp at the same time and therefore he is not offensively the spokesman of his author. In *The Well of the Saints* the fable of the blind beggars gives the play its shape and its significance. Yet Martin and Mary are so placed in a particular environment that we can enjoy their absurd vanity from a comic distance. By contrast even the jokes in *Waiting for Godot* are oppressed with the weight of meaning. The failure of *The Tinker's Wedding* stems from the fact that there

Synge did not succeed in giving us realistic figures who could tact-fully represent what he wanted to say. The ideal of the tinker's life shears away from the substance of the action. Generally, however, in the comedies Synge manages to present a form of dramatic experience which stops us from cutting through directly to an abstract level of understanding. Although when we look at it closely Synge's Irish setting may be as remote from our ordinary experience as the country road of *Waiting for Godot*, yet the initial recognition of reality which we grant to Wicklow or Mayo, makes the images something more than ideograms for the playwright's meaning.

Again and again in the twentieth century, the most serious dramatists have taken as the basis for their plays low rather than high forms. The successes of the modern theatre derive from the music hall, melodrama or operetta, whereas the repeated attempts to revive classical drama have resulted, for the most part, in papier mâché. Synge in common with several later playwrights works mainly with the lowest form of comedy – farce. Farce is an appro-priate form for twentieth-century drama, particularly in the theatre of the absurd. Beckett and Ionesco show us a world in which the cross-talk takes the place of communication, and the mechanical determinism of farce aptly represents man's situation. Where the classical comedy of Molière and Shakespeare presented a basically ordered society, farce in the hands of the modern drama-tists offers the reverse, a satiric and ironic view of the social pattern. The will of the individual in the great comedies of the past had found its expression finally in the corporate rhythm of social life. Synge is not alone in showing the very opposite, a dissident central character at odds with the role which his society offers him. In so far as the shape of the comic action mirrors the dramatist's and audience's agreed beliefs, twentieth-century farcical comedy gives us not an assured law of commonsense, but a sort of systematised nonsense.

Synge uses farce, as Beckett and Ionesco do, to express his suspicion and dislike of what society offers as normal. In the com-munity which idolises the father-killer he parodies the capricious social impulse to hero-worship. There is no need to explain *The Playboy* in Freudian terms, to account for its effect as a ritualised expression of the Oedipus complex. It is a quite simple technique of inversion, mocking the traditional family pieties by a situation where a father is merely a person 'you're used to, and you'd easy kill and make yourself a hero in the sight of all'. In the same way Beckett gives us a grotesque parody of parental relations in *Endgame*:

Hamm: Scoundrel! Why did you engender me?
Nagg: I didn't know.
Hamm: What? What didn't you know?
Nagg: That it'd be you.[11]

Neither dramatist has a specific point to make: Synge is not exposing a universal impulse towards parricide, any more than Beckett is making a plea for greater respect to one's parents. The point of the absurd logic of farce is that it should be seen to be absurd. The force of the distorted images which Synge and Beckett produce is to make us wonder whether what we ordinarily take to be reality is essentially more reasonable than the irrational action we are watching. They loosen our hold upon the normal and weaken our belief in a generally accepted code of human behaviour.

Synge's ironies, however, are not so totally destructive as those of Beckett. If the society he shows is an absurd one without real meaning or value, there is still at least one individual in each play who refuses to conform, and who expresses genuine beliefs. The heroes of Synge are anti-heroes, like those of so many twentieth-century playwrights – Beckett, Ionesco, O'Casey, Brecht, Pirandello. The extent to which we can sympathise with them is limited by their ironic place in the comedy. Martin Doul, the ragged beggar who imagines he is beautiful, is not an obvious figure with whom an audience might identify. Nor is Christy Mahon a swan thinly disguised as an ugly duckling, in spite of the Abbey tradition of playing him as conventionally good-looking. He must correspond, more or less, to the foolish fellow of his father's stories. But, all the same, at certain key moments Martin and Christy are permitted to speak out with eloquence and force, to defend their position as individuals against the requirements of their society. Synge is not afraid, as Beckett, Ionesco and Pinter so often seem afraid, of positive statement and frank emotion unhedged with irony. The characters who represent the last remnants of human value in the theatre of the absurd – Ionesco's Berenger, Vladimir and Estragon in *Waiting for Godot*, Aston in Pinter's *The Caretaker* – are shabby figures who are constantly denied full or direct self-expression.

It is Synge's language which makes all the difference here. There are words for Christy Mahon, Martin Doul or the Tramp, words which are fresh with meaning, and not subject to that deep distrust with which we listen to ordinary contemporary conversation on the stage. Eloquence is not impossible for people who are supposed still to have a 'popular imagination that is fiery and magnificent and tender'. It is not merely that Synge luckily came upon a language that was still poetic. It is a matter of credibility. An audience is prepared to accept that the Irish people do – or did – naturally use a vivid and unselfconscious dialect, and therefore the flow of language in Synge's characters does not seem false or inappropriate. This was why it was so important for Synge to stress the authenticity of his phrases, not simply in order to insist on a naturalistic ideal of accuracy, but to win belief for the substance and texture of his drama. He discovered in the Anglo-Irish dialect a medium which made it possible for Christy Mahon and Martin Doul to be adequate spokesmen for the imagination. The consistently high level of poetic language in the plays allows the central characters in the comedies to speak with an effectiveness which has been rarely seen elsewhere in the twentieth century.

For many readers Synge scarcely seems a very modern playwright. He stands so much apart from the mainstream of the drama that our sense of his historical position is very vague, but there is a general feeling that he is well back towards the beginning of the century, certainly a long way from the modernity of the absurdists. Ironically, it may be Synge's success which makes him so unobtrusive, where dramatists who have produced experimental failures look more significant. The techniques used in the comedies are simple and unostentatious so that the plays seem to be no more than they appear on the surface, realistic sketches of peasant life. Yet when we have considered their structure in detail, it is clear that they involve a complicated interplay between dramatic modes which links them with more obviously experimental plays of a later period. If the fragmented and disparate movements of modern drama can be said to have a central direction it is in the quest for an image of man – a man who can no longer fill the centre of a tragic universe, nor participate in an assured social order. It is in this context that the four 'unhappy comedies' of Synge may be seen as significantly the work of a modern dramatist.

9
Deidre of the Sorrows:
Unfinished or Unsuccessful

'Deirdre of the Sorrows' would have been his masterwork, so much beauty is there in its course, and such wild nobleness in its end, and so poignant is an emotion and wisdom that were his own preparation for death. (*Plays* II p. 180)

It makes some difference whether we agree with Yeats that *Deirdre of the Sorrows* would have been Synge's masterpiece had he lived to finish it to his satisfaction. Our perspective on his whole career must depend to some extent on what we make of this, his last play. For if we accept that *Deirdre* is unfinished, if we see it as a potential success which only needed the time which Synge was not permitted to give it, then an incalculable plus must be added to our sense of the importance of his work. It seems insensitive to analyse, judge and condemn the play as a failure; if nothing else, a pious respect for the dead leads us to give it the benefit of the doubt. The result, however, may be a sentimental blurring of Synge's stature as a dramatist. Our perception of the play itself loses sharpness, and in the pattern of Synge's career which ends with the incomplete *Deirdre* it is the tragically lost possibility rather than the creative achievement which is emphasised. There is something to be said for trying to establish just how unfinished the play was, and whether its shortcomings could have been put right. Obviously it is impossible to determine how Synge would have altered it, and so there can be no certainty about our conclusions. But we can look at what he was apparently aiming to do with the play, and trace the directions in which he was moving. We may then be able to judge *Deirdre* as it stands, to appreciate its merits and define its limitations and place it within the context of Synge's other plays.

so that it is no longer merely an epilogue to his work or the background to the moving story of his death.

Why should Synge have wanted to write a play about Deirdre? It seems an obvious question to ask. The epic story was quite outside his previous range of material, and it had been recently used by both Yeats and A. E. in plays which had been produced by the Abbey. A Dublin audience might have been expected to groan with boredom – 'not another Deirdre play'. This, however, is not the way Synge saw it; in fact, when he was considering doing a version of the Deirdre legend, he thought that it 'would be amusing to compare it with Yeats's and Russell's' (Plays II p. xxvii). Deirdre was started to some extent as an experiment in a different style. He wanted 'a change from Peasant Comedy', and while still hard at work on The Playboy, he wrote to Molly Algood: 'My next play must be quite different from the P. Boy. I want to do something quiet and stately and restrained and I want you to act in it' (Plays II p. xxvii). Obviously an added attraction of the Deirdre play was that it provided a major role for Molly. We can see from his letters that Synge had in mind a future in which both he and Molly moved on to a theatrical success independent of the Abbey,[1] and a starring tragic part for her would have been a good start. (The young unsophisticated Deirdre of Synge's first act was written for an actress who was only just over twenty.)

But if Synge began with arbitrary or pragmatic reasons for writing a play about Deirdre and the sons of Usna, it soon became much more than a self-conscious experiment in technique. By November 1907, within a month of starting work on the play, his letters to Molly show him so entirely absorbed he could think of nothing else. 'I am working myself sick with Deirdre or whatever you call it. It is a very anxious job. I don't want to make a failure.' (14 November); 'I am squirming and thrilling and quivering with the excitement of writing Deirdre and I daren't break the thread of composition . . .' (27 November)[2] By 1 December, he had already rewritten parts of it seven times. Looking at the earliest extant scenario, we can see something of Synge's intentions, and the reasons for his excitement.

Scenario Deirdre!!!
Act I Lavarcham House where D. has been put away by Conchubor. Old servant tells L. that C. is coming. They get ready

D.s needle work. He comes in looks at it. D. comes in shabby
with furze-sticks, and rather defies him. He goes. She hears a
hunt's man's horn, dresses herself magnificently. Thunder storm.
She comes back, spins and sings (left) women murmur (R). The
sons of Usnach come in. Naisi goes to Deirdre in the end they go
out both giving ominous curtain.
(Ps) (Determination for love and life in spite of fate)
II Scotland, woods. dawn, the brothers go out to visit their
trap. Lavarcham comes in to tell Deirdre the news and urge her
to stay in Scotland. Is Naisi happy? He is. Would anything take
him away? Ireland might. Brothers come back, Deirdre tries to
make them swear they will not leave Scotland. Fergus horn.
Scene with him. Strong climax in which Deirdre is over-ruled.
They all go out for Ireland. Curtain.
(Ps) (Inevitable sweeping into current of life)
III At Dawn after the death of the Sons of Usnach. Grave
being dug left. Deirdre alone. Conor comes. Final summing up
and death of Deirdre (Rider-like)   (MS 4342 f. i, *Plays* II
pp. 369–70)

Synge was to experiment at different times with a four-act
version, and a two-act version, but finally the structure of the play
remained much as it is in the scenario. The third act after the death
of Naisi, although it avoided the problem of on-stage murders, was
probably altered because it left out the only piece of dramatic action
in a play which was inclined to be static already. The management
of the return to Ireland caused Synge more problems than anything
else, and most of the fifteen versions of Act II are concerned with
this problem. In the scenario already, Synge is beginning to imagine
scenes on the stage, with the placing of the characters in Act I.
From the first, *Deirdre* was conceived in terms of a number of
spectacular scenes which would give the play its impact. The great
set-pieces – Deirdre receiving Naisi in state, the 'strong climax' in
Alban, the 'final summing-up' – are planned almost as tableaux, or
as operatic arias.
This sort of stylised action is what Synge took over from the epic
narrative. He had always admired the old Irish sagas, and had a
particular interest in the Deirdre legend. It was probably in 1900–1
that he made a literal translation of an eighteenth-century version
of the story by Andrew MacCurtin entitled *The Fate of the Children
of Uisneach*,[3] and in 1906 he suggested to Molly that she should

borrow a copy of Lady Gregory's *Cuchulain of Muirthemne*, and recommended her to read the chapter on 'The Sons of Usnach'. It is difficult to establish which Synge used as the basis for the play, Lady Gregory's or his own translation, as most of Lady Gregory's version seems to have been drawn from the same source as Synge's. Whichever version he used, the scenario is very much in the shape of the epic narrative. The saga is interspersed with short lyrics, in which a moment of high emotion is given expression in an impromptu 'lay'. The key 'scenes' on which the action turns are commonly given the stylised form of triple repetition – the horn of Fergus, for example, is heard three times before Deirdre's efforts to have it disregarded fail. It is these scenes of frozen tension with the ritualised evocation of the characters' feelings which Synge wanted to preserve in the play.

The poetry of the lyrics particularly attracted Synge. He spoke in an article written for *L'Européen* of the stories 'tel que le *Sort des Fils d'Uisneach*' which were filled with 'cette poésie particulièrement celtique qui réunit d'une façon inattendue une tendresse timide, un héroïsme rude et mâle et un amour infini pour les beautés de la nature.' (*Prose* p. 353) He tried to catch in the play what he found in the language of the saga, a simplicity which is yet strange and exotic, where emotion is expressed with the starkness of formula. Deirdre makes a 'complaint' when preparing to return to Ireland, naming over each glen where she and Naoise had been happy. The fourth verse, for example, in Synge's translation reads:

> [Wood] Forest of Cuan, alas! Forest of Cuan
> Where Ainle would come – oh my sorrow
> And [it was] the time was short to me there
> With Naoise [and] in the west of Alba. (MS 4341 f. 17r)

Through most of the versions of Act II Synge kept the repetitive lament of the original, but finally he limited it to a single phrase:

> *Deirde* (clasping her hands).   Woods of Cuan, woods of Cuan
> . . . It's seven years we've had a life was joy only and this day
> we're going west, this day we're facing death maybe . . . (*Plays* II
> p. 239)

He tried also to reproduce the spirit of the keen. He particularly admired Lady Gregory's version of Deirdre's lament for the death of the sons of Usna and quoted it in his review of *Cuchulain of*

Muirthemne. As always in the keen, the mourner will not long survive the loss of the dead:

> That I would live after Naoise let no one think on the earth; I will not go on living after Ainnle and after Ardan. After them I myself will not live; three that would leap through the midst of battle; since my beloved is gone from me I will cry my fill over the grave.[4]

The lines are taken over literally, the cadence very slightly modified to suit Synge's prose: 'It is not I will go on living after Ainnle and after Ardan. After Naisi I will not have a lifetime in the world.' (*Plays* II p. 263)

Single lines from the saga held Synge's imagination. In Lady Gregory's version Deirdre pursues Naoise who is out walking with his brothers. Ainnle and Ardan, who know of the trouble foretold, try to prevent Naoise turning to meet her, and three times Deirdre cries out, 'Naoise, son of Usnach, are you going to leave me?' The first meeting between Deirdre and Naisi in Synge is very different, but Synge engineers the situation so that he can use the line from the saga. Naisi and his brothers have been persuaded by Lavarcham to leave Deirdre's hut, and it is as Naisi is fumbling with the bolt of the door that Deirdre enters from the inner room: 'Naisi . . . Do not leave me, Naisi, I am Deirdre of the sorrows'. It is Synge's irony, as it is the irony of the original, to give to Deirdre at her most commanding, at her most magnetic, the words of a forsaken damsel in distress. Synge, however, goes on to give the line a structural purpose in the play, for Deirdre repeats it as she and Naisi quarrel by the grave. 'Do not leave me, Naisi. Do not leave me broken and alone.' (*Plays* II p. 255) It is poignant to hear the same words spoken again, but this time in real despair. Nothing can stop Naisi leaving her here, nothing can prevent the separation of death.

It is around these statuesque moments which he found in the saga that Synge built his play. The central heroic images are conceived on the grand scale. Deirdre, for instance, is again and again spoken of as a queen, although from a literal-minded point of view, she never actually had a right to that title. (In the original she is sometimes addressed as Princess – as the wife of Naisi who is a Prince in Alban – but never as queen.) She is a queen not by birth or by marriage, but by virtue of an innate authority.

Deirdre (gathering her things together with an outburst of excitement).   I will dress like Emer in Dundealgan or Maeve in her house in Connaught. If Conchubor'll make me a queen I'll have the right of a queen who is master, taking her own choice and making a stir to the edges of the seas . . . I'll put on my robes that are the richest for I will not be brought down to Emain as Cuchulain brings his horse to its yoke, or Conall Cearnach puts his shield upon his arm. And maybe from this day I will turn the men of Ireland like a wind blowing on the heath. (*Plays* II p. 199)

The word has a resonance for Synge which in itself adds to the stature of Deirdre. It is not merely the trappings of royalty that make the grandeur of a queen; she stands traditionally for an ideal of infinite splendour and vitality. It is in the spirit of Villon's famous 'Ballade', of Nashe's 'Brightness falls from the air', that Synge writes of Deirdre:

Queens get old Deirdre, with their white and long arms going from them, and their backs hooping. I tell you it's a poor thing to see a queen's nose reaching down to scrape her chin. (*Plays* II pp. 223–5)

Deirdre is not just a Very Important Person as the betrothed of a High King; she is everything that beauty can be.

Deirdre was planned as an heroic play on a scale different from anything Synge had done before. But there are also signs in that first scenario that he thought of it as building on much that he had already done, and that in *Deirdre* he was attempting a major synthesis. The final act of the play, we notice, was to be 'Rider-like', and the last scene of *Deirdre* is, in fact similar to the end of *Riders*. Deirdre mourns her dead with the same complete absorption that we saw in Maurya, oblivious to what is going on around her. The mood of sorrowful resignation, the restrained eloquence of grief is similar in tone and atmosphere to the famous last speeches of Maurya. But Synge in *Deirdre* was trying for something more complex than the single image of death which was *Riders*. It may be that one of the reasons for his excitement with the play was the idea of achieving a work greater than his much-praised one-act tragedy. In *Deirdre* he wanted to create a full tragic pattern, to set a positive force of life against the reality of death, a sense of life strong enough to stand in tension with it.

In the comments on the first two acts in the scenario, there are

two different values for the word 'life'. Naisi and Deirdre at the
end of Act I show a 'determination for love and life in spite of
fate', yet in Act II this resolution is set aside by the 'inevitable
sweeping into current of life'. The list of characters which Synge
jotted down on the back of the scenario brings out this antithesis:

> Characters
> Deirdre (very central and strong)
> Naisi ——
> Lavarcham (wisdom)
> Conor (Indifferent Life) (*Plays* II p. 370)

Conor, the opponent of the lovers, is the representative of life without positive commitment or direction, life as the way of the world.
In *Riders*, Maurya's intense feeling was set against such 'indifference', epitomised by Cathleen's flat statement 'It's the life of a
young man to be going on the sea'. For Synge the only existence
which could be opposed to both the annihilation of death and the
tedium of such indifferent life, was the passionate being-in-the-
world of the lovers in Alban.

The fulfilled love of Deirdre and Naisi is expressed in terms of
nature. The 'infinite love for the beauties of nature' in the poetry
of the saga attracted Synge because it was very much his own
poetic vein. In the comedies as in *Deirdre* the association of love
and nature is a constant:

> *Deirdre.*   It's a long time we've had, pressing the lips together,
> going up and down, resting in our arms, Naisi, waking with the
> smell of June in the tops of the grasses, and listening to the
> birds in the branches that are highest. (*Plays* II p. 231)

> *Christy* . . . when the air is warming in four months or five, it's
> then yourself and me should be pacing Neifin in the dews of
> night, the time sweet smells do be rising, and you'd see a little
> shiny new moon maybe sinking on the hills. (*Plays* II p. 147)

> *Martin Doul.*   Let you come on now, I'm saying, to the lands of
> Ivereagh and the Reeks of Cork, where you won't set down the
> width of your two feet and not be crushing fine flowers, and
> making sweet smells in the air. (*Plays* I p. 117)

Deirdre gave Synge a setting in which his own nature-worship
seemed appropriate. The wedding ceremony which he had invented
for *When the Moon Has Set* is used by Ainnle at the end of
Act I:

Colm.   In the name of the Summer, and the Sun, and the Whole World, I wed you as my wife. (Plays I p. 177)
Ainnle.   By the sun and moon and the whole earth, I wed Deirdre to Naisi. (He steps back and holds up his hands.) May the air bless you, and water and the wind, the sea, and all the hours of the sun and moon. (Plays II p. 215)

What is pretentious and embarrassing in a play about an Anglo-Irish Protestant marrying a nun seems plausible enough from the supposedly Druid Ainnle. The basic ideal, however, remains the same. The natural images which evoke the joys of love are not merely decorative; the pantheistic adoration of nature is for Synge an inseparable part of the intense enjoyment of 'love and life'.

If in some ways Deirdre looks like an expanded version of Riders, it could also be seen as a thematic continuation of the comedies. The Shadow and The Well of the Saints end at the point represented by Act I of Deirdre. Nora and the Tramp, Molly and Martin go out, as Deirdre and Naisi do, in defiance of predictions that they will come to no good. In The Well of the Saints the beggars have to face the 'deep rivers' in which Timmy the smith is sure they 'will be drowned together in a short while'. Nora has Dan's brutal vision of her corpse 'stretched like a dead sheep . . . in the butt of a ditch' to think of as she leaves. These scenes are in a very different mode from Deirdre and Naisi's choice of love and life 'in spite of fate'. Deirdre and Naisi go on to achieve their vision in some sort, whereas the central characters in the comedies are brought only to the possibility of a different richer life. But Synge expresses in all his plays his sense that the odds are against the fulfilment of his central characters' desire for a life of intensity and distinction. Against them is the weight of inertia represented by the indifferents; against them, too, is the prudential 'wisdom' of Lavarcham or of the Widow Quin. The ideal is still worth pursuing and the characters in the comedies go out hopefully, if not triumphantly. But the hope or the triumph is always threatened, and in Deirdre we see its destruction.

A great deal of personal emotion went into the creation of Deirdre. The most obvious reason why Synge should have been so excited with writing it, is that it was concerned with his own situation, his love for Molly and his fears of death. It is very easy to misread or sentimentalise here, to speak of the play in Yeats's words as Synge's 'preparation for death', a final statement within sight of the end. A remark of Synge's reported by Padraic Colum seems significant. They were discussing the progress of Synge's play and Colum expressed his doubts of the effect of the open grave on stage in the last act. Synge replied that 'he had been close to death, and that the grave was a reality to him, and it was the reality in the tragedy he was writing'.[5] This must presumably have been after his operation in May 1908 when his life had been in danger, but when he was apparently convalescing. There is a vivid awareness of death in the play, but it is not necessarily that of a man who knew himself to be facing death. To read *Deirdre* as though it was Synge saying goodbye to the world, rationalising his coming death by a romantic ideal of young love for ever unspoiled, is a mawkish misinterpretation.

The grave is the reality in *Deirdre*, it is the reality which makes everything else fade into insubstantial illusion. The play is not, however, a glorification of death. As Deirdre recognises, it is the one event which is beyond dignity and grace – 'and death should be a poor untidy thing, though it's a queen that dies'. Nothing could be more mistaken than the conception of the play as a celebration of the death-wish, with the death of Deirdre and Naisi an ecstatic consummation of their love. The end brings not an ultimate Wagnerian union, but the bitter separation of the quarrel by the grave.

> *Deirdre.*   For seven years you have been kindly, but the hardness of death has come between us. (*Plays* II p. 255)

The final scene between the lovers has all of Synge's characteristic honesty. He refuses to perpetuate the romantic myth, and insists that no relationship however intense can stand against this 'hardness of death'. If Deirdre comes finally to a mood of resignation, to the point where she can put away sorrow, it is, as with Maurya, through an anguished recognition of the power of death.

Deirdre's acceptance of her fate has led several critics to misunderstand the play. 'Deirdre . . . is not possessed by rage against morality; she accepts that the price to be paid for youth's splendour is its passing, and she triumphs in evading the miseries of age, as the lovers in Axel triumphed by choosing to die at the height of the intensity of their dream.'[6] 'Life for the old has been a long nightmare; for the young a brief, exquisite dream. [The old] have tried to bind to themselves a joy, and have destroyed it: the young kissed it as it flew, and they live in eternity's sunrise.'[7] But Deirdre does not choose death as a desirable alternative to life, she meets her fate because it is unavoidable. When she is asked to account for her decision to leave Alban, she suggests a variety of interpretations:

It may be I will not have Naisi growing an old man in Alban with an old woman at his side, and young girls pointing out and saying 'that is Deirdre and Naisi, had great beauty in their youth' . . . It may be we do well putting a sharp end to the day that is brave and glorious, as our fathers put a sharp end to the days of the kings of Ireland . . . or that I'm wishing to set my foot on Slieve Fuadh where I was running one time and leaping in the streams (to Lavarcham), and that I'd be well pleased to see our little apple-trees, Lavarcham, behind our cabin on the hill, or that I've learned Fergus, it's a lonesome thing to be away from Ireland always. (*Plays* II p. 237)

Any of these explanations are plausible, none of them, however, are definitive. Deirdre leaves, finally, not for any one of these reasons, nor even for the sum of all of them, but because there is no choice. The sorrows that are foretold will come true.

The sense of fate in *Deirdre* is conveyed through a variety of images. All the way through the play different futures are imagined for the lovers. Conchubor, for example, imagines Deirdre his queen at Emain or Fergus tries to woo them both from Alban with a vision of a distinguished old age – 'Let you be thinking on the years to come, Deirdre, and the way you'd have a right to see Naisi a high and white-haired Justice beside some king in Emain.' (*Plays* II p. 227) Lavarcham offers a view of Deirdre as an old woman 'with your grandsons shrieking round you', and Deirdre imagines herself and Naisi back in Ireland separated by a crowd of courtiers. As so often in tragedy the alternatives to the tragic action are presented as not essentially improbable. There is, however, only one set of images which has the compelling certainty of truth. Naisi hopes to escape – 'if our time this place is ended, come away without Ainnle and Ardan to the woods of the East, for it's right to be away from all people when two lovers have their love only. Come away and we'll be safe always' – but Deirdre knows that this is a mirage:

There's no safe place, Naisi, on the ridge of the world . . . And it's in the quiet woods I've seen them digging our grave, throwing out the clay on leaves are bright and withered. (*Plays* II p. 231)

This is not just a prophetic foreboding; Deirdre can see the grave being prepared, with every detail of the scene in the bare woods. It is an image which is too vivid to be resisted – it must be the truth; and given that truth, it is pointless to argue about whys and whens. As in the first act Deirdre decided to put on the role as queen for which she has been cast, so here she accepts her tragic destiny as a vocation. It is not a triumphant defiance of old age but a recognition of the violent death which is coming.

If Synge was excited by *Deirdre* and saw great possibilities in it, he was also worried by the fear of failure. In a letter to Frederick Gregg in September 1907, when he was still only considering the play, he said, 'I am a little afraid that the "Saga" people might loosen my grip on reality.' (*Plays* II p. xxvii) In January 1908 he complained to John Quinn:

> These saga people, when one comes to deal with them, seem very remote; one does not know what they thought or what they are or where they went to sleep, so one is apt to fall into rhetoric. (*Plays* II p. xxvi)

Synge here pinpoints the central difficulty he encountered in *Deirdre*, the need to give substance and immediacy to material which was essentially alien and remote. Much of our feeling of dissatisfaction with the play can be traced back to the sense of uneasy compromise between strikingly different levels, the heroic world of the saga, and the contemporary peasant life which was reality for Synge.

In the language of *Deirdre* we can see the problem at its most obvious. If Synge was uncertain where Deirdre and Naisi slept and what they thought, still less was he clear how they spoke. He decided to use as the basis for his dialogue the peasant speech he had developed in earlier plays, but as the characters in *Deirdre* were not twentieth-century Irish peasants, some awkward adjustments had to be made. For example, the opening greeting between Lavarcham and Conchubor in the earliest version of Act I, reads as follows:

Conor. God save you.
Lavarcham and *Old Woman.* God save you kindly. (*Plays* II p. 375)

Synge realised that this was an anachronism and altered it meticulously, so that in the final text we have:

> Conchubor and Fergus.   The gods save you.
> Lavarcham.   The gods save and keep you kindly, and stand between you and all harm for ever. (Plays II p. 185)

He keeps the ordinary Irish form of greeting – the first speaker blesses, the second replies with a more elaborate form of the same blessing – but 'the gods' instead of 'God' sounds artificial. The trouble is that Synge knows that Lavarcham and Conchubor are pagans, but the only language which is real to him is that of Christians. We saw him meeting the same difficulty with the language of the supposedly non-Christian tinkers in *The Tinker's Wedding*.

It is the self-consciousness with which Synge forced himself to transfer the narrative into the peasant idiom which is unfortunate. Nowhere else in the plays do we feel that he is simply translating ordinary English into dialect, as we do, for example, in Conchubor's speech to Deirdre in Act I:

> It's my wish to have you quickly, and I'm sick and weary thinking of the day you'll be brought down to me and seeing you walking into my big empty halls. I've made all sure to have you – and yet all said there's a fear in the back of my mind I'd miss you and have great troubles in the end. It's for that, Deirdre, I'm praying that you'll come quickly. And you may take the word of a man has no lies you'll not find with any other the like of what I'm bringing you in wildness and confusion in my own mind. (Plays II p. 195)

The clichés here are only barely concealed by dialect variants – 'I'm sick and tired', 'fear at the back of my mind', 'when all's said and done'. All the advantages of dialect are turned into disadvantages, for the underlying pattern of Conchubor's speech is standard English, and the necessity of using dialect forms only results in awkward syntax and meaningless circumlocutions. Where in the comedies Synge produced a language which was simpler and more fluid than its standard English equivalent, in *Deirdre* the dialogue is often clumsy and opaque.

It has been suggested that *Deirdre* revealed the limitations of Synge's use of dialect, that the play showed that he had exhausted its possibilities. The dialect forms seem to be applied mechanically and monotonously. The phrase 'the like of her', or 'her like', for example, which was always a favourite with Synge, turns up seven times in the first four pages of the play. Throughout we hear dialogue we have heard before. Conchubor, for example, tells how he used to imagine the life of the lovers in Alban, as the Tramp imagined his future with Nora:

> It's not long you'll be desolate, and I seven years saying, 'It's a bright day for Deirdre in the woods of Alban', or saying again, 'What way will Deirdre be sleeping this night, and wet leaves and branches driving from the north?' (*Plays* II p. 259)

> You'll be saying one time, 'It's a grand evening by the grace of God,' and another time, 'It's a wild night, God help us, but it'll pass surely.' (*Plays* I p. 57)

Naisi in the first act speaks to Lavarcham in words which were also the Tramp's:

> and it's not wine we're asking only. (*Plays* II p. 215)

> And it's none of your tea I'm asking either. (*Plays* I p. 45)

Nora's bitter parting shot to Dan is adapted for Deirdre's warning to Conchubor:

> it's not long, I'm telling you, till you'll be lying again under that sheet, and you dead surely. (*Plays* I p. 57)

> It's not long till your own grave will be dug in Emain . . . (*Plays* II p. 253)

But it is not necessarily because he had reached the inherent limits of what could be done with dialect that Synge was forced to self-plagiarism in *Deirdre*. It is rather because he was no longer working in immediate contact with his source. Synge was always prone to overwork favourite constructions, as we saw earlier, but in the comedies the richness and variety of idiom tended to counteract the dangers of monotony. While he was working on any of the other plays, Synge had a constant fund of real language which he could adapt for his purposes, with which he could strengthen or adjust the artistic effect of a scene. He could always have recourse to his notebooks or his memory to improve a speech of Christy Mahon or Martin Doul. It was because this was impossible in *Deirdre*, because he had no such fund of language to rely on, that he seems so often to be working at second hand on the basis of the dialogue of his own earlier plays.

One of the dangers with the play, Synge felt, was the tendency to 'fall into rhetoric', for want of a basic ground of reality. The advantage of using dialect as against, for instance, the blank verse of Yeats's *Deirdre*, should have been to counteract this artificiality and give a realistic substance to the language. Part of the problem, however, is that rhetoric, in the best sense of the word, is absolutely essential to the play. The great scenes in *Deirdre* are written in a high style which is fully rhetorical and which is noticeably different from Synge's ordinary dialect. Several critics of Synge's language have remarked that he uses a far less 'pure' Anglo-Irish in *Deirdre* than in the other plays. In particular, he makes repeated use of the Standard English perfect in preference to the Anglo-Irish alternatives. But if we look at the speeches in which the perfect is found and try substituting the normal dialect form, we can see why it was preferred:

> I am after putting away sorrow like a shoe that is worn out and muddy, for it is I am after having a life that will be envied by great companies.

The dialect construction would simply have made nonsense of the eloquence which Synge is giving Deirdre here. At the moments of greatest emotion in the play Synge does not limit himself to the convention of dialect, but breaks his own rules freely in the attempt to find a style dignified and powerful enough for the tragic action.

The high style of parts of *Deirdre*, particularly the final scenes, is quite different in effect from the dialect of the earlier plays. The range of language in the comedies includes eloquence and lyricism, but it is in many ways a 'low' style, and it tends to make the dialogue homely, familiar and realistic. Hyperbole is common, but it is frequently touched with a deflating irony: Christy's vision of Helen of Troy verges on the burlesque, although the emotion it expresses is genuine and intensely felt. It was a style wholly appropriate to Synge's comedy. But what he wanted to do in *Deirdre* was something very different, and the effect of the style which he imitated from the saga was to make strange rather than make familiar. Heroic poetry is often clear and simple, but it is a clarity and a simplicity which seems very alien, very remote from the way we normally apprehend reality. In so far as Synge uses dialect in *Deirdre* for the same sort of purposes as in the comedies it seems incongruous with the eloquent and formalised language of the key scenes.

At times Synge appears to be trying to convince us and himself that his characters are really real. At least this may account for the gratuitous brutality which we find, for example, in Lavarcham's speech, when she is urging Deirdre to accept a way of saving Naisi from Conchubor:

> *Deirdre* (a little haughtily).   Let you not raise your voice against me, Lavarcham, if you have great will itself to guard Naisi.
> *Lavarcham* (breaking out in anger).   Naisi is it? I didn't care if the crows were stripping his thigh-bones at the dawn of day. It is to stop your own despair and wailing, and you waking up in a cold bed, without the man you have your heart on, I am raging now. (*Plays* II p. 219)

The forced note here is part of Synge's shock-tactics to convince his audience that his characters are flesh and blood, as though by forcing us to imagine Naisi as carrion he might take us some way from thinking of him as a disembodied 'poetic' hero. Synge very much disliked what he called – or rather Stephen MacKenna called – the 'ideal, breezy-spring-dayish Cuchullainoid' atmosphere of most poetic plays based on the saga.[8] His reaction against their etherial other-worldly quality took the form of a crudely self-conscious 'earthiness'.

> Adieu, sweet Angus, Maeve and Fand,
> Ye plumed yet skinny Shee,
> That poets played with hand in hand
> To learn their ecstasy.
>
> We'll search in Red Dan Sally's ditch,
> And drink in Tubber fair,
> Or poach with Red Dan Philly's bitch
> The badger and the hare. (*Poems* p. 38)

Similarly in *Deirdre*, the decision to use dialect, to write a saga play in peasant dress, was part of a general effort to give a basic actuality to the drama.

The false tone which results is especially striking in the play's sexual references. Naisi and his brothers force their way into Lavarcham's hut – randy lads on the look-out for a girl:

At your age you should know there are nights when a king like Conchubor would spit upon his arm ring and queens would stick their tongues out at the rising moon. We're that way this night, and it's not wine we're asking only . . . Where is the young girl told us we might shelter here? (*Plays* II p. 205)

Lavarcham tries to make out that the hut is a love-nest: 'If you'd a quiet place settled up to be playing yourself maybe with a gentle queen, what'd you think of young men prying around and carrying tales?' (*Plays* II p. 205) Kings and queens, heroes and princes have bodies and bodily desires – the object of such passages seems to be to bring the point home to us. Because Synge had such difficulty imagining the everyday existence of his characters, he can only make for them an embodied life by deliberately stressing the complementary opposite of their heroism. It does not quite come together as dramatic reality.

Deirdre has weaknesses just where it most needs strength. The central situation which had to be real, Synge found it hardest to make convincing. The whole triangular relationship between Naisi, Deirdre and Conchubor is not successfully presented. Some critics have suggested that Synge may have been expressing his own feeling for Molly in Conchubor's jealous love for a girl much younger than himself, but if so he expresses it at times very badly. Conchubor resists Lavarcham's attempts to stop him meeting Deirdre on her return from Alban:

> *Lavarcham* . . . (Coaxingly.)   Come on to your Dun, I'm saying, and leave her quiet for one night itself.
> *Conchubor* (with sudden anger).   I'll not go, when it's long enough I am above in my Dun stretching east and west without a comrade, and I more needy maybe than the thieves of Meath . . . You think I'm old and wise, but I tell you the wise know the old must die, and they'll leave no chance for a thing slipping from them, they've set their blood to win. (*Plays* II p. 243)

Even in a burst of anger Conchubor is stiff and wooden – the dignity of the High Kingship sits ill upon him. He is pompous and ineffective, and the rather pathetic feelings he does have are always being distorted by Synge's need to express them in a High Kingly way.

An even more essential weakness, however, is the relationship between the lovers themselves. The life on Alban is suggested beautifully at times, particularly as Deirdre looks back to it.

Little moon, little moon of Alban, it's lonesome you'll be this night, and to-morrow night, and long nights after, and you pacing the woods beyond Glen Laid, looking every place for Deirdre and Naisi, the two lovers who slept so sweetly with each other. (*Plays* II p. 267)

In Act II we are given revealing glimpses of the seven years' happiness which they have had, as, for example, when Deirdre confesses to Lavarcham her fears for its loss:

It's well you know it's this day I'm dreading seven years, and I, fine nights, watching the heifers walking to the haggard with long shadows on the grass (with a thickening in her voice), or the time I've been stretched in the sunshine when I've heard Ainnle and Ardan stepping lightly, and they saying, 'Was there ever the like of Deirdre for a happy and a sleepy queen?' (*Plays* II p. 219)

This comes nearer suggesting a real everyday life for the characters than anything else in the play.

All the same, there is very little in the presentation of Deirdre and Naisi's life in Alban which convinces us that it has been seven years rather than, say, a long summer holiday. What have these characters been doing with their time in Alban? In the original saga there is some description of the service of the sons of Usna in battle for the King of Scotland, and there is an account of the children of Deirdre and Naisi – where they were sent for fosterage, and what happened to them afterwards. There are versions of the legend in which the king of Scotland tries to win Deirdre away from Naisi, or in which there is rivalry between a Scottish princess and Deirdre herself for Naisi's love. But in Synge there is none of this. The children are barely mentioned – it's time you should be settling down, says Fergus to Deirdre and Naisi, 'and getting in your children from the princes' wives'. There is no mention of fighting in Scotland. Fergus's taunt, as he goes out to find Ainnle and Ardan who are 'chasing otters by the stream', seems perfectly justified – 'It isn't much I was mistaken, thinking you were hunters only.' (*Plays* II p. 229) It is hard to see that Deirdre and the sons of Usna do much else with their time but hunting and fishing.

Obviously Synge did not want to get involved with extra characters in Scotland whom he could not use in Acts I or III. But the result of this lack of event in the life in Alban is to make the love of

Deirdre and Naisi to some extent unreal. After seven years it is still the lyrical romantic feeling which is appropriately expressed in images of natural beauty. It cannot be seen to have developed into a mature sexual relationship. Living in the woods, fishing salmon in Glen da Ruadh, is accepted as being synonymous with a full successful love. The imagery which would normally surround and support the central picture of passion here replaces the centre itself. This is perhaps a basic weakness in Synge's dramatic range. He is at his best with the dawning of love, with the radiant idealism of adolescence that we find in Christy and Pegeen. He can also express vividly sexual frustration and need, as with Martin Doul; if he fails with Conchubor, he comes nearer success with Owen. But where he approaches close to a continuing physical union, in Martin's description of watching Mary getting up in the morning, for example, or in Nora's life with Dan, we find a sort of revulsion. There is no such thing as an ordinarily happy married life in Synge. Not, of course, that this is what Deirdre and Naisi's life might have been, but we do feel that if these two people have been living together for seven years, their love in the second act should be different from the rapture of Act I. And it is not. The only form of change in love which Deirdre can conceive is decay.

To criticise the relationship of the lovers for its lack of develop-ment may appear to be an attack on what is an essential given of Synge's story. The love between Deirdre and Naisi is by definition a tragic ideal of the perfection which is cut short, and should not perhaps be submitted to the naturalistic criteria of psychological realism. But Synge does seem to invite such criticism by constantly trying to give his play a naturalistic basis. He is not content to leave his saga people in the remote Celtic twilight world. He wanted to make his audience feel the vigour of the epic characters, and to present them so that they were real for all their alienating heroic status. All through the drafts of the play Synge can be seen trying to 'make the whole thing drama instead of narrative', as he put it to Molly. From the manuscripts it may be possible to determine how far short of success he was when he died.

Synge's work on *Deirdre* was divided into two distinct periods, broken by the operation in May 1908. He worked very steadily at the play from October 1907 to March 1908, by which time he had produced nine drafts of Act I, ten drafts of Act II, and eight drafts of Act III. He was not able to do anything at it again until the

autumn of 1908, and from then on he worked fitfully on Acts II
and III until shortly before he went into hospital for the last time in
January 1909. Throughout the first period, the manuscripts show
that he stayed close to his source, using many of the phrases and
incidents which he found in the saga. He included even passages
which were extremely undramatic, for example, Lavarcham's
explanation to Deirdre of the circumstances in which Fergus was
sent to fetch her from Alban:

> There was a great dinner in Emain Macha, and the musicians
> were playing their music and the story-tellers telling tales. Then
> Conchubor hit on his silver bar. 'Is there a better house than
> Emain Macha, this night in the whole world?' says Conchubor.
> 'There is not,' says the people. 'Do any know of a great trouble
> and want, that is upon us?' says Conchubor. 'We do not,' says
> the people. 'It is this,' says Conchubor, 'that the three best men
> in the whole world, the three sons of Usna, should be put away
> from us, for the sake of any woman that is living.' 'We would
> have said that if we had dared,' says the people, 'For they are
> three wonders for hardness and bravery.' Then it was made up
> that Fergus should be sent to bring you . . . (MS 4342 f. 172r;
> *Plays* II p. 216)

This is admittedly a compressed version of an account which runs
to a full page and a half in Lady Gregory's version, but still it is
surprising that Synge had not realised by the time he reached the
'J' draft, that this sort of stylised question and answer with the
yes-men courtiers would be impossibly stilted for an actress to
report on stage. He may well have held on to the passage because
it afforded him a rare opportunity for showing the everyday lives
of his characters – describing a feast at Emain might stop the
palace seeming so alien and unreal. Paradoxically, however, the
effect of the extra detail is only to bring out the remoteness of
the society. The more clearly we see the epic world of Cuchulain
and the Red Branch, the wider the gap our dramatic sympathies are
forced to cross.

When Synge took up the play again after the long break caused
by his illness, this large-scale borrowing from the saga seems to
have dissatisfied him. In particular, the prophecies of Deirdre,
which he had used repeatedly in early drafts of Act II, now struck
him as out of place and artificial. He was so unhappy with the
second act, that he even thought he might cut it out altogether, and

take 'the good one scene in the II and run it into the third'. In his source, Deirdre is a Cassandra-like seer, who has dreams and visions which are always brushed aside by the others, and this is the way Synge presents her in the first drafts of Act II. But in the later revisions, her speeches are no longer overtly supernatural. An example from the 'L' draft of Act II, dated 2 November 1908, shows the sort of change involved:

> heard a story of
> I [ha]ve [seen] three birds coming from Ireland with drops of
> that
> honey in their mouths and it was drops of our own blood they
> heard   of your ending in a way
> took away with them. I [ha]ve [seen] Ainnle and Ardan going
> of troubles Fergus and
> to a grave where there was none to keen them. (MS 4342 f. 200)

The visionary who sees omens, and the woman who merely hears a story, are clearly very different.

Synge's main problem with Act II was the motivation of Deirdre. In the initial scenario as in the source, she is simply overruled by Naisi and the others, and returns to Ireland against her will. But quite early on Synge made the decision to leave Deirdre's own. While she was cast in the role of prophetess, there was, in a sense, less need for a motive; she saw her fate clearly, saw that it could not be avoided and thus resolved to go to meet it. But as she became increasingly an ordinary woman without more than normal fore-bodings, the part demanded some more clearly defined reason for her decision to risk accepting Fergus's offer. It seems to have been in the same 'L' draft in which the character of Deirdre's vision was changed, that Synge first introduced the scene of Deirdre overhear-ing Naisi and Fergus. This was a part of the process of 'strengthen-ing motives' which, as he told Lady Gregory, was one of his main concerns in his last month of work on the play. (See *Plays* II p. xxix) Deirdre goes in to the tent and comes out unseen to hear Naisi admit to Fergus that there have been times when 'I've had a dread upon me a day'd come I'd weary of her voice (very slowly) . . . and Deirdre'd see I'd wearied.' (*Plays* II p. 227) Even though he goes on to say that he has dismissed this anxiety, it is this line which stays with Deirdre and helps to convince her that their love is doomed.

This scene was intended to make the decision to return to Ireland more convincing and to add to the tension of the action. It was a part of Synge's effort to make the story psychologically real. In fact, it is a stagey device which weakens rather than strengthens the effect of the act. In how many melodramas does this sort of overheard misunderstood conversation lead to lovers' parting of the ways? In the attempt to present Deirdre's decision as dramatically plausible, Synge is forced back on the most implausible of stage mechanisms. The reason why it is so difficult to show a likely motive for Deirdre is because her actions do not arise in a world of likely motives. In a way, the earlier drafts of the act in which Deirdre was given a quite simple *volte-face* without any explanation, are more convincing than this contrived 'motivation'. The essence of the situation is that Deirdre and Naisi leave Alban because their heroic destiny demands it, not primarily for any internal emotional reasons.

Synge's principle of dramatic construction was always one of balance and contrast. He replied to someone who criticised *The Playboy* for its 'coarseness', that 'the romantic note and a Rabelaisian note are working to a climax through a great part of the play, and that the Rabelaisian note, the "gross" note, if you will, must have its climax no matter who may be shocked'. (*Plays* II p. xxv) It was Synge's instinct to offset romanticism with an earthy or grotesque reality, and in *Deirdre* just as in the comedies he tried to apply the same principle. He felt that what he needed to give body and weight to the heroics of his central characters was something equivalent to the 'Rabelaisian note' in *The Playboy*. This was the artistic reasoning behind the introduction of Owen, the most important single change he made in the play, and the most obviously unfinished alteration to its structure. If we are to conjecture as to how incomplete *Deirdre* is, Owen must be a central issue.

Ainnle makes clear Owen's purpose in the play: 'It's many times there's more sense in madmen than the wise'. Owen is like an Elizabethan wise fool, speaking unpalatable truths, supplying a reductive view of Deirdre's situation, questioning the romantic ideal of love. 'Tell me now . . . are you well pleased that length with the same man snorting next you at the dawn of day?' (*Plays* II p. 223) His conversation with Deirdre, Synge no doubt intended to be one additional cause of her decision to return to Ireland. What he says to her, although she rejects it contemptuously, yet gibes with her own anxieties, and gives them a new force. For Owen can speak to Deirdre harshly, crudely, brutally, as no one has spoken to her for years. He cuts through the protective insulation of adoring love and queenly dignity with which she has been surrounded:

> I tell you you'll have great sport one day seeing Naisi getting a harshness in his two sheep's eyes and he looking on yourself. Would you credit it, my father used to be in the broom and heather kissing Lavarcham, with a little bird chirping out above their heads, and now she'd scare a raven from a carcass on a hill. Queens get old Deirdre, with their white and long arms going from them, and their backs hooping. I tell you it's a poor thing to see a queen's nose reaching down to scrape her chin. (*Plays* II pp. 223–5)

Owen provides that sense of bodily reality which Synge felt was so necessary to the saga story.

Owen, however, was hardly the answer to all of Synge's problems. As far as we can make out, his part in Act II was to be prepared for in Act I: as Yeats tells us, there was to be a link scene involving a knife of Conchubor's with which Owen was finally to kill himself. But it is difficult to see how the figure of Owen, even if his part had been fully integrated into the action, could have changed the basic imbalance between realism and romanticism. Perhaps as significant evidence as any against the hypothesis that Synge could have made *Deirdre* into a complete success, is the fact that he did not seem to have been dissatisfied with the first act. Apart from the changes to prepare for Owen, he mentioned no plans for revision of Act I, and what was virtually the final version of this act was written in March 1908. Throughout the last six months, when he re-wrote Acts II and III again and again, he barely touched the first act. Yet the opening scenes are surely some of the weakest in the play, with the flabby speeches of Conchubor, and the badly off-key dialogue between Lavarcham and the sons of Usna. Perhaps Synge might have revised these, but there is no sign that he thought of putting them right.

It may well be that we have *Deirdre* at that stage of awkwardness and artificiality which we can find in the drafts of any earlier Synge play. All through the manuscripts of *The Playboy* there are scenes that are extremely clumsy and contrived, and that are redeemed as if by magic, often very late on in the process of composition. However, the pattern of strengths and weaknesses in *Deirdre* do seem to point to certain essential, perhaps insoluble difficulties. The play works best in the scenes of high tension in which the characters shed individuality and reach out for eloquence which is impersonal because universal. It is most ineffective where Synge has to manage exposition, motivation and character. It is often argued that *Deirdre* fails for lack of action, because it is static rather than dynamic. But in fact the greatest moments in the play – and they are perhaps as impressive as anything Synge ever wrote – are its scenes of stasis; we are much more often dissatisfied with what he intends to be the dynamics of the story. The best things in *Deirdre* burn holes in the rest of the play. The mechanics of the plot seem shoddy by contrast with the pure emotion of Deirdre's first meeting with Naisi, the leaving of Alban, or the keen by the graveside.

If Synge failed with *Deirdre*, it may not have been because his time was cut short; nor was it because there was too much emotion in it, or it was too close to his own situation. What went wrong, rather, was to do with the reality which Synge felt was necessary to any play of his. He needed to find for his subject a basis in that narrow patch of experience which he had made his own. One milieu and a few situations were for him intensely real. The Irish countryside and its people were bed-rock; the feeling of loneliness and frustration, the moment of first love, the thought of approaching death, most of all perhaps the enjoyment of the natural world – these were the areas in which Synge spoke with authority, where he was sure that what he was evoking was real. The writing of *Deirdre* took him outside the landscape he knew. The mode in which the saga people lived, and had to live in the play, was remote, strange and exotic, yet so imaginatively true that it was the texture of modern peasant life in which he tried to embed them which looked artificial. Again, the central relationship of the play, the love of Deirdre and Naisi, was not one of Synge's areas of certainty. The story of Deirdre, although it touched some of his deepest feelings, was not ultimately real to him as a whole, and it was not susceptible to translation into the terms of his reality.

10

Conclusion

A single statement brings us close to the centre of Synge's dramatic vision – 'on the stage one must have reality, and one must have joy'. As always with Synge's theorising he writes from the specific artistic position in which he finds himself, arguing here against both the joylessness of Scandinavia and the unreal poetic country of Maeterlinck and the early Yeats. But he speaks also for his deepest intuitions as a dramatist, and right through his plays the balance between reality and joy is essential. Reality began for him on Aran, and it began with the acute realisation of death. According to Padraic Colum, Synge once said that *Riders* was inspired by the recognition of his own mortality which came to him at the age of thirty. It seems almost absurdly banal as a motive for writing that play, but this urgent sense of death stayed with him all through the rest of his career. It is one of the reasons why it is unnecessary to see in *Deirdre* a prefiguration of his own death. The tragic awareness which is there both in *Deirdre* and in *Riders* is not simply the feeling of a man who knew that his own life was to be short. It is the horrified realisation of loss which we find at its most naked in his poetry:

> I read about the Blaskets and Dunquin,
> The Wicklow towns and fair days I've been in.
> I read of Galway, Mayo, Aranmore,
> And men with kelp along a wintry shore.
> Then I remember that that 'I' was I,
> And I'd a filthy job – to waste and die. (*Poems* p. 66)

The life of the senses in its very intensity carries for Synge always the fear of its ending. Any quietist emotion, any desire for reconciliation in death must struggle with this protesting indignant revulsion.

In the comedies, too, death is constantly present, but there Synge can entertain us with mock murder and mock resurrections. Although the four comedies are frequently sombre, even grim, there is always in them a comic delight in the richness and variety of language. This was part of what Synge meant by the joy he said the stage needed. The energy which we find in the speech of Mary Byrne, Martin Doul or Michael James – even Shawn Keogh at moments of inspiration – gives to the world in which these people live a special vitality and excitement. There is an exuberant pleasure in wildness for its own sake, in the vivid, striking and grotesque images which the popular imagination is continually coining. The Saturnalian function of comedy, however, works only through the language in Synge. There is little which is truly festive in the action of any of the four comedies and they end, as we have seen, with the denial of festivity. It is the speech of the characters which leavens these plays with the comic spirit.

In the comedies there is also the possibility of other sorts of joy – the shared harmony of love, or the life of the senses as a self-conscious encounter with the external world. These areas of experience are defined by a special attitude towards language, the use of words as sensitive instruments for the expression of emotion. In the Tramp of *The Shadow*, in Martin Doul and in Christy Mahon, there is something more than the generalised impulse to sport with highly coloured images. These characters recognise explicitly that with language they make themselves and their world, that words are positive gestures of meaning, giving shape and significance to their lives. It is this belief which differentiates them and ultimately sets them at odds with the other people in their community, who insist upon fixed social roles which cannot be displaced by the individual imagination.

Synge writes as one of the 'last Romantics' in his celebration of the imaginative attitude to life, in his view of the 'temperament of distinction' threatened by the ordinary social world. But he is not, as one critic has suggested, 'a luminary wholly attached to a nineteenth, not a twentieth century orbit'.[1] For the individualist stance in Synge which we could reasonably identify as Romantic, is constantly questioned by an ironic setting. Here, above all, we can see Synge's respect for reality, his capacity for holding in counterpoise the aspirations of the imagination and the social actuality in which they are grounded. The central characters of the comedies are not remitted from the general absurdity of the situation; they have no special extra-comic status. If they represent a truth denied by those around them, they can also be seen as freakish and ridiculous in comparison with their ordinary fellows. Synge does not compromise the ideals for which his imaginative heroes stand; but he submits them, as well as all the other characters, to a shifting perspective which encourages us to be sceptical of anything which calls itself the truth.

Synge did have a sense of humour; his comedies are not comedies by courtesy title only – they are very funny. But his sense of humour is certainly not a gay or light-hearted one. At his funniest he is deeply disturbing, showing us an absurdity which cuts into our most basic beliefs in what is normal. He can pursue a comic image wherever it may take him, even to the edge of tragedy. Yet his humour, satirical and black as it often is, can be distinguished from that of twentieth-century writers who followed him by an ultimate balance and sanity in his comic attitude. Synge's is not a neurotic vision, if by that we mean a view of the world plainly distorted by the obsessions of the individual artistic personality. There is a satirical spirit which seeks to justify its own diagnosis of man's ailments as incurable by the extremity of its images. Synge's delight in the absurd is more dispassionate than this. It is an almost impersonal perception of the incongruities of individuals in society, sceptical but not cynical, disenchanted but without an iconoclastic interest in disillusioning others.

When it comes to assessing the stature of Synge, the importance of the Irish background has tended to narrow down the dimensions of his work. The six plays do not bulk very large, and the overall impression is of a strictly limited and consistent body which can be conveniently labelled Irish peasant drama. We should no longer have to fight the old fight over whether Synge's main purpose was the realistic representation of peasant life. But his methods and techniques are similar throughout the six plays, and, as we have seen, he is weakest in those areas where he is not directly concerned with the realities of rural Ireland. Synge's critics were right – he was uninventive, although their charges of plagiarism were without foundation. His imagination worked always from what he knew, and any form of life in his plays which was invented rather than observed looks insubstantial or unconvincing.

For many readers all this adds up to a writer of limited significance, the interpreter of one specific place and time. By his setting and style he is removed from the main tradition of English literature; within his special field, it may be allowed that he is accomplished, but an artist who cannot transcend the circumstances of his art is not of major importance. These are difficult arguments to counter. It has been the object of this book to try to show that within the very definite limits of his work, it was yet possible for Synge to achieve plays of outstanding merit which can bear comparison with the best the twentieth century has to offer. The narrow dimensions of Synge's world did not preclude complexity; the foundations in a circumscribed reality which he required did not make imaginative profundity impossible. If he stands as an 'original', an awkward figure to fit into any hierarchy or chart of greatness, his anomalous position should not lead us to place him lower than he deserves.

Notes

Chapter 1

1. Quoted in David H. Greene and Edward M. Stephens, *J. M. Synge 1871–1909* (New York, 1959) p. 240.
2. Ibid., p. 265.
3. Ibid., p. 26.
4. Andrew Carpenter (ed.), *My Uncle John: Edward Stephens's Life of J. M. Synge* (London, 1974) between pp. 94 and 95.
5. Bernard Shaw, Preface to *Immaturity* (London, 1931) p. xxiv.
6. W. B. Yeats, *Wheels and Butterflies* (London, 1934) p. 7.
7. George Moore, *Parnell and his Island* (London, 1887) p. 99.
8. 'J. M. Synge and the Ireland of his Time', in *Essays and Introductions* (London, 1961) p. 319.
9. Quoted in Greene and Stephens, *J. M. Synge*, p. 63.
10. Mrs Synge, it seems, was not aware that her loud-voiced maid Ellen was an inspiration to her son. She wrote to Samuel on 9 September 1902, 'Johnnie has been so poorly here he thought it best to leave. I have been wanting him to go for some time his bedroom being over the kitchen he had no quiet. There are only rafters in the kitchen ceiling and everything can be heard plainly particularly with Ellen's extraordinary voice.' (MS 6221)
11. *The Collected Poems of W. B. Yeats* (London, 1963) pp. 120–1.
12. Ibid., p. 400.
13. E. OE. Somerville and Martin Ross, *Some Irish Yesterdays* (London, 1906) p. 23.
14. Daniel Corkery, *Synge and Anglo-Irish Literature* (Cork, 1966) p. 27.
15. Ibid., p. 19.
16. Ibid., p. 79.
17. Seamus O'Cuisin, 'J. M. Synge: His Art and Message', *Sinn Fein* (17 July 1909).
18. D. J. O'Donoghue, 'J. M. Synge: A Personal Appreciation', *Irish Independent* (26 Mar 1909).
19. D. J. O'Donoghue, 'The Synge Boom: Foreign Influences', *Irish Independent* (21 Aug 1911).
20. Somerville and Ross, *Some Irish Yesterdays*, p. 249.
21. I. S. Turgenev, *Collected Works*, Vol. IV (Moscow, Leningrad, 1963) p. 230 (my own translation).

22. Ibid., p. 11.
23. Corkery, *Synge and Anglo-Irish Literature*, p. 86.
24. George Moore, *Hail and Farewell: Vale* (London, 1914) p. 191.

Chapter 2

1. Greene and Stephens, *J. M. Synge*, p. 74.
2. W. B. Yeats, *Autobiographies* (London, 1955) p. 344.
3. J. M. Synge, 'A Story from Inishmaan', *New Ireland Review*, X (Nov 1898) 153.
4. Ibid.
5. Ibid.
6. Ibid.
7. John C. Messenger, *Inis Beag: Isle of Ireland* (New York, 1969) p. 136.
8. Ibid., p. 4.
9. Ibid., p. 41.
10. Ibid. Inis Beag is the fictitious name Messenger gives to the island on which he did his research. It is easy enough to identify.
11. Maurice O'Sullivan, *Twenty Years A'Growing* trans. M. L. Davies and G. Thomson (London, 1933) p. 128.
12. Walter Pater, *The Renaissance* (London, 1961) p. 221.

Chapter 3

1. Malcolm Pittock, 'Riders to the Sea', *English Studies*, 49 (1968) 448.
2. Ibid., p. 449.
3. *Revelation* VI 8. This interpretation is now so widespread that it is virtually accepted as a commonplace. See, for example, Donna Gerstenberger, *John Millington Synge* (New York, 1964) ch. III, or Robin Skelton, *The Writings of J. M. Synge* (London, 1971) p. 48, or David R. Clark, 'Synge's "Perpetual Last Day"; Remarks on *Riders to the Sea*', in *Sunshine and the Moon's Delight*, ed. S. B. Bushrui (American University of Beirut, 1972) p. 43.
4. *Revelation* XIX 8. This is suggested by Paul M. Levitt in 'The Structural Craftsmanship of J. M. Synge's *Riders to the Sea*', *Eire–Ireland*, IV (1969) 57.
5. T. R. Henn, '*Riders to the Sea*: a note', in Bushrui (ed.), *Sunshine and the Moon's Delight*, p. 35.
6. Letter from Stephen MacKenna quoted by Greene and Stephens, *J. M. Synge*, p. 169.
7. The original (MS 4424 no. 109) is as follows:

> do thit amac go bhfuair bean mo dearbhrathair Seaghán bás, agus bhi sí curtha an domhnaigh déirnach do mhí na nodlag agus feuc gurab brónac an sgeul é le radh, acht ma sadh féin caithfidh muid a bheith sasta mar nac féidir lé aon nduine a bheith beo go déo . . .

(The many mistakes of Gaelic transcription here are those of Martin MacDonough himself.)
I am most grateful to Declan Kiberd of Linacre College, Oxford, who translated this passage for me, and who discovered that the English version of Martin's letter given in Greene and Stephens, J. M. Synge, p. 105, is in fact an inaccurate translation of the Irish, rather than the actual words of the original letter, as the authors seem to imply. Mr Kiberd unearthed the original Gaelic letter from the Trinity College manuscript collection in December 1973. He is now working on some very interesting research on Synge's relation to the Irish language and Irish literature.
8. Corkery p. 77.

Chapter 4

1. Mícheál Ó Siadhail very kindly translated the whole of Mary's speech for me, and showed that it could be rendered almost literally back into Irish.
2. See Alan Bliss, 'A Synge Glossary', Bushrui (ed.), Sunshine and the Moon's Delight, p. 301, for the relative frequency of unusual vocabulary in the plays. He shows that The Playboy has many more 'unique' words on average, Riders has much fewer, and all the other four plays about the same proportion.
3. For example, P. W. Joyce, English As We Speak it in Ireland (London, 1910) ch. XIII, or M. Traynor, The English Dialect of Donegal (Dublin, 1953).
4. Not so unobtrusively, however, as to escape the notice of T. R. Henn, who senses something 'false' about both the 'moon of May' and the 'visage of the stars'. See The Plays and Poems of J. M. Synge (London, 1963) Introduction, p. 15.
5. Douglas Hyde, Love Songs of Connaught (London, 1893) p. 43.
6. Ibid., p. 41.
7. Jiro Taniguchi, A Grammatical Analysis of Artistic Representation of Irish English (Tokyo, [1956]), Nicholas Newlin, The Language of Synge's Plays – the Irish Element, Doctoral dissertation, University of Pennsylvania (1950). I am very grateful to Dr Newlin for permission to use his unpublished research findings.
8. P. L. Henry, An Anglo-Irish Dialect of North Roscommon (Dublin, n.d.) ch. VII.
9. Alan Bliss, 'The Language of Synge', J. M. Synge: Centenary Papers, 1971, ed. M. Harmon (Dublin, 1972) p. 48.
10. Spreading the News, Samhain (1905) 28.
11. Lady Gregory, Seven Short Plays (Dublin, 1909) p. 145.
12. Ibid., p. 56.
13. Ibid., p. 15. (A souper is someone who was converted to Protestantism by the proselytising power of the soup-kitchen.)
14. Sean O'Casey, Collected Plays, Vol. 1 (London, 1949) p. 218.
15. The point has filtered down to Gussie Fink-Nottle, who complains

of the script for the Pat and Mike cross-talk which Bertie Wooster gives him:

> in describing the incident [Pat] prefaces his remarks at several points with the expressions 'Begorrah' and 'faith and begob'. Irishmen don't talk like that. Have you ever read Synge's *Riders to the Sea*? Well, get hold of it and study it, and if you can show me a single character in it who says, 'Faith and begob', I'll give you a shilling.   P. G. Wodehouse, *The Mating Season* (Penguin, 1957) p. 88.

16. Henry, *An Anglo-Irish Dialect*, p. 161.
17. Maire Nic Shiublaigh and Edward Kenny, *The Splendid Years* (Dublin, 1955) pp. 42–3.
18. Grattan Freyer, 'The Little World of J. M. Synge', *Politics and Letters*, Vol. I, no. 4 (1948) 11.
19. Joyce, *English As We Speak it in Ireland*, p. 194.
20. Greene and Stephens, *J. M. Synge*, p. 15.
21. Joyce, *English As We Speak it in Ireland*, p. 129.
22. T. S. Eliot, *Poetry and Drama* (London, 1951) pp. 19–20.
23. P. L. Henry, 'The Playboy of the Western World', *Philologica Pragensia*, Vol. 8 (1965) 204.

Chapter 5

1. The incident on which the essay was based is described in Edward Stephens's unpublished *Life of J. M. Synge*, pp. 890–1. The reference here is not to the manuscript now in the Library of Trinity College Dublin, but to Stephens's own typescript copy which is now in the possession of Dr Andrew Carpenter. I am most grateful to Dr Carpenter for making it available to me.
2. Mr Thomas O'Neill of Ballinanty, Ballinaclash, has suggested to me that the original of 'Patch Darcy' as described in 'The Oppression of the Hills' may have been a man named Winterbottom who lived in one of the remote Wicklow glens at the end of the last century. He apparently had a lot to drink at a threshing and set out over the hills and was lost. When they found his body it was only identifiable by the buttons on his shirt, which had been sewn on with black thread rather than white.
3. Rathnew, from Synge's time to the present, has always had a bad reputation:

> Rathnew, Rathnew!
> As I passed through,
> Without a church or steeple,
> In every door
> There stands a whore
> To mock the decent people.

The traditional rhyme is curiously close to Synge's description.
4. Although the term 'tinker' is generic, only a small proportion of the travelling people are actually tinsmiths. In fact, in recent years, the

tinker's trade has almost died out, and many of the itinerants have been assimilated into the ordinary population. The 'rich tinkers of Meath' are often now the prosperous owners of studs or riding-stables, and the equivalent of Michael Byrne drives a large car and sells transistor radios by the roadside.

5. For much of this information I am indebted to Mr Thomas Cullen of Ballinaclash.
6. Synge included the story in The Aran Islands, see Prose pp. 70–2. It is identified by Sean Ó Súillebháin as International Tale-Type 1350 in 'Synge's Use of Irish Folklore', Harmon (ed.), J. M. Synge: Centenary Papers, pp. 18–34. Ó Súillebháin, we may hope, has finally laid the ghost of 'the Widow of Ephesus', which, he points out, is quite unrelated to this tale-type.
7. Corkery, Synge and Anglo-Irish Literature, p. 124.
8. The second title for the play, The Shadow of the Glen, makes this more obvious than the original In the Shadow of the Glen.
9. Corkery, Synge and Anglo-Irish Literature, p. 152.
10. David H. Greene, 'The Tinker's Wedding; A revaluation', PMLA, Vol. LXII (1947) 827.
11. Skelton, The Writings of J. M. Synge, p. 73.
12. Ibid., p. 79.
13. Carpenter (ed.), My Uncle John, pp. 156–7.
14. Report of the Commission on Itinerancy (Dublin, 1963) p. 88.
15. Ibid., pp. 89–90.

Chapter 6

1. 'Doul', is of course not a surname, but a nickname derived from the Irish word for 'blind': they are 'Blind Martin' and 'Blind Mary'. It is therefore incorrect to refer to them as 'the Douls'.
2. Timmy was not often so shamed into a concern with his appearance. The man who was probably the original of Timmy, George Smith of Ballinaclash, is remembered going down from his forge to the pub without washing, with a great white beard, and 'white eyes staring out from a blackened face'. Synge was familiar with several smiths in the area – Edward Stephens mentions Darcy of Moneystown and Mooney of Avoca – but it seems likely that the unusual appropriateness of name and trade in George Smith struck Synge, and gave him the cue for 'Timmy the smith'.
3. Joseph Holloway's Abbey Theatre, ed. Robert Hogan and Michael J. O'Neill (Carbondale, 1967) p. 53.
4. Ibid., p. 111.
5. 'The Passing of Anglo-Irish Drama', An Claideamh Soluis (9 Feb 1907). The article is unsigned, but as it is the leading editorial we may assume that it was written by Pearse who edited the paper.
6. M. Gorki, Plays (Moscow, 1969) pp. 164, 168.
7. Maxim Gorki, 'Observations on the Theatre', English Review, Vol. xxxviii (1924) 494–8.

Chapter 7

1. *The Irish Times* (30 Jan 1907).
2. M. J. Sidnell, 'Synge's *Playboy* and the Champion of Ulster', *Dalhousie Review*, Vol. 45 (1965) 51–9.
3. Mary Rose Sullivan, 'Synge, Sophocles, and the Un-Making of Myth', *Modern Drama*, Vol. XII (1969) 242–53.
4. Hugh H. MacLean, 'The Hero as Playboy', *University of Kansas City Review*, Vol. XXI (1954) 9–19.
5. Stanley Sultan, 'A Joycean Look at *The Playboy of the Western World*', in *The Celtic Master*, ed. M. Harmon (Dublin, 1969) pp. 45–55.
6. Henn, *The Plays and Poems of J. M. Synge*, p. 59.
7. Alan Price, *Synge and Anglo-Irish Drama* (London, 1961) p. 162.
8. Una Ellis-Fermor, *The Irish Dramatic Movement* (London, 1939) p. 177.
9. Patricia Meyer Spacks, 'The Making of the Playboy', *Modern Drama*, IV (1961) 314–23; reprinted in *Twentieth Century Interpretations of The Playboy of the Western World*, ed. T. R. Whitaker (Englewood Cliffs, N.J., 1960) pp. 75–87.
10. Howard D. Pearce, 'Synge's Playboy as Mock-Christ', Whitaker (ed.), *Twentieth Century Interpretations*, pp. 88–97.
11. Ronald Peacock, *The Poet in the Theatre* (London, 1946) p. 95.
12. R. R. Sanderlin, 'Synge's Playboy and the Ironic Hero', *Southern Quarterly*, Vol. 6 (1968) 289–301.
13. J. F. Kilroy, 'The Playboy as Poet', *PMLA*, Vol. 83 (1968) 439–442.
14. Arthur Ganz, 'J. M. Synge and the Drama of Art', *Modern Drama*, Vol. X (1967) 57–68.
15. Carpenter (ed.), *My Uncle John*, p. 188.
16. *All's Well that Ends Well*, Act IV, sc. iii, ll. 335–9.
17. Nic Shiublaigh and Kenny, *The Splendid Years*, p. 83.
18. Padraic Colum, *The Road Round Ireland* (New York, 1926) p. 368.
19. Ibid., pp. 268–9.
20. Nic Shiublaigh and Kenny, *The Splendid Years*, p. 81.

Chapter 8

1. T. R. Henn, *The Harvest of Tragedy* (London, 1956) p. 204.
2. Price, *Synge and Anglo-Irish Drama*, p. 138.
3. See J. L. Styan, *The Dark Comedy: The Development of Modern Comic Tragedy* (Cambridge, 1962).
4. Carpenter (ed.), *My Uncle John*, p. 174.
5. Induction ll. 80–4, *Ben Jonson*, Vol. VI, ed. C. H. Herford, P. and E. Simpson (Oxford, 1938) p. 15.
6. Northrop Frye, *The Anatomy of Criticism* (Princeton, N.J., 1957) p. 48.

7. See, for example, Styan, *The Dark Comedy*, or Ann Saddlemyer, *J. M. Synge and Modern Comedy* (Dublin, 1968).
8. Thomas Kilroy, 'Synge and Modernism', in *J. M. Synge Centenary Papers 1971*, p. 170.
9. Sean O'Casey, *Collected Plays*, Vol. 1 (London, 1949) p. 87.
10. Donna Gerstenberger, 'Bonnie and Clyde and Christy Mahon: Playboys All', *Modern Drama*, Vol. XIV (1971) 227–31.
11. Samuel Beckett, *Endgame* (London, 1964) p. 35.

Chapter 9

1. See *Letters to Molly, John Millington Synge to Maire O'Neill 1906–1909*, ed. Ann Saddlemyer (Cambridge, Mass., 1971) p. 218.
2. Ibid., pp. 214, 220.
3. This translation is now in the Trinity College manuscript collection, MS 4341.
4. Lady Gregory, *Cuchulain of Muirthemne* (Gerrards Cross, 1970) p. 113.
5. Colum, *The Road Round Ireland*, p. 370.
6. Skelton, *The Writings of J. M. Synge*, pp. 139–40.
7. Price, *Synge and Anglo-Irish Drama*, p. 215.
8. Greene and Stephens, *J. M. Synge*, p. 156.

Conclusion

1. Peacock, *The Poet in the Theatre*, p. 89.

Sources

1. *Synge: Primary Sources*

Henn, T. R. (ed.)   *The Plays and Poems of J. M. Synge* (London, 1963).

Saddlemyer, Ann (ed.)   'Synge to MacKenna: the Mature Years', *Massachusetts Review*, Vol. v, pp. 279–95.

Saddlemyer, Ann (ed.)   *Letters to Molly: John Millington Synge to Maire O'Neill 1906–1909* (Cambridge, Mass., 1971).

Skelton, Robin (Gen. Ed.)   *J. M. Synge: Collected Works* (Oxford, 1962–8):

> Volume I: *Poems*, ed. Robin Skelton, 1962;
>
> Volume II: *Prose*, ed. Alan Price, 1966;
>
> Volumes III and IV: *Plays*, ed. Ann Saddlemyer, 1968.

Synge, J. M.   'A Story from Inishmaan', *New Ireland Review*, x (1898) 153–6.

2. *Unpublished Material*

Synge Collection of manuscripts in the Library of Trinity College, Dublin. Contains the bulk of Synge's worksheets of plays, notebooks, diaries and letters. For a detailed catalogue see *The Synge Manuscripts in the Library of Trinity College Dublin* (Dublin, 1971).

Newlin, Nicholas B.   *The Language of Synge's Plays – The Irish Element*, Doctoral dissertation (University of Pennsylvania, 1950).

Stephens, Edward M.   *Life of J. M. Synge*, unpublished manuscript now in the Library of Trinity College, Dublin.

3. *Synge: Secondary Sources*

Bushrui, S. B. (ed.)   *Sunshine and the Moon's Delight: J. M. Synge 1871–1909* (Beirut, 1972).

Bourgeois, Maurice   *John Millington Synge and the Irish Theatre* (London, 1913)

Carpenter, Andrew (ed.)   *My Uncle John: Edward Stephens's Life of J. M. Synge* (London, 1974).

Corkery, Daniel   *Synge and Anglo-Irish Literature* (Cork, 1966).

Eliot, T. S.   *Poetry and Drama* (London, 1951).

Ellis-Fermor, Una   *The Irish Dramatic Movement* (London, 1939).

Freyer, Grattan   'The Little World of J. M. Synge', *Politics and Letters*, Vol. 1, no. 4 (1948) 5–12.

Ganz, A.   'J. M. Synge and the Drama of Art', *Modern Drama*, X (1967) 57–68.

Gerstenberger, Donna   'Bonnie and Clyde and Christy Mahon: Playboys All', *Modern Drama*, Vol. XIV (1971) 227–31.

Gerstenberger, Donna   *John Millington Synge* (New York, 1964).

Gorki, Maxim   'Observations on the Theatre', *English Review*, Vol. XXXVIII (1924) 494–8.

Greene, D. H.   '*The Tinker's Wedding*; A Revaluation', PMLA, LXII (1947) 824–7.

Greene, D. H. and Stephens, E. M.   *J. M. Synge 1871–1909* (New York, 1959).

Harmon, Maurice (ed.)   *J. M. Synge Centenary Papers 1971* (Dublin, 1971).

Harmon, Maurice (ed.)   *The Celtic Master*, being contributions to the first James Joyce symposium in Dublin (Dublin, 1969).

Henn, T. R.   *The Harvest of Tragedy* (London, 1966).

Henry, P. L.   'The Playboy of the Western World', *Philologica Pragensia*, Vol. 8 (1965) 189–204.

Kilroy, J. F.   'The Playboy as Poet', PMLA, LXXXIII (1968) 439–442.

Levitt, Paul M.   'The Structural Craftsmanship of J. M. Synge's *Riders to the Sea*', *Eire-Ireland*, iv (1969) 53–61.

MacLean, Hugh H.   'The Hero as Playboy', *University of Kansas City Review*, XXI (1954) 9–19.

O'Cuisin, S.   'J. M. Synge: His Art and Message', *Sinn Fein*, 17 July 1909.

O'Donoghue, D. J.   'J. M. Synge: A Personal Appreciation', *Irish Independent*, 26 Mar 1909.

O'Donoghue, D. J.   'The Synge Boom – Foreign Influences', *Irish Independent*, 21 Aug 1911.

Peacock, R.   *The Poet in the Theatre* (London, 1946).

Pearce, H. D. 'Synge's Playboy as Mock-Christ', *Modern Drama*, VIII (1965) 303–10.

Pittock, Malcolm 'Riders to the Sea', *English Studies*, 49 (1968) 445–9.

Price, Alan *Synge and Anglo-Irish Drama* (London, 1961).

Saddlemyer, Ann *Synge and Modern Comedy* (Dublin, 1968).

Sanderlin, R. R. 'Synge's Playboy and the Ironic Hero', *Southern Quarterly*, VI (1968) 289–301.

Sidnell, M. J. 'Synge's Playboy and the Champion of Ulster', *Dalhousie Review*, XLV (1965) 51–9.

Skelton, Robin *The Writings of J. M. Synge* (London, 1971).

Spacks, P. M. 'The Making of the Playboy', *Modern Drama*, IV (1961) 314–23.

Stephens, E. M. *see* Carpenter, Andrew

Sullivan, M. R. 'Synge, Sophocles and the Un-Making of Myth', *Modern Drama*, XII (1969) 242–53.

Synge, Samuel *Letters to my Daughter: Memories of John Millington Synge* (Dublin, 1931).

Taniguchi, Jiro *A Grammatical Analysis of Artistic Representation of Irish English* (Tokyo, [1956]).

Whitaker, T. R. (ed.) *Twentieth Century Interpretations of The Playboy of the Western World* (Englewood Cliffs, N.J., 1969).

Yeats, W. B. *Essays and Introductions* (London, 1961).

4. Related Material

Beckett, Samuel *Endgame* (London, 1964).

Colum, Padraic *The Road Round Ireland* (New York, 1926).

Eliot, T. S. *Selected Essays* (London, 1951).

Frye, Northrop *The Anatomy of Criticism* (Princeton, N. J., 1957).

Gorki, Maxim *Plays* [Russian] (Moscow, 1969).

Gregory, Augusta *Spreading the News*, in *Samhain*, 1905.

Gregory, Augusta *Seven Short Plays* (Dublin, 1909).

Gregory, Augusta *Our Irish Theatre* (New York and London, 1914).

Gregory, Augusta *Cuchulain of Muirthemne* (Gerrards Cross, 1970).

Henry, P. L. *An Anglo-Irish Dialect of North Roscommon* (Dublin, n.d.).

Hogan, Robert & O'Neill, Michael J. (eds) *Joseph Holloway's Abbey Theatre* (Carbondale, Ill., 1967).

Hyde, Douglas   *Love Songs of Connaught* (London, 1893).

Joyce, P.W.   *English As We Speak it in Ireland* (London, 1910).

Messenger, John C.   *Inis Beag: Isle of Ireland* (New York, 1969).

Moore, George   *A Drama in Muslin* (London, 1886).

Moore, George   *Parnell and His Island* (London, 1887).

Moore, George   *Hail and Farewell: Vale* (London, 1914).

Nic Shiublaigh, Maire and Kenny, Edward   *The Splendid Years* (Dublin, 1955).

O'Casey, Sean   *Collected Plays*, Vol. 1 (London, 1949).

O'Flaherty, Tom   *Aranmen All* (Dublin, 1933).

O'Sullivan, Maurice   *Twenty Years A'Growing* Trans. M. L. Davies and G. Thomson (London, 1933).

Pater, Walter   *The Renaissance* (London, 1961).

Report of the Commission of Itinerancy (Dublin, 1963).

Shaw, G. B.   *Immaturity* (London, 1931).

Somerville, E.OE. & Ross, Martin   *Some Irish Yesterdays* (London, 1906).

Styan, J. L.   *The Dark Comedy* (Cambridge, 1961).

Traynor, M.   *The English Dialect of Donegal* (Dublin, 1953).

Turgenev, I. S.   *Collected Works* [Russian] Vol. IV (Moscow, Leningrad, 1963).

Wodehouse, P. G.   *The Mating Season* (Penguin, 1957).

Yeats, W. B.   *Autobiographies* (London, 1955).

Yeats, W. B.   *Collected Poems* (London, 1963).

Yeats, W. B.   *Wheels and Butterflies* (London, 1934).

Index

Abbey Theatre, 3, 16, 103, 150, 158, 161
A. E. (George Russell), 161
Aeschylus, 57
Algood, Molly, 3, 77, 161, 175, 177
Algood, Sarah, 42
All's Well that Ends Well, 139
Anna Karenina, 15
Aran, x, 7, 10, 18, 19–40 passim, 53, 54, 55, 58, 59, 61, 62, 86, 90, 151, 183
Aranmen All, 30
A Rebours, 20, 23
Aristophanes, 150
Aristotle, 56, 116
As You Like It, 148
Autobiographies, 3

Bartholomew Fair, 149
Baudelaire, Charles, 21
Beckett, Samuel, 146, 154, 155, 156, 157, 158
Behan, Brendan, 76
Bergson, Henri, 136, 137
The Birds, 150
The Birthday Party, 155
Blasket Islands, 14, 18, 32
Bliss, Alan, 67
Boccaccio, 34
Boticelli, 20
Boucicault, Dion, 69
Le Braz, Anatole, 21, 29
Brecht, Bertolt, 158
Brodzky, Leon, 24, 27

La Cantatrice Chauve, 154

The Caretaker, 154, 158
Castle Kevin, 2, 6
La Cathédrale, 20,
Les Chaises, 146
Colum, Padraic, 144, 168, 183
Connemara, 16, 18, 38, 41, 51, 53, 55
Corkery, Daniel, 10, 11, 13, 16, 30, 58
Costello, Michael, 42
Cuchulain of Muirthemne, 163

Daily Express, 2, 21
Deirdre (Yeats), 173
De la Vigne, Andrieu, 110
Dirane, Pat, 21, 24
A Drama in Muslin, 5

L'Ecole des Femmes, 148
Edgeworth, Maria, 5
Eliot, T. S., 78, 133
Ellis-Fermor, Una, 134
Emmet, Robert, 9
Endgame, 158
English As We Speak it in Ireland, 72
English Dialect Dictionary, 63
L'Européen, 163

The Fate of the Children of Uisneach, 162
Fay, W. G., 9, 110, 120, 127, 145
France, Anatole, 20
Frye, Northrop, 180

Gaelic League, 9
Galway, 10

Ganz, Arthur, 135
Gautier, Théophile, 39
Glenmalure, 84, 85
Goethe, J. W. von, 4
Gorki, Maxim, 128, 129, 130
Grattan, Henry, 9
Greene, David H., ix, 6, 19
Gregg, Frederick, 170
Gregory, Lady Augusta, 66, 68, 69, 136, 144, 163, 178, 179
Griffith, Arthur, 8, 34

Hail and Farewell, 17
Henn, T. R., xi, 146
Henry, P. L., 67, 71, 79
Henry IV Part I, 137
Holloway, Joseph, 127
Huntsman's Sketches, 13, 15
Huysmans, J.-K., 20, 21
Hyacinth Halvey, 68, 136
Hyde, Douglas, 63

Ibsen, Henrik, 8, 78, 128, 130
The Iceman Cometh, 127, 128, 129, 130
Inishmaan, 42, 53
Inishere, 42
Ionesco, Eugène, 146, 154, 155, 156, 157, 158
Irish Times, 2, 132

John Bull's Other Island, 5
Jonson, Ben, 148, 149
Joyce, James, 3, 57, 133
Joyce, P. W., 72, 74
Juno and the Paycock, 151, 152

Keats, John, 133
Kerry, 16, 18, 41, 59, 60, 62
Kilroy, J. F., 135
Kilroy, Thomas, 150
King Lear, 141
Kipling, Rudyard, 13

La Légende de la Mort en Basse Bretagne, 21
Leonardo da Vinci, 20
Lever, Charles, 69
Loti, Pierre, 21, 29

Love Songs of Connaught, 64
The Lower Depths, 127, 128, 129

MacCurtain, Andrew, 162
MacDonough, Martin, 7, 10, 55
MacKenna, Stephen, 1, 7, 9, 10, 53, 174
McNeice, Louis, 17
Maeterlinck, Maurice, 22, 183
Mallarmé, Stéphane, 20, 23
Manchester Guardian, 4, 9, 62
Martin, Violet (Martin Ross), 10
Mattheson, Cherrie, 4
Mayo, 1, 5, 10, 61, 62, 150, 155, 157
Measure for Measure, 149
Messenger, John C., 29, 30, 32
A Midsummer Night's Dream, 63
Milton, John, 56
Le Misanthrope, 149
Molière, 8, 146, 148, 149, 157
Moore, George, 5, 17
Moralité de L'Aveugle et du Boiteux, 110

Nashe, Thomas, 165
New Ireland Review, 21, 24, 27
Newlin, Nicholas, 65, 66, 67, 68, 69
Nic Shiublaigh, Maire, 71, 144

L'Oblat, 20
O'Casey, Sean, 72, 151, 152, 154, 158
O'Connell, Daniel, 2
Ó Cuisin, Seamus, 12
O'Donoghue, D. J., 12
O'Donovan, Fred, 145
Oedipus at Colonus, 56
Oedipus Rex, 133
O'Flaherty, Tom, 30
O'Neill, Eugene, 128, 129, 130
O'Sullivan, Maurice, 33
Owen, Wilfrid, 152

Parnell, Charles, 9
Parnell and his Island, 5
Pater, Walter, 20, 23, 39
Peacock, Ronald, 134

Pearce, Howard D., 134
Pearse, Padraig, 128, 152
Pêcheur d'Islande, 21
Pelléas et Mélisande, 22
Petrarch, 4
Petronius, 34
Pinter, Harold, 154, 155
Pirandello, Luigi, 158
Pittock, Malcolm, 51, 52
The Plough and the Stars, 69, 151, 152
Price, Alan, x, 7, 133, 134, 146

The Quare Fellow, 76
Quinn, John, 170

Racine, Jean, 19
Raphael, 22
The Renaissance, 20, 23
Report of the Commission on Itinerancy, 106
Revelation, 52, 53
Rhinocéros, 156
Ronsard, 4
Russell, George (A. E.), 161

Samson Agonistes, 56
Sanderlin, R. R., 134
The Shadow of a Gunman, 151, 152
Shakespeare, William, 8, 34, 139, 148, 157
Shaw, G. B., 3, 5
Sinclair, Arthur, 127
Sinn Fein, 12
Skelton, Robin, 103
Soldiers Three, 13
Somerville, E. OE. and Ross, Martin, 10, 13
Sophocles, 56, 57
Spacks, Patricia, 134
The Speaker, 20
Spreading the News, 69, 136
Stephens, Edward M., ix, 3, 6, 19, 106, 135
Symons, Arthur, 19
Synge, J. M.,
 Individual works cited:
 The Aran Islands, 10, 11, 12, 19–40 *passim*, 43, 53, 58, 60, 70, 72, 142
 'At a Wicklow Fair', 86
 'Autobiography', 20
 'An Autumn Night in the Hills', 84, 90
 Deirdre of the Sorrows, 17, 41, 66, 160–82 *passim*, 183
 'Etude Morbide', 20, 23
 'In West Kerry', 10, 16
 'A Landlord's Garden in Co. Wicklow', 4, 7
 'Letter to the Gaelic League', 8
 'National Drama', 8, 13
 'The Oppression of the Hills', 84, 85, 90
 'The People of the Glens', 7, 86, 87
 The Playboy of the Western World, 1, 7, 9, 11, 41, 58, 60, 61, 62, 64, 65, 72, 74, 77, 79, 80, 83, 95, 103, 105, 106, 109, 110, 113, 132–45 *passim*, 146, 147, 148, 153, 154, 155, 157, 161, 180, 181
 Riders to the Sea, 11, 32, 41–59 *passim*, 61, 67, 103, 165, 166, 167, 183
 The Shadow of the Glen, 7, 8, 11, 21, 34, 41, 58, 66, 68, 70, 73, 74, 80, 84–103 *passim*, 109, 110, 113, 126, 136, 146, 147, 156, 167, 184
 'A Story from Inishmaan', 21, 24
 The Tinker's Wedding, 58, 61, 66, 68, 75, 80, 84–9, 103–9 *passim*, 110, 146, 156, 171
 'The Vagrants of Wicklow', 87, 107
 'Vita Vecchia', 23
 The Well of the Saints, 9, 19, 26, 30, 35, 58, 72, 74, 75, 76, 82, 89, 103, 105, 109, 110–31 *passim*, 136, 146, 147, 148, 153, 156, 167
 When the Moon has Set, 4, 23, 90, 135, 166

Synge, Mrs Kathleen, 2
Synge, Robert, 2
Synge, Samuel, 2, 3
Synge and Anglo-Irish Literature, 10, 11

Taniguchi, Jiro, 65, 66, 67
The Three Sisters, 146
Tolstoy, Leo, 15, 16, 39
Turgenev, Ivan, 13–16
Twenty Years A'Growing, 33

Villon, François, 165
Volpone, 149

Wagner, Richard, 23
Waiting for Godot, 146, 156, 157, 158
Wicklow, x, 2, 7, 15, 18, 24, 41, 59, 61, 62, 84–90 *passim*, 135, 156, 157
The Wild Duck, 127, 128, 130, 146
Wilde, Oscar, 20

Yeats, Jack B., 62
Yeats, W. B., 1, 4, 5, 6, 8, 9, 19, 20, 23, 91, 144, 160, 161, 167, 173, 181, 183